HEALING FAITH

HEALING FAITH

An Annotated Bibliography of Christian Self-Help Books

Compiled by **ELISE CHASE**

Bibliographies and Indexes in Religious Studies, Number 3

Greenwood Press

Westport, Connecticut • London, England

4-21-86

Copyright Acknowledgments

The following entries have been reprinted from *Library Journal*, Published by R. R. Bowker Co. (a Xerox company), copyright © 1979-84 by Xerox Corporation : 003, 011, 023, 036, 047, 053, 054, 055, 060, 064, 074, 080, 089, 091, 098, 099, 103, 104, 105, 106, 114, 115, 119, 125, 134, 137, 140, 141, 157, 164, 189, 191, 205, 206, 208, 216, 221, 233, 234, 235, 245, 246, 260, 266, 288, 299, 321, 340, 353, 375, 391, 393, 399, 400, 404, 418, 426, 428, 443, 479, 488, 491, 492, 499, 506, 507, 508, 511, 512, 518, 525, 529, 534, 549, 552, 568, 569, 570, 573, 578, 586, 599, 606, 623, 625, 637, 647, 648, 654, 656, 657, 658, 678, 680, 702, 713, 714, 723.

Library of Congress Cataloging in Publication Data

Chase, Elise.
   Healing faith.

   (Bibliographies and indexes in religious
studies, ISSN 0742-6836 ; no. 3)
   Bibliography: p.
   Includes indexes.
   1. Christian life—Bibliography.
2. Christianity—Psychology—Bibliography.
3. Sociology, Christian—Bibliography. I. Title.

II. Series.
Z7776.5.C48 1985   016.2484   85-929
[BV4501.2]
ISBN 0-313-24014-0 (lib. bdg.)

Library of Congress Catalog Card Number: 85-929
ISBN: 0-313-24014-0
ISSN: 0742-6836

First published in 1985

Greenwood Press
A division of Congressional Information Service, Inc.
88 Post Road West
Westport, Connecticut 06881

Printed in the United States of America

10 9 8 7 6 5 4 3 2 1

For my parents,
Aurin and Patty Chase

CONTENTS

viii   Contents

PREFACE

A. BACKGROUND AND PURPOSE

The 1970s, popularly dubbed the "Me Decade," spawned an outpouring of popular self-help books with roots in humanistic psychology whose social repercussions have proved very significant. Less widely noticed, but also of great importance, has been the publication during the same period of numerous self-help books from a Christian perspective: some integrating psychology and Christian theology, some critiquing psychology in the light of faith, and some merely letting the two perspectives stand side by side in an uneasy tension.

In an effort to gain greater bibliographic control over this vast amount of material, much of which is never reviewed in standard library journals, the present bibliography brings together 723 titles published in America since 1970 and representing a range of theological perspectives. Most are straight self-help books, but some (such as reflective and devotional works, guides to social action, or first-person narratives) offer material that could usefully serve a self-help function for the Christian reader even though their formats, strictly speaking, would exclude them from the self-help genre. The bibliography is divided into three long chapters--"Spiritual Psychodynamics," "Family and Developmental Issues," and "In the Wider Community"--each subdivided according to more precise thematic topics. Annotations touch on features such as thesis, scope, and style. They are intended as aids to librarians making selection decisions in church, divinity school, college/university or public library settings; as guides for pastors/counselors; as resources for study in the fields of religion/psychology and religion/sociology; and as tools for the interested general reader.

B. THE BIBLIOGRAPHIC PROBLEM

Religious books have unquestionably gained in popularity in recent years; William Griffin of Publishers Weekly, for instance, has reported that the 1984-1985 edition of Current Christian Books includes 25,000 titles by 13,000 authors from 300 publishers. This contrasts the 1975 edition which encompasses 13,000 titles by 5,000 authors from 150 publishers. It is quite surprising, then, that the field of popular Christian writing in general, and the genre of Christian self-help books in particular, should still be so problematic for many librarians. Recent articles in Library Journal have testified to an awareness of high reader demand for such titles and to the need for more reviews in this area. (See, for example, Susan Avallone's "Receptivity to Religion," in which she reports on results of a follow-up survey to earlier investigations into librarians' attitudes toward popular Christian material.[2]) Yet at the same time, one often finds a distaste or suspicion expressed by librarians toward this type of book.

This implicit (and sometimes explicit) hostility has almost certainly been intensified by recent linkages between Christian conservatives and right-wing political activism. As a result of the Moral Majority's highly publicized efforts, for instance, the term "Christian" now suggests to the "secular" popular mind something quite different from what many members of the full Christian community understand it to signify. It is thus all the more important for librarians to become better versed in the whole range of popular Christian literature which has been for many, until now, a "terra incognita."[3]

Part of the problem is simply one of access. Even though Publishers Weekly (PW) and Library Journal (LJ) now have monthly columns devoted to reviews of popular religious books and offer special religious issues twice a year (in the fall and early spring), respondents to LJ's surveys have consistently complained that there are simply not enough reviews in standard selection tools for them to be adequately informed about this material.

Other resources do exist, but they tend to be geared toward specialized subgroups. In spite of its brief stint as Christian Bookseller and Librarian, for instance, Christian Bookseller—which bills itself the trade magazine of religious publishing—seems largely aimed at and used by Christian bookstores. Church and Synagogue Libraries (published by the Church and Synagogue Library Association), which also reviews assorted titles in the popular Christian vein, has as its primary audience librarians in the church or synagogue settings. Before its recent demise, Religious Book Review, earlier titled Religious Book Guide and Religious Book Guide for Booksellers and Librarians, was a good resource available for divinity schools and larger libraries. This offered a wide range of reviews for both scholarly and more popular works, plus a subject index to current books and annotated lists of new releases. Now, however, there is really no equivalent tool. To be sure, if one reads widely in Christian periodicals one can find reviews for a cross-section of books for the general reader; still, this is not a very efficient method.

If one turns to the field of actual bibliographies dealing with current Christian self-help writing, the situation is even more bleak. Save for Mark Lau Branson's very useful Reader's Guide to the Best Evangelical Books (Harper, 1982), this compiler could not identify any related book-length bibliographies that have appeared during the fifteen years covered by the present work. Even Branson treats inspirational/self-help books quite scantily in a brief opening section, devoting most of his attention to titles on biblical interpretation and doctrine, church and ministry, Christianity and culture, and so forth. Church and Synagogue Library Association has made a fine contribution with its various bibliographies on assorted topics, but these are generally quite short and are not intended as resources for extensive research or as indepth selection tools

for the larger public or divinity school library. Interestingly enough,
Bill Katz and Linda Sternberg Katz have just produced a substantive new
bibliography on "secular" self-help titles: Self-Help: 1400 Best Books
on Personal Growth (R. R. Bowker Co., 1985). Because they specifically
exclude religious titles, however, their book and the present work are
complementary rather than overlapping in the material they cover.

Healing Faith, then, attempts to fill a very real gap in this literature. Christian self-help books, by their very nature, bring theological attitudes to bear on such a wide range of practical problems in
daily life that to become familiar with them is to get a good overview of
the Christian faith and its grass-roots influence on American society.
Their popularity with general readers, then, while clearly important, is
but one of many reasons to explore perspectives they have to offer.

C. SCOPE OF THE PRESENT WORK

"Christian self-help." At first glance, the concept seems built on
a massive internal contradiction: the image of a comfortable, self-serving
kind of faith in which God is "used" by His "believers" for their own
autonomous ends. Indeed, such a strain does run through much popular
Christian literature and frequently has been analyzed, in the context of
its historical antecedents, by scholars in the field. (See, for example,
Roy M. Anker's discussion-cum-bibliographic essay , "Popular Religion
and Theories of Self-Help," in which he examines the characteristically
American tension between worldly success and personal piety, from its
roots in colonial Puritan society, where economic success was considered
desirable but entailed the obligation of responsible stewardship, to
more contemporary manifestations [Norman Vincent Peale, Robert H. Schuller],
in which God's power is sometimes viewed as little more than a vehicle
for success, often seen as an end in itself.[4]) A number of titles annotated in these pages do, indeed, reflect this latter attitude; other
entries, however, suggest a very different interpretation of what "Christian self-help" might actually mean.

If one understands the Christian message to be embodied in the two
central commandments,--to love God with all of one's heart, soul, and
mind, and to love one's neighbor as oneself--one accepts an enormous
challenge: namely, how to reach a level where one begins to be capable
of such a humanly "impossible" sort of love. Christian self-help books,
at their best, seek to guide the reader on his or her path toward just
such a goal: to become grounded in an understanding and love of God, in
the person of Jesus Christ, and then, in this context, to grow into a
redeemed integrity, a new ability to bring reconciliation into personal
and family relationships, and a new concern with problems and suffering
in the wider community. This pattern is conceived, for instance, by the
ecumenical Church of the Saviour in Washington, D.C., where emphasis is
equally placed on the "journey inward" and the "journey outward." It is,
in addition, the theological context in which this bibliography (if not
every book it contains) is also conceived.

The title--Healing Faith--suggests, on the one hand, the value of
religious faith in coping with personal / social difficulties, and, on
the other, that faith itself, as it has sometimes been understood, can
also be enriched--its occasionally neurotic distortions "healed"--by

insights of modern psychology. The bibliography brings together a selection of Christian books published in America since 1970 that represent a broad range of theological perspectives and that, in very general terms, can be seen to serve a self-help function: by exploring spiritual psychodynamics; by suggesting guidelines for Christian living in a variety of developmental and family circumstances; and by offering encouragement and counsel to those wishing to move into areas of Christian social action, according to the mandates of their faith as they perceive it. Most of the titles are straight books of advice and guidance, some are personal narratives by individuals who have undergone crisis experiences and wish to share what they have learned, still others might more strictly be termed devotional works or books on spirituality. In these latter cases, however, titles with an essentially psychodynamic (rather than doctrinal) approach have been favored. Books on Bible study or theological reflection are included only when a central purpose is to explore modes of concrete response to dilemmas of daily living and when the topics covered fit naturally into the thematic sequence of the bibliography itself. All annotated entries are appropriate for the general reader; some titles may be aimed toward professionals as well, but in such cases the style is not restrictive. Books for pastors or counselors that are clearly intended only for this audience—books, for instance, on counseling techniques to be used in the office setting or on service projects to be implemented as part of formal church programs—have been left out.

Inclusion of a title does not necessarily constitute a recommendation; it does indicate that the theological viewpoint expressed by the author reflects a key stance in the Christian community today: fundamentalist, conservative evangelical, neo-evangelical, charismatic, or liberal. Very broadly speaking, the most conservative titles tend to be grounded (explicitly or implicitly) in the belief that a conscious choice to receive Christ as savior must precede any redemptive growth; from there, they generally move on to offer behavioral and attitudinal guidelines for daily living, frequently taken from Paul's epistles to the early churches. This advice is often quite precisely detailed, verging, in the less sensitive books, on a kind of new legalism. At the same time deeper, more intimate personal feelings may be viewed with a kind of distrust, as forces to be mastered and controlled rather than explored in growing toward integration and understanding. The preference, therefore, is often for cognitive and behavioral therapeutic techniques rather than for approaches that draw on the insights of depth psychology; analogously, directive methods are favored over client-centered ones.

The very liberal titles, in contrast, emphasize faith as a process. Words like "journey" and "story" tend to predominate words like "plan" or "design," and biblical passages are cited, if at all, to illustrate a point already made rather than as justification for making it in the first place. Christ is viewed as the embodiment of God's love—a love accessible to all people rather than to only those who have made a conscious decision to accept Him as savior. There is a greater tolerance for ambiguity, an expectation that faith and doubt may coexist side by side. The preference is often for Jungian approaches to psychodynamics and considerable use is made of tools like Ira Progoff's intensive journal. Finally, detailed behavioral instructions given by Paul to the early churches tend to be seen as culturally specific rather than permanently binding.

Between these two extremes one sometimes finds books in which a
genuine effort is made to integrate an orthodox understanding of the biblical message with an openness to all schools of psychology, depth psychology as well as directive, behavioral approaches as well as those more
introspective. My own preference, I should acknowledge, is often for
titles like these in which the author struggles honestly and openly with
the tensions between orthodox faith, on the one hand, and psychological
insights, on the other, and, in particular, seeks to use psychological
principles to facilitate growth consistent with the entire range of Jesus's
teachings.

There is, of course, yet another category of "Christian" books:
those issued by denominational publishers and written by theologians or
pastors/counselors but which make virtually no mention of God or faith
in their discussions, resting instead on psychological theory, pure and
simple. A related category includes popular titles (like those by Leo
Buscaglia) and more theoretical ones (like James W. Fowler's Stages of
Faith) which treat spirituality in general terms without explicit reference to Christian doctrine. Books like these have usually been excluded,
since this bibliography explores ways in which Christianity and psychology openly intersect each other. On rare occasions such a book is included because it addresses a topic of practical importance in human living
(choosing and adjusting to a nursing home, for example) which was not
readily covered in the more explicitly Christian works. Sometimes, too,
a theologically eclectic author is included because he or she represents
an ecumenical institution of influence in the Christian community.

Most of the titles selected were listed as being in print in the
1983-84 edition of Books in Print (BIP)--87 percent, to be precise. Those
not so listed, and published prior to 1983, are marked "o.p." at the end
of the citation. Since the bibliography is intended as a research tool
as well as for librarians making selection decisions, out-of-print titles
are included to show representative views on a variety of issues, even if
the books cannot be currently purchased. It is interesting to see where,
in some cases, a sudden run of "o.p." designations suggests that a certain
subject may have been quite fashionable a short time ago yet today is
somewhat passe. The first section of Chapter One offers an example of
this where several listed titles explore transactional analysis from a
Christian perspective; most are now out of print, yet less than a decade
ago, this topic was obviously all the rage. Thus even in the short
fifteen-year span covered by the bibliography it is possible to see something of the ebb and flow of interest in special subjects.

Many titles, of course, are still in print, but today exist as different editions from those originally seen by the compiler. In cases
like these, discrepancies between 1983-84 BIP entries and copies examined
in the library are briefly noted in the citations. Minor variations in
pagination may also exist in cases where the book was examined in galley
format prior to publication.

To aid in the acquisition of titles through interlibrary loan, OCLC,
LC and ISBN numbers are provided. When the examined edition was not on
OCLC's data base, the OCLC number for an alternate edition of the same
title is instead given. A key to various elements of a typical entry
is provided at the end of the Preface.

Finally, given authors' affiliations reflect situations and activities at the time the book was written and do not necessarily correspond to present circumstances.

D. METHODOLOGY

The bibliography is clearly selective, and the final decision on which titles to include was preceded by a lengthy search. First, about 4,000 possible candidates were identified on the basis of reviews and publishers' ads/announcements appearing between 1970 and 1984 in Library Journal, Publishers Weekly, Booklist, Kirkus, Religious Book Review (in its various incarnations), and Church and Synagogue Libraries. Additional resources were also randomly used: Christian periodicals reflecting a variety of theological positions (Sojourners; Christianity Today); assorted issues of Christian Bookseller; exploratory walks down the aisles of Christian bookstores and divinity school libraries; and personal familiarity with several hundred books previously examined in connection with reviewing activities for Library Journal.

The next step was to seek out the most promising titles judged on the basis of annotations and reviews already seen (if any), implications of the title and subtitle, subject matter covered, and identity of the author; some 1,500 books were examined and considered at this stage of the process--in bookstores, divinity school libraries, and the Library of Congress. Not until this investigation had been completed was the final selection of the 723 titles listed here actually made. Of the annotations themselves, 13 percent originally appeared in whole or in part as reviews I wrote for Library Journal between 1979 and 1984. The remaining 87 percent are published here for the first time.

Selection criteria were as follows: that the author attempt to bring Christian doctrine (conservative or liberal) explicitly into the discussion; that the book cover a topic relevant to the subject at hand; that it be accessible to and appropriate for the general reader; and that, if a range of other titles on the same subject was readily available, the work make some new contribution in terms of method or approach or be written by a noteworthy author whose views deserved representation. There were, of course, some final trade-offs. For example, a book dealing with a topic otherwise inadequately covered was occasionally included even though its theological discussion was minimal, and in two or three instances titles discovered through publishers' ads just before the annotations went to press were used even though the books themselves were not yet available for direct examination. Exceptions to the regular guidelines are noted in the annotations.

Inevitably, in a work like this, there are bound to be some unfortunate omissions. As an illustrative case, consider the topic of abusive behavior in families. One title on abusive marriages, Turning Fear to Hope by Holly Wagner Green, scheduled for publication in November 1984 by Thomas Nelson, would certainly have been included except that it crossed my desk in galley format one week after the annotations had already gone to press. Two other titles also appeared promising: Marie Fortune's Sexual Violence: The Unmentionable Sin (Pilgrim, 1983), and Margaret O. Hyde's Sexual Abuse: Let's Talk about It (Westminster, 1984). Since I was unable to obtain copies of either title in any bookstore or library and because it was

unclear from the write-ups whether they would actually have satisfied all
criteria for inclusion, neither appears in the bibliography. One example
of a related title which I did see, but ultimately rejected, is Christine
Comstock Herbruck's Breaking the Cycle of Child Abuse (Winston, 1979).
This work, while excellent, turned out to be geared mainly toward the
professional counselor, sharing case material from Parents Anonymous groups.
Moreover, since its perspective was not explicitly theological, it failed
to qualify on two separate counts.

Sometimes the year of publication alone was enough to exclude a title
that would otherwise have been an ideal choice. For instance, Charlie
Shedd's well-known books of counsel, Letters to Karen and Letters to Philip,
were both originally published in the late 1960s and therefore do not
appear. The same is true of his excellent book on sex education for teens,
The Stork Is Dead. In a few instances where a book has been substantially
rewritten and issued as an essentially new work, exceptions to the 1970
cutoff date have been made. The later edition is included in the annotations with a note indicating that the original version appeared prior
to 1970.

E. ORGANIZATION

The bibliography is organized into three chapters. The first, "Spiritual Psychodynamics," deals with books that seek to relate Christianity
and psychology explicitly to one another or that offer guidance for mental
health or a deeper spiritual life. These are titles whose topic is,
broadly speaking, the individual psyche or soul in relation to itself and
to God, rather than relationships in the context of family or community
life. Chapter Two, "Family and Developmental Issues," brings together
works that discuss experiences characteristic of different stages of the
life cycle or arising in the challenges of family living. Chapter Three,
"In the Wider Community," presents titles that offer guidance in extending
Christian relationships beyond the realm of nuclear family and personal
friendship and in becoming actively involved with the wider world. These
three areas of living, considered sequentially, thus trace a course that
might naturally be followed in a process of spiritual deepening, with
healing and transformation on the individual level facilitating more
loving relationships with family members and close friends and, ultimately,
leading to a deeper involvement with the whole "family of God."

In each of these main categories, books are further subdivided according to their specific subjects. In Chapter One we have, first, "Psychological Theories and Therapies," titles that tilt toward the theoretical
as their authors (many of whom are active both in self-help writing and
in more scholarly pursuits) explore ways to integrate Christianity with
the broad discipline of psychology, or with particular theoretical or
therapeutic approaches. The next division confronts "Self-Image and
Success," while the third, "Emotions, Sin and Guilt," offers advice on
working with difficult emotions (especially anger), with feelings of
guilt, and with the reality of sin. "Psychological Disturbances, Addictions and Pain" is the most explicitly "clinical" section, presenting
works of counsel or experiential narratives on coping with disorders like
severe anxiety, schizophrenia, depression, alcohol or drug addiction;
this category closes with several titles on the general problem of suffering.

"Varieties of Prayer" concerns psychodynamics in the individual's prayer life as well as particular techniques and styles of prayer,--meditation, contemplation, prayer for inner healing--while "Inner Exploration and Wholeness" includes works on journaling, introspection, dreamwork, the use of spiritual direction, and dynamics of personal integrity. Finally, "Conversion and Personal Spirituality" presents titles that explore the "human side" of Christian doctrine, often with a "how to do it" approach: how to be born again, for example, or how to seek Baptism in the Spirit. These are really works of "applied spirituality" in the sense that they incorporate doctrines of faith into daily life.

By far the longest part of the bibliography, Chapter Two's "Family and Developmental Issues," takes a generally chronological approach to the issues covered, in the order that they might be faced over the life cycle. Thus, the opening section contains books of spiritual/psychological guidance for "Pre-teens, Adolescents, and College-Age Youth." (Books for younger children are grouped later under the heading "The Growing Child," presuming parental involvement in the titles' selection, use, or both·) Next come works on "Being a Man, Being a Woman," which discuss various Christian perspectives on male and female identities and roles in general terms, apart from the specific context of marriage.

"From Loneliness to Intimacy" includes books on the dynamics of relationship building,--again in general terms rather than within a context of committed partnership--with particular attention to techniques for conflict resolution and communication and for strengthening the capacity to forgive and to care. "Singles, Sexuality and Forming Commitments" brings together books on single living and romantic/sexual issues, prior to or leading up to marriage. This section also includes books written for homosexual individuals who are struggling to cope with this orientation. Works on homosexuality in a family member or as a focus of social concern are examined later.

The universe of books on marriage and family living is so enormous that it is nearly overwhelming. To get a handle on the potential chaos, the whole subject was broken down into broadly developmental themes. Thus, "Marriage and Marriage Dynamics" concerns the marital relationship per se: the early years, sexuality, roles of husband and wife vis-a-vis one another, communication skills, and some "special situations" that can arise such as marriage to a pastor, religiously mixed marriage, or marriage to a nonbeliever. The next heading, "Family Planning, Pregnancy and Childbirth," seems fairly self-evident, though it should be noted that works on out-of-wedlock pregnancy are included here too. "Being a Parent" covers childrearing from the mother's or father's perspective: attitudes and parenting styles that might be called for at different stages of the whole process, such as in rearing small children, in rearing teens, and even , at the other end of the spectrum , in being an in-law. Taking a slightly different approach to similar issues, "The Growing Child" contains books that explore children's needs or developmental potential in terms of the child's own perspective and experience: a child's need for help with feelings, with starting school, sex education, religious training, handling money, and so on. As mentioned earlier, some of the books included here are written specifically for young children themselves, though parental involvement is assumed either in selection, use, or both.

"Special Situation Parenting" contains books on rearing strong-willed children, handicapped children, adopted or foster children, etc., while "Styles of Family Life" presents titles that deal with the configuration and dynamics of family living in its entirety: role relationships among the various members (emphasized by conservatives), family life as a school-house for nurturing social responsibility (emphasized by liberals), dual career families, styles of handling money, and so on. Next are books on "Facing Crisis" in the family: problems with troubled children, run-away teens; drug addiction, cult involvement, or pregnancy; abusive activity; mental disturbance or suicide in family members; and, finally, marital problems of a serious nature, including adultery and estrangement. Di-vorce is covered in "Divorce, Single Parenting, and Remarriage," along with works on forming new partnerships and coping effectively with newly blended families.

We leave the realm of family dynamics, temporarily, in the next section, "Health and Illness." These books are generally similar to some of the titles in Chapter One, since they deal with personal health in its own right rather than in terms of the family constellation, but because of the link between serious illness and the crisis of facing death (covered in the conclusion of Chapter Two) it seemed appropriate to group them there. They are followed by titles on coping "When a Loved One Dies" and by works on "Mid-life, Aging, and Facing Death."

We come, finally, to Chapter Three, "In the Wider Community." The opening section, "Spirituality for Service," emphasizes books exploring the tensions between contemplation and action, between caring for others and caring for oneself: titles on prayer or spiritual reflection whose thrust is toward living as a servant, living more simply, or becoming spiritually prepared for a deeper involvement in issues of peace or social concern. "The World of Work," the next section, is included here because these books do, after all, deal with the world beyond the home, seeking in many cases to link spiritual priorities with one's personal vocation. "Toward a Wider Call" continues this same process but goes beyond job issues per se. This section presents works that guide the reader in identifying opportunities or aptitudes for personal ministry, and in affirming spiritual gifts and using them for the good of the whole fellow-ship.

"Evangelism and Discipling" brings together books on sharing one's faith with others and leading groups for prayer or Bible study, while "Dynamics of Fellowship" contains titles that deal with relationship building in the context of small fellowship groups or church life. Some of the works in this section describe specific congregations, such as the ecumenical Church of the Saviour in Washington, D.C., and the Peninsula Bible Church in Palo Alto, but they have been chosen not as guides for professionals leading church programs but rather because they illustrate so effectively fellowship dynamics that can arise in any gathering of believers.

"Counseling One Another" offers books of guidance for lay helpers, while "Toward a Simple Lifestyle" shares works that prod readers to shed "false securities" and to move into simpler, more vulnerable ways of living, with specific reference to issues of peace and social justice. "Living in Christian Community" is quite similar; here, however, the

books deal with dynamics specific to intentional religious residential
communities, shared living situations designed to embody "kingdom living"
on a small scale. Once again, several titles are included which are more
in the nature of illustrative case histories than straightforward "how
to" guides.

Because of the political nature of many of its titles, "Christian
Social Action" incorporates statements and attitudes that may, at times,
be openly hostile to other Christians who see things differently. (As a
case in point, see annotation 675 on Franky Schaeffer's Bad News for Modern
Man.) Opening with a few theoretical statements that illustrate conservative and liberal perspectives on social action in general, this final
section then brings together a variety of works addressing a range of
concerns. Homosexuality, pornography, abortion, the population problem,
world hunger, the housing and energy crises, racism, human rights, and,
of course, the threat of nuclear war and modes of peacemaking are but some
of the topics covered. Here probably more than anywhere else, the "self-
help" label admittedly gets stretched a good deal, at times beyond easy
recognition! The rationale for including these guides for social action
is that true self-fulfillment, for the Christian, seems to involve some
active concern for the wider community that transcends the purely personal.

I have made an effort to find books that stress the individual's
response to problems rather than titles that merely analyze issues on
the social or political level, though in a few cases it did seem necessary to include works that were almost entirely analytical, simply for
purposes of "showing the other side." For instance, innumerable books
are available, and several are annotated here, encouraging Christians to
become active in the anti-nuclear movement; in the interests of even-
handedness, in spite of its failure to offer guidelines for personal action, I have also included one by Francis Schaeffer and others, Who Is
for Peace?, which presents theological arguments for a strong nuclear
deterrent.

This brief overview suggests, I hope, something of the book's general
organization. Within each topical category, the arrangement of titles
has been designed to create a smooth narrative flow between annotations
and to juxtapose books with diverse theological views on similar subjects.
While this sacrifices the alphabetical sequence commonly found in bibliographic works, it will, hopefully, allow readers to appreciate more clearly
the patterns of theological and psychological debate unfolding in Christian self-help literature today.

The reader should understand that the thematic arrangement is not
intended to serve as a precise indexing device. At times it was a very
moot question as to where a particular title best belonged. Chapter
One, "Spiritual Psychodynamics," for instance, includes books on private
prayer and on personal spirituality, while Chapter Three, "In the Wider
Community," includes titles on prayer as a resource for community involvement and social service. Theoretically, books in the first category emphasize individual psychodynamics, while books in the second stress the
process of moving creatively into the public realm. Readers already
familiar with this literature, however, will surely realize that lines
like these simply cannot be clearly drawn. Specifically, what about those
titles that explore the creative tension between personal contemplation
and action in the world? By rights, they might go in either place,

depending on which aspect one chooses to emphasize. For the most part, though, they have been placed in Chapter Three, on the grounds that their overall thrust is toward a deeper involvement with others. Similar ambiguities arise in such overlapping categories as "Dynamics of Fellowship" and "Living in Community," or "Toward a Simple Lifestyle" and "Christian Social Action."

Then, too, some topics may be treated in more than one place, depending on the perspective from which a title approaches its subject. Take books on such crisis issues as drug abuse, homosexuality, or abortion, for instance. Works offering guidance to the individual caught in a personal struggle in one of these areas will likely be found in either Chapter One or Chapter Two, while those that approach the topic as a target for social action will be grouped in Chapter Three.

Quite obviously, a subject index was needed to located more precisely works on a given topic, and readers are urged to use this index actively in order to get a solid grasp on the material available. Author and title indexes are provided, too, with references to relevant Christian titles mentioned in the annotations by way of comparison as well as to the annotated entries themselves.

Because organization is by specific topic rather than by theological viewpoint, it will frequently happen that a conservative evangelical author may, for instance, be placed alongside one who is steeped in Jungian spirituality. The result is a kind of ongoing internal dialogue among the different ideological and doctrinal schools in today's very pluralistic Christian community. So often, it seems, Christians with different political or theological views tend to view each other with suspicion, distrust, or even outright hostility. By juxtaposing these alternative voices against each other, I hope that this bibliography can make some small contribution toward a time when Christians of differing views might come together more openly to hear one another's concerns, and to learn from one another's insights.

NOTES

1. William Griffin, brief review of Current Christian Books in his "Religious Books" column, Publishers Weekly, June 15, 1984, p. 48.
2. Susan Avallone, "Receptivity to Religion," Library Journal, October 15, 1984, pp. 1891-93.
3. Patty Campbell, "The Young Adult Perplex," Wilson Library Bulletin, June 1982, pp. 772-73.
4. Roy M. Anker, "Popular Religion and Theories of Self-Help," in Handbook of American Popular Culture, vol. 2, ed., M. Thomas Inge (Westport, Conn.: Greenwood, 1980), pp. 287-316.

ACKNOWLEDGMENTS

I wish to thank the many people who helped make this bibliography a reality. First, I am most grateful to Anneliese Schwarzer, Associate Editor,
The Book Review, Library Journal, for her many helpful comments and suggestions and for her deeply valued support and friendship.

Gai Carpenter, Director of Hampshire College's Harold Johnson Library,
kindly gave me permission to use the computer terminal in gaining access
to OCLC numbers and other bibliographic data, and everyone there with
whom I worked was unfailingly cheerful and helpful.

The background research for this project would have been quite impossible were it not for the gracious cooperation of the managers and
salespeople in numerous Christian bookstores in Massachusetts, Maine,
Connecticut, New Jersey, and the Washington, D.C. area, all of whom let
me browse through their material for hours and even days at a time.

Mary R. Sive, Acquisitions Editor at Greenwood Press, and Michelle
Aucoin, Assistant Production Editor, have been consistently thoughtful
and helpful, and I give them many thanks.

My thanks, too, to the Reverend David McDowell, Pastor of College
Church in Northampton, Massachusetts, for offering several useful suggestions regarding the Preface, and to my good friend Karen Gale for
sharing thoughts on promising titles in the project's early stages.

Friends and colleagues at the West Springfield Public Library and
the Forbes Library in Northampton have been very patient with my over-
worked condition and my overcrowded schedule, for which I am most appre-
ciative.

I am grateful, also, to Elise Bruml, her husband Gary Burtless, and
their son Andrew, special friends who opened their home to me so that I
might have a base of operation while working at the Library of Congress.

My typist, Mary Kansog, was indefatigable; she truly gave of herself
to this project at a time when she was under enormous pressure in other
areas of her life.

Finally, I appreciate more than I can say, all of the support, on so
many different levels, which my parents extended to me during this time.

ABBREVIATIONS AND
ENTRY ELEMENTS

Standard abbreviations used in bibliographic citations are as follows:

bibliog(s). = bibliography(ies)   o.p. = out of print
BIP = Books in Print   p. = pages
ed(s). = edition(s); edited   pap. = paperbound
illus. = illustrations; illus-   photogs. = photographs
   trated   rev. ed. = revised edition
introd. = introduction   tr. = translated

Two-letter postal abbreviations for the states
are used in the citations.

Possible elements of an entry are as follows:

Author. Title: subtitle. Place of publication: Publisher (Series,
if any), date. Pagination. Miscellaneous information (e.g., photographs or illustrations; bibliography; notes; index; etc.). LC
number. ISBN number. OCLC number. "pap." if edition cited is
paperbound. (Information re other BIP entries or discrepancies
between 1983-84 BIP entry and edition actually examined). ("o.p."
if the title was out of print according to the 1983-84 edition of
BIP).

Occasionally in an annotation cross-reference may be given to another title which is itself included in the bibliography. On such
occasions, the parenthetical phrase "see annotation" is frequently
used to direct the reader to the Author/Title Indexes, and thence
to the title in question.

HEALING FAITH

1.
SPIRITUAL
PSYCHODYNAMICS

A. PSYCHOLOGICAL THEORIES AND THERAPIES

001. Narramore, Bruce and John D. Carter. The integration of psychology
   and theology. Grand Rapids, MI: Zondervan (Rosemead Series), 1979.
   139p. bibliog. notes. index. LC 79-16125. ISBN 0-310-30341-9. OCLC
   5126275. pap.
Aimed at professionals, but included because of Narramore's extensive work
in popular Christian self-help writing, this explores possibilities for
the integration of psychology and theology. It examines barriers (anti-
pathy to biblical absolutes among psychoanalytic, Rogerian, existentialist
and behavioral thinkers), the scope of possible integration, some models
of how the two fields intersect ("against," "of," "parallels" and "integrates" models), and suggestions for future directions.

002. Collins, Gary R. The rebuilding of psychology: an integration of psychology and Christianity. Wheaton, IL: Tyndale, 1977. 211p. bibliog.
   notes. index. LC 76-47299. ISBN 0-8423-5315-1. OCLC 7855074. pap.
A clinical psychologist with theological training at a Baptist seminary
surveys difficulties currently confronting the discipline of psychology
(overspecialization, fragmentation, dubious methodology, etc.) and propo-
ses as solution a specifically theistic psychology, grounded in Christian
faith and a belief in the Bible as God's unique revelation. Collins urges
that "raw" natural data be viewed in the light of faith when drawing
conclusions, and while his book is clearly intended for professionals and
students, motivated general readers should be able to use it also.

003. Myers, David G. The human puzzle: psychological research and Christian belief. San Francisco: Harper/CAPS (with the Christian
   Association for Psychological Studies), 1978. 256p. notes. LC
   77-15873. ISBN 0-06-065558-5. OCLC 3710845. pap.
Myers, who is both a committed Christian and a professional psychologist,
does a good job of comparing and integrating biblical insights and current research findings that touch on controversial themes like the mind-
body relationship, the influence of attitudes on action and vice versa,
how superstitious thinking is related to prayer, and the problem of
human freedom. Believing that religious faith and the scientific method
can be fruitful partners provided each respects the other's domain, Myers

concludes that in most cases the implications of the two perspectives are mutually compatible; still, he does not shy away from facing threatening contradictions when these emerge (as in his discussion on prayer). Lucid and engaging.

004. Heaney, John J., ed. Psyche and spirit: readings in psychology and religion. Revised ed. New York: Paulist, 1984. 252p. bibliog. notes. LC 83-63111. ISBN 0-8091-2610-9. pap.
While designed for use in courses on the psychology of religion, this is included because of the excellent overview it offers into a cross-section of efforts at bringing Christianity and psychology into dialogue. Excerpts from the writings of Freud, Kung, Fromm, Vitz, Fowler, Jung, Maslow and others are topically arranged according to issues addressed (of ego psychology, self psychology, and theology). Heaney's goal is to help readers understand the nature of psychological and theological approaches to religion and to gain insight for personal development.

005. Stern, E. Mark and Bert G. Marino. Psychotheology. New York: Paulist, 1973. 146p. LC 79-128142. ISBN 0-8091-1782-7. OCLC 89736. pap. (1970 ed. examined).
Billed by the publishers as a "how to grow" book based on the psychological challenge of Jesus, this argues that despite some apparent contradictions, Christianity and psychology actually speak in the same voice, and that "the individuation of God takes place through Christ in us" as barriers are removed. Discusses human freedom and development, sin, implications of the Incarnation for human consciousness, love, identity, time, authority, and sins of authority. Strongly influenced by Jungian theory.

006. Sall, Millard J. Faith, psychology and Christian maturity. Grand Rapids, MI: Zondervan, 1977. 181p. bibliog. index. LC 74-25354. ISBN 0-310-32431-9. OCLC 1676043. pap. (o.p.).
For the "knowledgeable layman," this discusses what psychology and the Bible, respectively, teach about human nature, then proceeds to harmonize the two views. Touches on issues of ego and ego development, value formation, anxiety, and identity, showing how Christianity advocates a "balanced" life, healing the wounded ego but rejecting pride. Very practical in its implications, stressing that psychotherapy is a fine resource when needed and seeking to reassure readers that using professional help is compatible with their faith. At the conservative end of the spectrum, theologically.

007. McLemore, Clinton W. The scandal of psychotherapy: a guide to resolving the tensions between faith and counseling. Wheaton, IL: Tyndale, 1982. 191p. illus. notes. LC 81-84288. ISBN 0-8423-5852-8. OCLC 8260210. pap.
A psychology professor at Fuller, Presbyterian in background, discusses the relationship between Christianity and psychotherapy in a book aimed mainly at mental health workers but also at lay readers. More an exploration of key questions than a set of packaged answers, this compares concepts of regeneration and mental health (the two don't always go together, and law-breaking can sometimes, in the short run at least, facilitate "mental health") and looks at psychotherapy itself vis-a-vis evangelism. Advocates an openness to all therapeutic schools (discussed individually) but underlines essential differences between the biblical focus on faith and the therapist's focus on personality.

008. Peck, M. Scott. The road less traveled: a new psychology of love, traditional values and spiritual growth. New York: Touchstone-Simon and Schuster, 1980. 316p. illus. notes. LC 79-15410. ISBN 0-671-25067-1. OCLC 5101604. pap. (1978 ed. examined).
Organized into four sections--on discipline, love, growth/religion and grace--this offers thoughts drawn from Peck's psychiatric practice on the nature of spiritual growth as an integral part of full mental development. Emphasizes the process by which such growth occurs over a lifetime, and how hidden religious beliefs about God (and even disbelief) can be influential. While certainly not evangelical,--it was written just before Peck became a Christian--this still emphasizes that growth is always assisted by a force that transcends conscious will, regardless of our personal concepts. Includes illustrative clinical material.

009. Larson, Bruce. No longer strangers. Waco, TX: Key Word-Word, 1976. 145p. LC 74-146675. ISBN 0-87680-827-5. OCLC 130685. pap. (1971 ed. examined).
A presentation for the general reader of "relational theology" and its implications, this explores the importance of effective communication and a vulnerable, affirmative style in one's relationships with God, with one's inner self, with "significant others," and with the world at large. A good introduction to the "relational Christianity" movement which emphasizes mutual ministry and advocates "discovering" Christ with other people rather than simply "bringing" Him to them. Larson, a Presbyterian minister and former president of Faith at Work, also describes his approach in The relational revolution (Word, 1976).

010. Vitz, Paul C. Psychology as religion: the cult of self-worship. Grand Rapids, MI: Eerdmans, 1977. 149p. notes. indexes. LC 77-3403. ISBN 0-8028-1696-7. OCLC 2818016. pap.
A psychology professor argues that psychology has become a religion in itself, a form of "secular humanism based on worship of the self." Excludes experimental psychology, behaviorism, psychoanalysis and transpersonal theory from the discussion to focus on schools emphasizing "the self": especially theories of Fromm, Rogers, Maslow and May. The critique includes the argument that "selfism" is bad science (we aren't intrinsically that good) and that it has been destructive of family relations and social responsibility. A look, too, at opportunities for Christianity as an alternative, including some thoughts on Christian politics.

011. Kilpatrick, William Kirk. Psychological seduction. Nashville, TN: Thomas Nelson, 1983. 239p. bibliog. notes. LC 83-12151. ISBN 0-8407-5843-X. OCLC 9644652. pap. (also cloth).
Kilpatrick argues that psychology--by which he really means the self-centered thrust of certain "pop psych" schools--constitutes a new religion in competition with Christianity, and he examines ethical/attitudinal problems it raises such as an amoral emphasis on self-esteem, excessive avoidance of pain, etc. His writing is so graceful and his arguments so convincing one is tempted to forget what he fails to stress, namely that many psychological theories (e.g., of Jung, Erikson) can actually nurture spirituality. One-sided, but extremely well done, with specific discussion on the burden involved in deifying the self, ways a permissive self-acceptance can be destructive, cross-cultural evidence of people's intuitive knowledge that rebirth is necessary, and "secular temptations" that are making in-roads into the Christian community.

012. Bobgan, Martin and Deidre Bobgan. The psychological way/the spiritual
     way. Minneapolis:Bethany House, 1979. 219p. notes. index. LC 79-17884.
     ISBN 0-87123-026-7. OCLC 5239751. pap.
The Bobgans, who are active in education and counseling and co-direct a
counseling ministry, claim that secular psychotherapy has become a religious belief system antagonistic to Christianity; it consists of man-made
techniques, whereas the Bible, God's revelation, contains all the guidance
needed to deal with nonorganically caused mental-emotional disorders.
Moving from a general critique of psychotherapy, they proceed to examine
and criticize popular therapeutic schools one by one (psychoanalysis,
scream therapy, est, TA, client centered therapy, etc.). A central goal
is to help lay people decide how to deal with their own problems; at the
extreme conservative end of the spectrum.

013. Price, Eugenia. Leave your self alone. Grand Rapids, MI: Zondervan,
     1982. 127p. LC 79-16461. ISBN 0-310-31431-3. OCLC 5171663. pap.
With the flood of self-help books on the market, says Price, it is all too
easy to become mired in the "paralysis of analysis." She advocates instead putting ourselves and our circumstances into God's hands, focusing
on Him and on others and, as much as possible, letting oneself alone.
Chapters deal with ways of taking this approach vis-a-vis past and future
experiences, prayer, conversation, adversity, illness, grief, and transitions.

014. Hulme, William E. Your potential under God: resources for growth.
     Minneapolis, MN: Augsburg, 1978. 158p. notes. LC 77-84092. ISBN
     0-8066-1618-0. OCLC 3771759. pap. (also cloth). (o.p.).
Pastoral counselor Hulme visited a number of humanistic growth institutions
and movements on the West Coast. Rather than a specific critique, he
offers here a description of how growth occurs, as he sees it, within
Christianity (God's grace breaking through our sin and psychological obstacles) and touches, where relevant, on similarities or differences between this process and the processes facilitated by movements like Gestalt,
est, TM, Silva Mind Control, etc.

015. Larson, Roland S. and Doris Larson. Values and faith: value-clarifying
     exercises for family and church groups. Minneapolis, MN: Winston,
     1976. 255p. illus. bibliog. LC 76-9549. ISBN 0-03-018046-5. OCLC
     8583265. pap.
Organized according to the broad themes of valuing one's faith, one's
family, one's self/gifts, others, and old/new truths, this offers practical
exercises to help people formulate their beliefs and integrate attitudes
with behavior. The context is explicitly Christian; the aim is to explore
areas of uncertainty or struggle as well as who Christ is and what He means
in daily living. Includes prayer and resources from the Bible as well as
exercises/games.

016. Walter, James Lynwood. Body and soul: gestalt therapy and religious
     experience. Nashville, TN: Abingdon, 1971. 208p. bibliog. index.
     LC 74-148077. ISBN 0-687-03634-8. OCLC 146192. (o.p.).
For professionals and "seekers" alike, this attempts to relate the bibli-
cal/ancient Hebrew view of personhood (in which spirit and body are fully
integrated, not intended to be dualistically divided) to the contemporary
emphasis in Gestalt therapy on naturalism and holism. Theological concepts are sometimes viewed metaphorically (e.g., in discussing the "creation myth") as Walter explores change and growth, death and rebirth, sex-

uality and spirituality, and moving beyond utopianism. Appendixes contain statements from Perls, Maslow, and others.

017. Skousen, Max B. Christianity and est. Marina del Rey, CA: DeVorss &
     Co., 1978. 176p. LC 77-91635. ISBN 0-87516-250-9. OCLC 4499386. (o.p.).
The author, who took the "est" training in 1976, argues here that the essential messages of Christianity and of "est" are quite similar (the need
to be transformed), but that Christianity has not been able to fulfill its
potential because the nature of and need for this transformation has been
improperly understood. The bulk of the book is a rather esoteric interpretation of Christianity and scriptural passages which will probably
interest est advocates but may offend (or just plain bewilder) traditional
Christians.

018. Bontrager, John Kenneth. Free the child in you: take an adventure
     into joyful living through Transactional Analysis. Philadelphia:
     Pilgrim, 1974. 192p. illus. bibliog. LC 73-22120. ISBN 0-8298-0272-X.
     OCLC 796982. (o.p.).
A rather superficial attempt to "transactionalize" Christianity by arguing
that one of Jesus' main attractions was His "I'm OK-You're OK" position:
his "Adult" effectively filtered out undesirable "Parent" messages, allowing his "Natural Child" to become liberated and free. Bontrager spends
much time citing Scriptures and parables to prove his point (writing off
some of the "hard sayings" on the grounds that Jesus had not yet properly
transcended the inner "Parent" when he spoke such words). Closes with
advice on applying TA in church, home, and community.

019. Batey, Richard A. Thank God I'm OK: the Gospel according to T.A.
     Nashville, TN: Abingdon, 1976. 112p. illus. notes. index. LC
     76-14358. ISBN 0-687-41389-3. OCLC 2224978. (o.p.).
Another attempt to integrate the methods and theory of Transactional Analysis with the Gospel. Batey compares the New Testament message of freedom with TA's emphasis on growing beyond original "not-OK" feelings: in
both cases one needs to transcend legalism (only "OK if...") and attain an
"Adult" faith realization that grace is real, God is love (Christianity),
thus updating "Parent law" and freeing the "Natural Child" (TA). More
clear and straightforward than Bontrager, with less defensive-sounding
theological justification. Still, the message is essentially the same,
with seemingly little attention paid to any need for hard work or self-
discipline as one grows into "Kingdom living."

020. Reuter, Alan. Who says I'm OK?: a Christian use of Transactional Ana-
     lysis. St. Louis, MO: Concordia, 1974. 125p. illus. notes. LC 74-13756.
     ISBN 0-570-03187-7. OCLC 984166. (o.p.).
Compared to other TA books, this has more of a simple "how to" emphasis
than Bontrager's, say, and seems much more oriented to working with the
full Gospel message. Of course we are guilty, Reuter says (e.g., guilt
feelings are not just parental scripting), but we need not remain so: once
the "Adult" understands the Gospel, a new identity is possible via repentance, confession, and forgiveness. This basie message is presented with
helpful charts, questions for reflection, illustrative biblical passages,
and examples from Christian and secular literature (C. S. Lewis, Shakespeare)
that make the text ideal for the general reader. Reuter's conclusion: TA
can be very useful as a tool, but when it is offered as a kind of total
salvation, it compromises Christianity.

021. Murphree, Jon Tal. When God says you're OK: a Christian approach to
   Transactional Analysis. Downers Grove, IL: InterVarsity, 1975. 130p.
   notes. LC 75-21452. ISBN 0-87784-716-9. OCLC 2330927. pap.
Of the many books integrating TA and Christianity, this is one of the most
faithful to the full Gospel message. Murphree, an evangelical counselor,
stresses that what is missing in TA is the dimension of a relationship with
God. When this context is added, the original conflicts between Parent/
Adult/Child can be resolved: confession by the Adult and acceptance of
God's forgiveness by the Child dissolves guilt, setting the Adult free from
the Parent's prejudicial attempts to control; thereafter the Child is free
to experience, and the Adult to understand, God's true nature. An interesting synthesis.

022. Umphrey, Marjorie and Richard Laird. Why don't I feel OK? Irvine, CA:
   Harvest House, 1977. 160p. bibliog. LC 77-24826. ISBN 0-89081-041-9.
   OCLC 3327151. pap. (o.p.).
Of the many books on TA and Christianity, this emphasizes, more than most,
concrete application and an analysis of how various unproductive styles of
Christian thinking or behavior can be unmasked by TA. Umphrey looks at
"scripts" that can be used to "program losers" (e.g., certain interpretations of "let go and let God"), plus "games Christians play," to avoid responsibility. She advocates daring to re-evaluate decisions, self-disclosure, and vulnerability, stressing that if one is in a right relationship
with God, rescripting will be fruitful, not subversive.

023. Kraft, William F. Achieving promises: a spiritual guide for the transitions of life. Philadelphia: Westminster, 1981. 131p. bibliog.
   LC 81-10496. ISBN 0-664-24384-3. OCLC 7573129. pap.
Kraft's newest book posits a theory of adult spiritual development which
draws on Erikson's concept of the life cycle (each stage contains a characteristic crisis offering the potential for deeper growth when courageous-
ly confronted) and Gail Sheehy's notion of specific adult "passages" within
marriage, work, child-rearing, aging, etc. Kraft's originality lies in his
emphasis on the healing potential of seemingly regressive situations;
rather than opting for the "normal madness" of psycho-social adjustment,
we can, in our pain, seek transcendence and a deeper relationship with God.
For spirituality collections in large public and seminary libraries.

024. Gleason, John J., Jr. Growing up to God: eight steps in religious development. Nashville, TN: Abingdon, 1975. 141p. notes. LC 74-17093.
   ISBN 0-687-15972-5. OCLC 1009737. pap. (o.p.).
While more professionally than popularly oriented, this is included because
it is one of the few titles seen working specifically with Eriksonian
theory and attempting to integrate his "eight stages" of human development
with religious faith. Stressing that each crisis of growth provides the
chance to incorporate a particular mode of faith on the experiential level,
Gleason also discusses cultural manifestations of faith (e.g., animism represents a focus on the first developmental period of trust vs. mistrust).
Certainly not a complete statement on the subject, but a start, at least.

025. Sanford, John A. The kingdom within: the inner meaning of Jesus' sayings. New York: Paulist, 1970. 226p. bibliog. notes. index. LC
   77-105548. ISBN 0-8091-2329-0. OCLC 10632936. pap.
Christianity, says Sanford, is often seen as primarily relevant to the social scene. Seeking to redress the balance, he explores here ways in which
Jesus' teachings are also deeply relevant to the inner life. Looking at

Jesus' own personality as the paradigm of wholeness in the Jungian sense,
he goes on to explore a number of teachings/parables on the nature of the
Kingdom, the cost of discipleship, our "inner pharisee" and "inner adver-
sary," the role of evil and sin (Satan/evil always seeks to destroy wholeness), and more. A landmark integration of Christianity and Jungian theory,
clearly stated.

026. Kelsey, Morton T. Christo-psychology. New York: Crossroad, 1982. xii,
     154p. illus. notes. LC 82-14888. ISBN 0-8245-0630-8. OCLC 8709491.
     pap.
Intended as a practical aid for people wishing to combine Christian insights with those of depth psychology, this surveys Freud's contributions
on ego development (a strong ego is needed for the spiritual pilgrimage
if one is not to become lost in the inner world), Jung's life and thought
(psychological types, the idea of individuation, dreams and archetypes,
the process of active imagination, etc.), and how Jungian concepts can be
integrated with Christian counterparts. Kelsey is an Episcopalian priest,
a marriage and family counselor, and shares aspects of his personal quest
as well as theoretical views. For serious lay readers and pastors/coun-
selors.

027. Miller, William A. Make friends with your shadow: how to accept and
     use positively the negative side of your personality. Minneapolis,
     MN: Augsburg, 1981. 142p. LC 80-67793. ISBN 0-8066-1855-8. OCLC
     8032656. pap.
Arguing that those who deny or repress their shadow side end up projecting
their own evil onto others or even being swallowed up by it, a supervisor
of clinical pastoral education and a Christian counselor discusses the
nature of the shadow (those collective traits not allowed as a recognized
part of the "persona"), its reflections in myth, Jesus as an advocate of
befriending one's shadow, the destructiveness of an innocence that cannot
recognize its own evil counterparts, the Pauline striving for righteousness
as essentially different from Jesus' way, the dynamics of projection, and
the shadow in relation to control, discovery, wholeness. Illustrative
anecdotes.

028. Littauer, Florence. Personality plus. Old Tappan, NJ: Revell, 1982.
     192p. illus. LC 82-10228. ISBN 0-8007-1323-0. OCLC 8533559.
Littauer deals with the four temperaments (choleric, sanguine, melancholy
and phlegmatic), stressing that every person is actually a blend and that
each particular temperament has its characteristic assets and liabilities.
The point is to identify one's own tendencies and then capitalize on the
strengths. In relationships, Littauer explains, opposites do attract, and
with Christ as catalyst, differences can be used creatively to nurture a
greater wholeness.

029. LaHaye, Tim. Transformed temperaments. Wheaton, IL: Tyndale, 1983, 1971.
     150p. LC 77-152120. ISBN 0-8423-7306-3. OCLC 156128. pap.
LaHaye's book Spirit-controlled temperament (Tyndale, 1966) introduced his
thinking on the four temperaments and their place in his conservative evangelical approach to psychology. This present book continues examining the
strengths and weaknesses of each type, using as models detailed portraits
of four representative biblical characters (Paul the Choleric, Moses the
Melancholy, etc.) and stressing how the types can become transformed when
they are "Spirit-filled." Some thoughts, too, on using the concept of
the types in one's own growth and development.

030. Sullivan, Barbara A. First born, second born. Lincoln, VA: Chosen-
    Zondervan, 1983. 156p. bibliog. index. LC 83-2011. ISBN 0-310-60381-1.
    OCLC 9323327. pap.
Based on research from secular psychology, the Bible, and experiences of
members of her own faith fellowship, Sullivan looks at ways birth order
may correlate with personality traits. Her tone is conversational, with
many illustrative cases, shared anecdotes, and biblical examples (e.g.,
Jacob as the typical second-born, inclined to spot weaknesses in the older
sibling). The aim is to foster self-acceptance and show how, once accepted,
weaknesses can be transformed into strengths.

031. Powell, John. Fully human, fully alive. Niles, IL: Argus, 1976. 189p.
    illus. LC 76-41586. ISBN 0-913592-77-3. OCLC 3011309. pap. (other
    eds.).
The popular priest/author discusses "vision therapy," closely linked to
Albert Ellis' rational-emotive therapy. Powell believes that emotional
reactions grow out of how we perceive reality; hence, emotional growth requires revision of faulty attitudes, recognition of how our perceptions
are defective, and serious efforts to correct them or round them out.
Stressing that God loves us unconditionally, Powell closes with a final
chapter integrating "vision therapy" with religious faith.

B.   SELF-IMAGE AND SUCCESS

032. Schuller, Robert H. Self-esteem: the new reformation. Waco, TX: Word,
    1982. 177p. illus. notes. LC 82-8356. ISBN 0-8499-0299-1. OCLC
    8452157.
Written more for religious communicators than as a straight self-help book,
this is still noteworthy for its explicit statement of the philosophy
underlying all of Schuller's writing. When reaching out to the "un-
churched," he says, it is better to focus on the human, felt needs of the
audience--for dignity and self-esteem, say--than to take a "theocentric"
approach. With this assumption, he looks at the Lord's Prayer as an expression of concern for peoples' human well-being.

033. Narramore, S. Bruce. You're someone special. Grand Rapids, MI: Zonder-
    van, 1980. 173p. notes. index. LC 78-5423. ISBN 0-310-30331-1. OCLC
    3844923. pap. (1978 ed. examined).
An evangelical psychologist argues that a healthy self-love is essential
since lack of it distorts one's God-concept. Narramore deals with hindrances to a good self-image and ways to work them through: by realizing
we cannot be perfect anyway, and that God's acceptance is never deserved
or earned but is freely offered in Christ. "Conviction" is simply God
bringing to our attention weaknesses we need to deal with, but not with
the intention we should become mired in guilt. The aim is to be surren-
dered fully to God's sovereignty and to live by His pattern, loving one
another and communicating a sense of mutual value.

034. Skoglund, Elizabeth. Loving begins with me. San Francisco: Harper,
    1979. x, 98p. notes. LC 78-3364. ISBN 0-06-673933-1. OCLC 5553740.
    (o.p.).
Psychologist Skoglund concentrates here on questions of self-image. A
sense of self-worth is important, she says, if we are to have a good relationship with God, and she stresses that responsible behavior is crucial
in building such a positive self-concept. Sympathetic to TA methods

("God says I'm OK" is the title of one chapter), she considers commandments
as guidelines to point us in the right direction, not standards to be
immediately achieved. Common sense in a spiritual vein.

035. Kinzer, Mark. The self-image of a Christian: humility and self-esteem.
     Ann Arbor, MI: Servant (Living as a Christian), 1980. 106p. ISBN
     0-89283-088-3. OCLC 7480647. pap.
One of the "Living as a Christian" series, this focuses on one aspect of
the self-image question: how Christ's words on humility have been dis-
torted to create, in many, a false humility that makes them doubt their
real worth. Actually, Kinzer argues, authentic Christian humility should
free us to act with "holy boldness" as we look at ourselves truthfully,
recognizing both strengths and weaknesses. Includes discussion of the
distinction between timidity and humility, Jesus as a model, and concrete
steps toward freedom in servanthood.

036. Baldwin, Stanley C. A true view of you. Ventura, CA: Regal, 1982.
     186p. notes. LC 81-84569. ISBN 0-8307-0779-4. OCLC 8176734. pap.
Baldwin suggests orienting oneself to God rather than comparing oneself
with others while building a self-concept, dealing with various put-downs
and failures, and working toward solid achievements. He also draws some
sensible distinctions between unhealthy pride and guilt, say, and their
more fruitful counterparts, self-esteem and constructive sorrow. The style
is friendly and informal as Baldwin shares both personal anecdotes and
experiences of others. An additional item for public, church libraries.

037. Osborne, Cecil G. The art of learning to love yourself. Grand Rapids,
     MI: Zondervan, 1976. 154p. notes. LC 76-23231. ISBN 0-310-30572-1.
     OCLC 2332047. pap.
Osborne's message is that all people need acceptance and loving experiences
to discover that God loves them; a sense of identity, the basis for healthy
self-love, comes with honest self-disclosure in caring relationships with
others. Explicitly Christian but very gentle and reassuring advice re
letting go of all guilt after honest repentance, developing the capacity
for authentic communication, and distinguishing real self-love from its
false counterparts. Sensible and useful.

038. Hoekema, Anthony A. The Christian looks at himself. Grand Rapids,
     MI: Eerdmans, 1975. 152p. bibliog. indexes. LC 75-1285. ISBN
     0-8028-1595-2. OCLC 1176722. pap.
Leaning toward the theoretical, this argues that Christianity does have
resources for building a positive self-image, since the Gospel emphasizes
the hope of redemption over the bleakness of the Fall. However, it is
necessary that people be continually transformed over time, since the
natural inclination is to fall back into habits of the "false self."
Hoekema offers some useful advice to those entrusted with training others
(especially parents); he advocates complete acceptance, freedom within
limits, and certain "Parent Effectiveness Training" techniques like active
listening, though he disagrees with PET's humanistic thrust.

039. Brownback, Paul. The danger of self-love: re-examining a popular myth.
     Chicago: Moody, 1982. 157p. notes. LC 82-12543. ISBN 0-8024-2068-0.
     OCLC 8628703. pap.
Though this is more theoretical than straight "self help," it is accessible
to the general reader, and its message is significantly different than most
put forth in other books on the question of self-image. Noting the em-

phasis placed on self-esteem in current evangelical writing, Brownback
argues that this runs counter to the thrust of scripture, which is actually
that we are to pay no attention to our self-image at all, one way or the
other. He argues, too, that an over-emphasis on God's love as unconditional errs in causing us to forget that even after justification, perform-
ance does matter (though God relates to us as Father, not as Judge). A
smattering of criticism toward Rogers, Fromm, Maslow, Adler, the "me generation," and those Brownback considers tainted evangelicals.

040. Peale, Norman Vincent. The positive principle today: how to renew
    and sustain the power of positive thinking. New York: Fawcett-Crest,
    1978. notes. LC 76-4068. ISBN 0-449-23260-3. OCLC 2048207. pap.
    (Prentice-Hall ed. examined).
Another variation on the positive thinking theme, this addresses the problem of how to keep the positive principle going in one's life over the
long haul, through the ups and downs. Twelve chapters present twelve
different guidelines toward this end ("Take a new look at that word 'impossible'" or "Let seven magic words change your life"). Innumerable inspirational anecdotes ("Janitor moves up," "Pilot's arm cut off") illustrate
how the techniques work--aided, of course, by prayer and "in-depth" faith.

041. Peale, Norman Vincent. Positive imaging: the powerful way to change
    your life. Old Tappan, NJ: Revell, 1982. 192p. LC 82-10179. ISBN
    0-8007-1278-1. OCLC 8533446.
One more variation on positive thinking, positive imaging consists of con-
sciously visualizing a desired goal till the image taps into unconscious
resources, coupled with prayer and thanks for success in advance of actual
attainment. Peale shares how he learned of the technique and his first
tentative attempts to use it, then discusses (with many examples) its
value for bolstering a shaky ego and conquering problems with finances,
loneliness, worry, doubt, lack of forgiveness, illness, etc.

042. Schuller, Robert H. You can become the person you want to be. Old
    Tappan, NJ: Spire-Revell, 1976. 160p. LC 72-7783. ISBN 0-8007-8235-6.
    pap. (also Dutton ed.).
Asking questions like whether a cerebral palsied quadriplegic can learn
to walk, Schuller answers with a resounding yes, offering readers an "in-
visible ladder" with which to climb up from despair and revive their dreams.
A standard Schuller pep-talk on setting goals, developing self-confidence,
eliminating fear of failure, and, generally, employing "possibility thinking" to maximum advantage.

043. Hart, Archibald D. The success factor. Old Tappan, NJ: Power-Revell,
    1984. 188p. illus. LC 83-23065. ISBN 0-8007-5138-8. OCLC 10147102.
    pap.
True success, says psychologist Hart (Fuller Theological Seminary) does
not mean achieving in every area (we all have some weaknesses) but rather
finding and fulfilling God's purpose for our lives with the art of "reality
thinking," an alternative to "positive thinking." Reality thinking begins
when we accept the "givens" of our lives. Discusses the nature and implications of reality thinking (it puts God in control), working with one's
mind via discipline and straight thinking, and using reality thinking to
control stress, the stream of thought, and destructive self-feelings. Very
clearly written, with occasional Scripture references to demonstrate specific points and helpful suggestions for reflective exercises; a common-sense
approach in the context of an essentially conservative biblical message.

044. Raines, Robert A. Success is a moving target. Waco, TX: Word, 1975.
152p. illus. notes. LC 75-10091. OCLC 1818136. (o.p.).
Objective goals, says Raines, may lose meaning as soon as we attain them;
likewise, God's will is not something external and pre-specified that we
must find and follow. Rather, as we grow and change (and make mistakes),
our "targets" shift, but God meets us wherever we are, especially in places
of brokenness. Here he explores, within this context, various dimensions
of "success": becoming a new creation, living corporate visions, becoming
more humane "losers" and "wounded healers."

045. Forbes, Cheryl. The religion of power. Grand Rapids, MI: Zondervan,
1983. 164p. LC 82-24711. ISBN 0-310-45770-X. OCLC 9110406.
Beginning with a look at how power is emphasized in "secular" self-help
books (e.g., Michael Korda), this goes on to discuss ways in which evangelical writing has also become contaminated by excessive stress on achievement. Many Christian books, says Forbes, seem to view God mainly as a
means toward personal wealth and power. She explores some behavioral areas
within which power plays are often camouflaged (e.g., sex or piety) and
looks at Jesus' and Paul's understanding of genuine spiritual power as
opposed to the world's way.

C. EMOTIONS, SIN AND GUILT

046. Baars, Conrad W. Feeling and healing your emotions. Plainfield, NJ:
Haven-Logos, 1979. iii, 277p. notes. index. LC 79-53629. ISBN
0-88270-510-5. OCLC 5943116. pap. (available through Bridge).
Baars, a psychiatrist, discusses the function and purpose of human emotions
in the context of a spiritual dimension. The text is in question/answer
format (lengthy responses to brief questions) and addresses topics like
"the feeling revolution," or "emotions: man's psychic motors," with specific sections as well on anger, forgiveness, repression, and such commonly
discussed themes. Considerable space is devoted to theologically oriented
speculation--humane vs. "utilitarian" emotions, the role of free will vis-
a-vis the emotions, etc. The language is sometimes less than clear, though
this is aimed at general readers.

047. Roberts, Robert C. Spirituality and human emotion. Grand Rapids, MI:
Eerdmans, 1982. ix, 134p. bibliog. LC 82-13774. ISBN 0-8028-1939-7.
OCLC 8826560. pap.
This "exercise in therapeutic Christian reflection" aims to help readers
experience desired emotions which, Roberts argues, always grow out of concerns, or passions. Faith's central passion is a yearning for God's kingdom, seen in the wish for immortality, a worthy life, and fellowship among
equals. By attending to our perceptions and interpretations of reality and
dwelling on right concerns, we can nurture emotions like gratitude, hope,
and compassion. An orthodox approach for motivated readers.

048. Backus, William D. and Marie Chapian. Telling yourself the truth.
Minneapolis, MN: Bethany House, 1980. 185p. notes. LC 80-10136. ISBN
0-87123-562-5. OCLC 5992352. pap. (study guide available).
In a clear style suited to a popular audience, the authors offer advice on
growing beyond depression, anxiety, anger, lack of self-control, etc., via
the principles of "misbelief therapy." The aim--since feelings are ultimately caused not by present circumstances but by attitudes toward them--

is to locate "misbeliefs" that create undesirable feelings and to remove them, via self-talk, with "Truth." God, we are told, wants us to be positive, not negative (though simplistic triumphalism is not desirable either). The "truths" put forth have a heavy scriptural emphasis. Study guide also.

049. Stoop, David. Self-talk: key to personal growth. Old Tappan, NJ: Power-Revell, 1981. 159p. LC 81-12136. ISBN 0-8007-5074-8. OCLC 7731855. pap.
Stoop, a clinical psychologist, says people often get trapped by either losing control or remaining over-controlled. Instead, the goal should be comfortable self-control. He believes that since thoughts create feelings, we can learn to grow by directing our thinking along fruitful channels, and he looks here at ways of releasing faith, dealing with anger, and transcending guilt, anxiety and stress. His method draws on Albert Ellis' "ABC" technique, as expounded in books on rational-emotive therapy, and he discusses "Activating events," "Belief systems," and "Consequences emotionally." (See also David and Jan Stoop's Refresh your marriage with self-talk, Revell, 1984.)

050. Hart, Archibald D. Feeling free. Old Tappan, N J: Revell, 1979. 191p. illus. notes. index. LC 78-26474. ISBN 0-8007-0973-X. OCLC 4493359.
The author, a psychotherapist, says Christians often fall into the trap of thinking their emotions are incompatible with their faith, and either over-control them or, failing in that, find themselves overwhelmed. Hart believes people need to control emotions up to a point by controlling their streams of thought, and he looks at specific areas of difficulty clients often have (e.g., with anger, depression, guilt). Beyond this constructive control, however, it is important to recognize and accept feelings so as to be free to love authentically. Includes discussion of how a false "God concept" can inhibit people emotionally.

051. Wilder, Garnett M. Using your emotions creatively. Valley Forge, PA: Judson, 1984. 76p. notes. LC 83-19568. ISBN 0-8170-1020-3. OCLC 9946369. pap.
Pointing out in the introduction that neither total self-expression nor total eradication of desire can work, Wilder advocates submission of our wills to God so we can use our emotions in the context of His guidance. Focuses particularly on potentially negative emotions--e.g., discouragement, anger, anxiety, boredom and fear--with illustrative anecdotes from his own and others' experiences showing how "clean anger," for instance, can be used creatively.

052. Jacobs, Joan. Feelings!: where they come from and how to handle them. Wheaton, IL: Tyndale, 1976. 143p. LC 76-27573. ISBN 0-8423-0856-3. OCLC 3051661. pap. (o.p.).
Jacobs, the wife of a minister and mother of five, became aware of the importance of working with feelings when she noticed a discrepancy between her own depression and guilt, on the one hand, and the doctrines about her value as God's child, on the other. She writes here about the need to befriend her own negative feelings, not to bury them, and to use all our feelings as raw material in growing toward deeper faith, since if we are alienated from ourselves we will be alienated from God. She advocates approaching Scripture holistically, not legalistically, and offers thoughts on family relationships, choosing a counselor, etc.

053. Ghezzi, Bert. The angry Christian: how to control--and use--your
     anger. Ann Arbor, MI: Servant (Living as a Christian), 1980. 108p.
     notes. ISBN 0-89283-086-7. OCLC 7135713. pap.
One of the "Living as a Christian" series designed to offer practical biblical advice on current problems, this excellent little book by a coordinator of Ann Arbor's interdenominational "Word of God" community holds that
"anger is supposed to be a useful emotion, one that supports our Christian
lives." Avoiding the pitfalls of pop psychology (express anger freely)
and of traditional Christianity (repress it), Ghezzi suggests ways to use
controlled anger fruitfully. Ideal for paperback collections in public
and church libraries.

054. Lester, Andrew D. Coping with your anger: a Christian guide. Phila-
     delphia: Westminster, 1983. 114p. illus. bibliog. LC 82-24730.
     ISBN 0-664-24471-8. OCLC 9133420. pap.
Pastoral counselor Lester writes for Christians anxious about and/or unconscious of their anger, explaining why anger makes us uncomfortable, what
its underlying causes are, what the Bible says on the subject (e.g., it is
mismanaged anger, not the experience itself, that is destructive), and how
it can be used for ill or for good as an opportunity for spiritual insight
and growth. A good introduction to the subject for public, church libraries.

055. Walters, Richard P. Anger: yours, mine and what to do about it. Grand
     Rapids, MI: Zondervan, 1981. 160p. LC 81-12997. ISBN 0-310-42601-4.
     OCLC 7739532. pap.
There are, psychologist Walters argues, three main forms of anger. Two of
these (rage and resentment) are prohibited by Scripture and are psychologically counterproductive. The third (indignation) is an appropriate response to injustice "if it energizes our physical and emotional systems to
oppose evil." Walters shares case histories to show how modes of anger
differ from each other and how they grow out of internal and external circumstances. He also offers both stop-gap and long-range solutions for
dealing with them, the most important of which is forgiveness. Will be
useful for public and church libraries.

056. Ketterman, Grace H. You can win over worry. Old Tappan, NJ: Revell,
     1984. 160p. LC 83-24488. ISBN 0-8007-1391-5. OCLC 10163170.
Practical advice by a Christian physician that begins with a brief look
at the nature of worry (how it differs from anxiety, say), how we learn
the habit, internal/external causes, and tangible manifestations. Most
of the book is devoted to advice on winning over worry: pitfalls to avoid,
spiritual resources, conquering related feelings (anxiety, depression),
dealing with troubled relationships and job factors, etc. Down-to-earth
advice, illustrative examples, and low-key biblical references.

057. Hulme, William E. Am I losing my faith? Philadelphia: Fortress
     (Pocket Counsel Books), 1971. vii, 56p. notes. LC 71-133035. ISBN
     0-8006-0154-8. OCLC 122428. pap.
One of the "Pocket Counsel" series (brief, non-technical works intended as
adjuncts to a real-life counseling relationship), this is written for people having a crisis of belief. Hulme stresses that faith grows deeper
through the process of questioning, wondering and doubting, and he looks
at various modes of doubt--intellectual and emotional--which are all reflections of the limits of our minds and hearts to encompass truth as a

perfect whole. Ultimately, he suggests, faith becomes an act of will in
spite of human doubts, and we must all begin where we are. Reassuring
and clearly written.

058. Mann, Gerald. The seven deadly virtues. Waco, TX: Word, 1979. 115p.
   notes. LC 78-65809. ISBN 0-8499-2853-2. OCLC 5195412. pap.
What many Christians regard as virtues, says Mann, are actually poisonous
to spiritual growth because they serve as "repellants" to other people
rather than as "magnets" to bring them to Christ. Examines such unrecog-
nized sins as censoriousness, permissiveness, childishness and exhibition-
ism, which often masquerade beneath a hypocritical piety. A somewhat off-
beat, interesting warning that the worst behavior can spring from seemingly noble motives.

059. Menninger, Karl. Whatever became of sin? New York: Hawthorn, 1973.
   viii, 242p. notes. index. LC 72-7776. ISBN 0-8015-8554-6. OCLC 813140.
Defining sin as "transgression of the law of God" and as "moral failure,"
psychiatrist Menninger bewails the disappearance of the word from the American vocabulary and its virtual elimination as a concept due to increasing
clinical sophistication and sociological analysis, "groupthink," and a new
social morality that views as mere "crime" what used to be viewed in moral
terms. Menninger's concept of sin is clearly corporate as well as private
(the Vietnam War hovers as spectre, background to all his comments), and
he offers a call to a new sense of accountability on the personal, social,
and international scenes.

060. Grant, Brian W. From sin to wholeness. Philadelphia: Westminster,
   1982. 173p. notes. LC 81-16122. ISBN 0-664-24399-1. OCLC 7925042.
   pap.
A psychologist looks developmentally at the Seven Deadly Sins. Sloth and
gluttony (e.g., apathy and overindulgence) reflect unresolved early childhood difficulties; anger and lust (vengefulness and sexual problems) indicate residual adolescent struggles; avarice, envy, and pride (greed, jealousy, and conceit) are distinctively "adult" sins. Churches, Grant suggests, should not teach parishoners to try and avoid sin entirely (an impossible task) but should encourage people to identify the human need beneath
the behavior and find better ways of meeting it. Highly recommended for
public, church, seminary libraries.

061. Kennedy, Eugene. A sense of life, a sense of sin. Garden City, NY:
   Image-Doubleday, 1976. 200p. LC 74-25110. ISBN 0-385-12070-2. OCLC
   1253966. pap.
By a priest/psychology professor/author, this departs from traditional
theological concepts to reformulate the question of sin in a more humanistic fashion. Kennedy offers thoughts on "moral living" (not "moral
theology") for the layperson who finds himself or herself wondering, does
sin exist anymore? The title is significant, for it is the enduring sense
of sin (and its counterpart, the sense of life) that Kennedy affirms, not
some preconceived definition or understanding of what, precisely, constitutes sin. He favors taking ourselves seriously, listening to our emotional responses as valid indicators, and testing prior notions against
experience. He believes also that maturity and conscious responsibility
are necessary before a person can be said to "sin" in his or her acts. A
particularly interesting chapter is that in which Kennedy suggests some op-
erational ways to practice self-examination and come to terms with sinful-
ness by considering the Ten Commandments in the context of modern life.

062. Peck, M. Scott. People of the lie: the hope for healing human evil.
New York: Simon and Schuster, 1983. 269p. notes. LC 83-13631. ISBN
0-671-45492-7. OCLC 9732209.
The different, and disturbing, element here (and Peck fully acknowledges
it) is that an attempt is made not just to identify abstract "evil," but
to describe "evil people"--what they are like, the things they do, illus-
trated at length in case histories. The key is in the consistency of sin-
ning, and the refusal to call it sin; in scapegoating, avoidance, cowardice.
Since writing The road less traveled (see annotation), psychiatrist Peck
has become a firmly committed Christian. Rightly, he tells the reader his
book is potentially dangerous (it is also very important), and he urges
that it be handled with great care.

063. Sanford, John A. Evil: the shadow side of reality. New York: Crossroad,
1981. 161p. notes. index. LC 81-625. ISBN 0-8245-0526-3. OCLC 7205485.
pap.
Acknowledging that threatening questions can arise when one tries to integrate orthodox Christian and Jungian views on evil, Sanford nonetheless
attempts such integration here. He explores ego-centered vs. "Divinely"-
centered perspectives, the dimension of evil in mythology, differing views
on evil in the Old and New Testaments and in Jesus' vs. Paul's teachings,
and he suggests, paradoxically, that were it not for evil, human feeling
responses and thus inner wholeness could not fully emerge. He closes with
a challenging summation, focusing on the dangers of a "split off" shadow
side and on the question of whether evil can ever be completely integrated
and transformed.

064. Myers, David G. The inflated self: human illusions and the biblical
call to hope. New York: Seabury, 1980. 189p. notes. index. LC
80-16427. ISBN 0-8164-0459-3. OCLC 6305188. (also pap.).
Myers, winner of the 1978 Gordon Allport Prize in social psychology,
argues with a wealth of supporting data that the twin evils of selfishness
and greed are realities to be reckoned with in human nature. The problem
is compounded by our tendency to all manner of illusory and self-deceptive
thinking: perceiving patterns in mere randomness, etc. Despite the subtitle, Myers' focus is more on the problem and on our false hopes (pop
psych, mass therapies, "self-serving" religion) than on what he deems
authentic biblical hope in a God who created and accepts our creatureli-
ness.

065. McNulty, Frank J. and Edward Wakin. Should you ever feel guilty?
New York: Paulist, 1978. 91p. notes. LC 78-70627. ISBN 0-8091-2149-2.
OCLC 4834264. pap.
Aimed mainly at Catholic readers who grew up in pre-Vatican II days when
the emphasis was on specific laws, on "do's" and "don'ts," this encourages
people to steer a middle way between excessive guilt and no guilt at all.
Guidelines for differentiating between superego and conscience, focusing
on process rather than on isolated acts; suggestions on "writing our own
scripts," understanding reconciliation, and growing in self-conscious
awareness. Includes discussion of Kohlberg's stages of moral development.

066. Warner, Paul L. Feeling good about feeling bad. Waco, TX: Word, 1979.
87p. illus. LC 78-59431. ISBN 0-8499-0104-9. OCLC 5103249. pap.
If we are genuinely guilty, says psychiatrist Warner, then we need God's
forgiveness, but often we suffer from what he terms "irrational" guilt.
Feelings and temptations, for instance, are not in themselves sin, and if

we do not give in to the temptation, then we should not feel guilty for
having experienced it. In this context, he offers some encouraging words
on how to learn from all our feelings rather than simply fearing or denying them.

067. Kinzer, Mark. Living with a clear conscience: a Christian strategy
     for overcoming guilt and self-condemnation. Ann Arbor, MI: Servant
     (Living as a Christian), 1982. 160p. ISBN 0-89283-115-4. OCLC
     8968377. pap.
Another brief, simple book in Servant's series offering practical Christian advice, this explains that there is a kind of "counterfeit virtue"
that appears as self-condemnation, an overscrupulous conscience that
masks as righteousness. Just as it is necessary to overcome actual wrong-
doing, so it is necessary to grow beyond such self-condemnation, and
Kinzer suggests ways of doing so by taking charge, caring about the other
person, drawing on God's power, etc.

068. Abata, Russell M. Helps for the scrupulous. Liguori, MO: Liguori
     Pubs., 1976. 127p. LC 76-21430. ISBN 0-89243-061-3. OCLC 2616066.
     pap.
Written by a priest/counselor and intended for people whose fear of sin
has paralyzed them, this stresses the importance of taking final responsibility for what one believes to be right and wrong. Beyond this, Abata
explains, we can only be held accountable for what we know and are able
to accomplish; and indeed, we cannot always immediately do everything we
know. Offering specific counsel in the areas of sex, anger, stealing
and confession, this encourages more openness to feelings and stresses
that God's is a "loving" judgment for our own good rather than a negative,
vindictive process.

069. Becker, Arthur H. Guilt: curse or blessing? Minneapolis, MN: Augsburg,
     1977. 144p. LC 77-72455. ISBN 0-8066-1588-5. OCLC 3388124. pap. (o.p.).
A professor of ethics and pastoral care argues that guilt, like pain, has
a positive side. It is a two-edged sword in that, while it causes acute
discomfort, it is actually grounded in love, reminding us when sinful
behavior is causing damage to ourselves or others. Like conscience,
guilt can either enslave us or liberate us, depending on how we approach
it; a proper response resolves conflict and leads to new self-acceptance.

D. PSYCHOLOGICAL DISTURBANCES, ADDICTIONS, AND PAIN

070. Anderson, George Christian. Your religion: neurotic or healthy?
     Garden City, N Y: Doubleday, 1970. 191p. LC 74-123682. OCLC
     101636. (o.p.).
The thesis here is that some religious styles are neurotic and trigger
unnecessary anxiety and guilt, but a healthy religion can nurture maturity,
creativity, and independence. After a look at some frankly pathological
cases, Anderson briefly discusses psychiatry's influence on religion, then
looks at problem areas: sin vs. sickness (they are not the same), guilt
and suffering (don't tilt toward masochism), emotional problems of clergymen, and sex in a religious context. Closes with a profile of a healthy
religion. The author founded the Academy of Religion and Mental Health.

071. Miller, William A. Why do Christians break down? Minneapolis, MN:
     Augsburg, 1973. 124p. illus. LC 73-78260. ISBN 0-8066-1325-4. OCLC
     701028. pap.
A look at some negative aspects of Christianity as it is often preached:
ways it can inhibit the expression of real feelings or the recognition of
one's "shadow side," causing the presentation of a false face and the experience of a deteriorating self-image. Miller calls for a greater emphasis on the reconciling, forgiving presence of Jesus in the Gospels, in
contrast to purely abstract doctrine.

072. Roe, John E. A consumer's guide to Christian counseling. Nashville,
     TN: Abingdon, 1982. 143p. LC 81-12790. ISBN 0-687-09480-1. OCLC
     7773511. pap.
This, in large measure, is designed as reassurance for Christians ashamed
of needing help in the first place. While some problems do stem from sin,
says Roe, others spring from physical, intellectual, emotional or social
circumstances. He advises, then, that people beware of counselors who see
all mental illness as the result of immediate sin, and he suggests a
"shopping process" together with an understanding of different kinds of
counselor training and different specialties--all of which he reviews
for the reader.

073. Hyder, O. Quentin. Don't blame the Devil. Old Tappan, NJ: Power-
     Revell, 1984. 163p. illus. bibliogs. LC 83-13864. ISBN 0-8007-5132-9.
     OCLC 9759560. pap.
An evangelical psychiatrist and lay preacher on the faculty of the New
York School of the Bible discusses a variety of psychological problems/
disorders from a clinical and biblical perspective, accent on the biblical.
Discussions are in the form of conversations between himself and hypothetical patients who suffer from, or wonder about, phobias, mood swings,
depression, behavioral habits, relationship difficulties, psychosis, anxiety, etc.; they include considerable attention to scriptural verses and
concepts (e.g., God's sovereignty vis-a-vis human responsibility) as well
as some explanation of clinical terms. For the conservative reader.
Appendixes contain Scripture references plus data on nutrition and exercise.

074. Hoffman, Joy. With wandering steps and slow. Downers Grove, IL: Inter-
     Varsity, 1982. 140p. LC 81-18566. OSBN 0-87784-804-1. OCLC 7924479.
     pap.
True-to-life in its broad outline but with names and details altered, this
documents through a series of letters between graduate student "Hope" and
Christian psychologist "Mark" a young woman's growth in the Christian faith
as she struggles with physical illness and a doomed sexual passion. Honestly depicting anxiety, bitterness, sexual yearning and rage as well as
faith, love and joy, this makes a real contribution, and "Mark's" responses
embody a genuine "agape." For libraries serving college/graduate students
and pastoral counselors.

075. Bennett, James W. A quiet desperation. Nashville, TN: Thomas Nelson,
     1983. 191p. LC 83-11400. ISBN 0-8407-5847-2. OCLC 9576272. pap.
A very honest personal account of the author's prolonged battle with severe
generalized anxiety. It struck suddenly--acute unexplained terror--and
persisted over years in spite of Bennett's determination to conquer it,
his growth in Christian faith and work in therapy, etc. This is no simple

story of triumph--indeed, a key message is that faith may not resolve all
problems or provide miracle cures, but that nonetheless God is present in
the midst of on-going struggles.

076. Abata, Russell M. and William Weir. Dealing with depression: a whole-
     person approach. Liguori, MO: Liguori Pubs., 1983. 143p. LC 82-84045.
     ISBN 0-89243-170-9. OCLC 9719781. pap.
The authors discuss the nature and roots of depression, explaining that it
generally reflects unsatisfied needs on the social, emotional, physical,
or spiritual levels--including a person's failure to get in touch with God.
Stressing the importance of being loved and of loving others, and the resource available in God's love for us, they conclude with some practical
aids for dealing with the problem in a "whole-person" fashion: hope,
humor, new habits, and accepting imperfections.

077. Minirth, Frank B. and Paul D. Meier. Happiness is a choice: a manual
     on the symptoms, causes and cures of depression. Grand Rapids, MI:
     Baker Book House, 1978. 248p. notes. indexes. LC 78-62442. ISBN
     0-8010-6062-1. OCLC 4424835. pap.
This team of Christian psychiatrists suggests that while behavior/response
patterns are deeply rooted in early childhood, it is still possible to
change. Here they aim to encourage such a choice and offer guidelines for
seeking happiness fruitfully. First comes a discussion on the nature of
depression (symptoms, suicidal clues, grief dynamics). Then we have a
look at causes (largely psychological and spiritual; the authors recognize
a physical component but do not stress it) and personality syndromes, with
numerous self-rating scales. Finally come guidelines for overcoming depression, handling anger and anxiety, and (very brief) the role of hospitalization and medication. Includes Scripture and subject indexes.

078. Littauer, Florence. Blow away the black clouds: a woman's answer to
     depression. Eugene, OR: Harvest House, 1981. 136p. bibliog. LC
     80-85334. ISBN 0-89081-285-3. OCLC 7770537. pap.
The author, who had her own bouts with depression when she lost two brain-
damaged sons, discusses what the condition is like, who is vulnerable, and
how to begin steps toward healing. Recognition of the problem, setting
priorities, checking one's physical health, reaching out to someone else,
etc., can all be helpful, she suggests, and these are things a person can
do on his/her own (though often professional help is necessary, too).
Includes a section on living with and helping someone else who is depressed.
A practical, behaviorally-oriented guide for those with some motivation
toward self-help.

079. Smith, Nancy Covert. Journey out of nowhere. Waco, TX: Word, 1973.
     124p. notes. LC 72-96351. (o.p.).
A gracefully written personal narrative with helpful counsel for others by
a woman, active in church work, who suffered an acute depressive breakdown.
Smith shares the experience of the breakdown itself, entering a hospital,
her family's responses, the challenge of returning home, the struggles
involved in facing friends and associates, and, of course, the process of
therapy. She has achieved a remarkable balance between emotional immediacy
and objective distance; her stress is on faith, hope, and the healing value
of caring involvement with others, and her words should be useful to relatives and friends of those who have suffered mental breakdowns, as well as
to the mentally troubled themselves.

080. Baker, Don and Emery Nester. <u>Depression: finding hope and meaning</u>
    <u>in life's darkest shadow</u>. Portland, OR: Multnomah (Critical Concerns
    Series), 1983. 197p. index. LC 82-24609. ISBN 0-88070-011-4. OCLC
    9133240.
Jointly written by a minister who suffered a period of depression and a
Christian psychologist who counseled him, this first gives us Baker's own
memoir, which effectively conveys the despair and hopelessness he underwent,
aggravated by his prior self-image as a minister who "should" embody only
Christian triumph. Then, Nester deals briefly with types of depression,
therapy, the roles of patient and family in effecting cure, etc. Evangelical as well as clinical in its thrust and tone.

081. Smith, Nancy Anne. <u>All I need is love</u>. Downers Grove, IL: InterVarsity,
    1977. 120p. LC 77-6036. ISBN 0-87784-723-1. OCLC 7155542. <u>pap</u>.
Originally published under the title <u>Winter past</u>, this is a personal account
by a woman who suffered severe rejection and sexual abuse when she was
young and later, as an adult, succumbed to hysteria and depression. Smith
writes with detachment but deep sensitivity of the process of therapy, her
special struggles as a Christian who felt she should be instantly victorious, other people's difficulties in understanding her inevitable turbulence, etc. Very well done. (The author herself is now a professional
psychologist.)

082. Hosier, Helen. <u>Suicide: a cry for help</u>. Irvine, CA: Harvest House,
    1978. 142p. notes. LC 78-65124. ISBN 0-89081-178-4. OCLC 4956618.
    (o.p.).
Written by one who herself made a failed suicide attempt, this explores
causes of suicide among children, young people, men and women, drawing on
personal statements and research findings. Then Hosier looks at attitudes
toward suicide characteristic of various historical eras and of the Christian community, contemporary ministries and resources for suicidal people,
biblical cases of suicidal depression (e.g., Elijah), faith as a strength,
and ways others may respond. More appropriate for the suicidal person
him/herself than some books on the subject, this includes appendixes with
telephone ministries and suicide prevention centers.

083. Keller, John E. <u>Drinking problem?</u> Philadelphia: Fortress (Pocket
    Counsel Books), 1971. 56p. LC 75-133036. ISBN 0-8006-0155-6. OCLC
    123161. <u>pap</u>.
Keller is administrative director of an alcoholism rehabilitation center
connected with a Lutheran hospital. While very brief, this is a strong,
clinically clear and spiritually oriented discussion on recognizing whether
or not one is an alcoholic, coming to the point of accepting that reality,
surrendering to God in recognition of one's own helplessness, and beginning
the process of recovery. Case histories and factual discussion of symptoms
and stages, with a final chapter on how one's spouse can help.

084. Costales, Claire with Jo Berry. <u>Alcoholism: the way back to reality</u>.
    Glendale, CA: Regal, 1980. 157p. notes. LC 79-93018. ISBN
    0-8307-0742-5. OCLC 6666483. <u>pap</u>. (Rev. ed. <u>Staying dry</u>, 1983).
An alcoholic from the ages of 17 to 31, Costales shares experiences from
her alcoholic "career" and how she found her way back to sobriety. The
turning point came when she called on God to help her; complete recovery,
she believes, depends on willingness to ask another's help, and she explains the "one-to-one" treatment system she developed and how it harmo-

nizes with key Christian principles. Included is a discussion of seven
steps for deprogramming, relationships with family members, and predictable family reactions.

085. Deane, Philip and Lola Deane. Is this trip necessary? Camden: Thomas
     Nelson (Youth Forum), 1970. 88p. LC 70-127077. OCLC 138996. (o.p.).
Books in Nelson's "Youth Forum" series are collaborations between the publisher and the Youth Research Center, Inc. of Minneapolis which deal with
concerns of young people as indicated by the Center's surveys. The Deanes
are a pediatrician/nurse team with experience as foster parents and as
counselors with youthful addicts. Here they share stories of young people
they have known who became involved with drugs—tragically, in some cases,
only temporarily in others. Most of the narrative is written directly to
young people, clearly addressing their concerns, peer pressure, and fears,
and explaining why it is important to stay drug free or—in the case of
users—where they can go for help. Includes thoughts on Christianity as
a resource and closes with advice for parents.

086. Adair, James R., ed. Unhooked. Grand Rapids, MI: Baker Book House,
     1971. 159p. LC 71-152901. ISBN 0-8010-0017-3. OCLC 163160. pap.
     (o.p.).
True personal stories of former addicts who transcended their addiction
through a personal relationship with Jesus Christ, mainly told via first
person narratives that testify to the personal transformation in their
lives. Includes resource lists of agencies offering help to addicts
(mainly evangelical; in many cases Teen Challenge centers).

087. Barrile, Jackie. Confessions of a closet eater. Wheaton, IL: Tyndale,
     1983. 199p. LC 83-50238. ISBN 0-8423-0438-X. OCLC 10762423. pap.
Bulimia is an eating disorder characterized by a binge/purge cycle, closely
related to anorexia nervosa. Barrile, now active as a counselor and speak-
er on the subject, herself a recovered bulimic, combines personal sharing
with guidance for the reader in this clear, honest account. To illustrate
the principles under discussion she cites other cases, too, as well as her
own experience, and offers many concrete suggestions such as the "Get Well"
cards she made for herself and used in the recovery process (cards with
affirmations, expectations, tips for dealing with anger, etc.). Includes
discussion of the role of biblical principles in her cure.

088. O'Neill, Cherry Boone. Starving for attention. New York: Continuum,
     1982. xvi, 187p. photogs. LC 82-10600. ISBN 0-8264-0209-7. OCLC
     8688668. (also Dell ed.).
A graphic but sensitively written account by one of Pat Boone's daughters
telling of her long and ultimately successful struggle with anorexia nervosa. Includes a look at the darker side of Boone family life,—emphasis
on strict standards and anguished efforts at perfection in a sometimes
rigid Christian context—but mainly this is an important look at the dynamics involved in the syndrome of anorexia, which Cherry finally over-
came through Christian counseling and her husband's empathic involvement.
Letters from family members, searching for perspective, conclude the
volume, together with some thoughts on characteristic dynamics of anorexia
by the therapist who worked with Cherry and her husband. Finally, an appendix lists several national organizations in various parts of the country
which readers can contact for further information.

089. Lee, Judy. Save me!: a young woman's journey through schizophrenia
     to health. Garden City, NY: Galilee-Doubleday, 1980. x, 176p.
     LC 78-22365. ISBN 0-385-15101-2. OCLC 5555562. (o.p.).
Judy Lee's story is one of overwhelming pain: an unhappy childhood in a
troubled, then broken, home; periodic attempts at suicide; an abortive
college career spent bombed out on acid; destructive relationships; finally,
diagnosis at age 19 as an incurable paranoid schizophrenic. But it is also
a story of dramatic victory: not only did Judy grow beyond her clinical
symptoms, but, with the help of her gut level faith in Jesus and the skills
of a reality therapist, she came to the point where she could hold down
a job in New York's advertising world and write this quite remarkable
book. The narrative is honest and direct; the pace rapid; the tale en-
grossing. There is forgiveness here--for herself and others--but also a
sound critique: of judgmental Christians; of the early 1970's youth
culture; of some traditional psychiatry. Ideal for the general reader.

090. Yancey, Philip. Where is God when it hurts? Grand Rapids, MI: Zonder-
     van/Campus Life, 1977. 187p. notes. LC 77-12776. ISBN 0-310-35411-0.
     OCLC 3420039. pap.
While preparing to write these reflections on the problem of suffering,
Yancey talked to many people struggling with different types of pain.
First he looks at pain "through the microscope," to see the role it plays
in life; then he explores suffering on a global scale, asking what God
seems to be up to; finally he looks closely at real individuals and their
personal responses. Because he is writing with a degree of distance (his
raw material is others' suffering, not his own), this has somewhat less
moral authority than books like Clarkson's or Eareckson's, below. But as
practical Christian philosophy it makes some useful points.

091. Clarkson, Margaret. Destined for glory: the meaning of suffering.
     Grand Rapids, MI: Eerdmans, 1983. 132p. LC 83-1704. ISBN 0-8028-1953-2.
     OCLC 9323253. pap.
An author, poet, and hymn writer shares her own strategies for coping with
pain over the years and offers an in-depth look at how she has reconciled
her faith in God with human suffering. Clarkson's is an orthodox Christi-
anity--she stresses the Fall and Satan's activity in the world as she affirms God's ultimate sovereignty and ability to use all pain for eventual
glory--but it is her compassionate empathy with others and her own deeply
grounded peace that, in the end, persuade us.

092. Eareckson, Joni and Steve Estes. A step further. Grand Rapids, MI:
     Zondervan, 1978. illus. photogs. bibliog. notes. LC 78-12084. ISBN
     0-310-23972-9. OCLC 4211181. pap.
In her highly acclaimed autobiographical tale Joni (see annotation), the
author told how she was paralyzed from the neck down in a diving accident
and shared her long battle with despair and bitterness prior to growing in
the Christian faith with the help of young evangelist Steve Estes. This
second book is written in response to the many letters she has since received asking questions about the problem of suffering, and offers various
"reasons" for pain (suffering can help us empathize, can build the body of
Christ, provides chances for glorifying God, breaks us of willfulness,
etc.). This also tackles head on the problem of why certain healings do
not happen (Joni and a group of supporters once claimed a healing for her
in faith; there was no result). A conservative evangelical statement.

093. Price, Eugenia. No pat answers. Grand Rapids, MI: Zondervan, 1972.
      145p. LC 72-83880. ISBN 0-310-31331-7. OCLC 658085. pap.
Addressing the problem of human suffering in its various manifestations--
failure, bereavement, disappointment, disillusionment, handicaps and the
seeming wastefulness of life prematurely cut off--Price challenges her
readers to look beyond "pat" answers to such tragedy (e.g., that suffering
is to punish the disobedient, or to test and perfect us with trials) and
simply to rest with the comfort of Christ's presence in the midst of unex-
plainable mystery. For what suffering people ultimately need, she asserts,
is not an intellectual explanation, but hope. Price stops short of Harold
Kushner's explicit statement (in When bad things happen to good people,
Schocken, 1981) that God's power is limited, but she does stress that
"fortune," good and bad, is also a factor, and that God, as she sees it,
does not directly decree illness and death.

094. Wolff, Pierre. May I hate God? New York: Paulist, 1979. 76p.
      LC 78-70815. ISBN 0-8091-2180-8. OCLC 4859141. pap.
Spiritual guidance for those who, because of acute suffering or apparent
injustice, feel alienated from God. Citing biblical examples (Job's
speeches, vengeful psalms) Wolff stresses the importance of bringing to
God all that we are--including our rage--and letting go of it in honest
communication, which will always be a step toward reconciliation. Our
protest, he suggests, may even be an expression of God's "revolt" through
us, as in Christ's righteous indignation. Brief and simple, with one
appendix for spiritual directors and another containing scriptural references on adversaries, suffering, trials, etc.

095. Tournier, Paul. Creative suffering. San Francisco: Harper, 1983.
      146p. bibliog. LC 82-48939. ISBN 0-06-068296-5. OCLC 9323008.
More in the vein of personal reflection than straight "self-help" advice,
this starts with the paradox of highly achieving orphans and the implied
link between deprivation and creativity, then goes on to speculate about
the relationship between good and evil and the ways creativity can spring
from such painful emotions as anger, frustration, etc. Valuable musings
from a physician/counselor interested in synthesizing psychology, classical
medicine, and religious faith.

096. Kennedy, Eugene C. The pain of being human. Garden City, NY: Image-
      Doubleday, 1972. 277p. LC 73-159651. ISBN 0-385-06888-3. OCLC 688387.
      pap.
Here are about 80 brief reflective essays (an average of three to five
pages each) offering thoughts and counsel on growing through the ordinary
experiences of pain that people necessarily encounter if they move at all
deeply into life and love. Topics include psychodynamics (reaction formation, rationalization), specific painful feelings and circumstances (loneliness, discouragement), how to sort out misunderstandings, and a host of
other issues--including some specifically Christian concerns, e.g., is it
really the Spirit one is hearing? More explicit integration of psychology
and Christianity than in many of Kennedy's books.

097. Herhold, Robert M. The promise beyond the pain. Nashville, TN: Abing-
      don, 1979. 111p. LC 79-895. ISBN 0-687-34331-3. OCLC 4664608. (o.p.).
Herhold, a Lutheran pastor, believes that God wishes us all to know his
"strange joy" and that while we should not seek or desire pain in a maso-
chistic way, the pain which does come to us (physical, emotional, or spiritual) can be used by God for our welfare. He intends his book more as

reflective testimony to this fact than as a straight "how to" sort of
guide and touches on listening to our pain, opportunities for daily rebirth, the joy of surrendering to God, the healing value of laughter, etc.

098. Bishop, Joseph P. New beginnings. Lincoln, VA: Chosen Books, 1980.
     123p. LC 79-23104. ISBN 0-912376-49-X. pap. (o.p.). (You can have a
     new beginning in BIP Supplement, 1983-84).
With illustrative examples from his own life and the lives of others--
friends, parishioners, figures from church history and Scripture--Bishop
shares with moving simplicity his faith that God uses pain and sin as raw
material for spiritual rebirth. The author's candor in revealing such
personal struggles as a near nervous breakdown early in his own ministry
adds immeasurably. Intelligent and compassionate.

E. VARIETIES OF PRAYER

099. Davidson, Graeme J. with Mary MacDonald. Anyone can pray: a guide
     to methods of Christian prayer. New York: Paulist, 1983. vii, 193p.
     illus. bibliog. LC 82-62921. ISBN 0-8091-2542-0. OCLC 10084102. pap.
Davidson calls this a "recipe book" of prayer techniques, and the description is apt. The variety is striking, from traditional Christian approaches (the Jesus prayer, praying the Rosary, praying in tongues, etc.)
to Eastern techniques (TM, Zen, Yoga). Davidson tries to "Christianize"
the latter, reminding readers, for instance, to use TM for involvement not
for withdrawal, and he warns people to be alert to medical implications of
methods like fasting. Yet the discussions are so brief, this seems more
like a kind of reference tool than a real "how to" book.

100. Murphey, Cecil. Prayerobics: getting started and staying going. Waco,
     TX: Word, 1979. 187p. LC 79-63934. ISBN 0-8499-0146-4. OCLC 5678335.
Here are simple, easy to follow thoughts on getting into "spiritual shape"
together with reflective questions at the end of each chapter. Contrary
to what the title might imply, Murphey has not just written a superficial
book on techniques; instead, he looks at some spiritual concepts and their
application as well as at prayer behavior per se. Includes discussion on
accountability, dreaming as a mode of prayer, contract praying, personal
attitudes toward prayer, etc.

101. Bloom, Anthony. Beginning to pray. New York: Paulist, 1970. 114p. LC
     70-169613. ISBN 0-8091-1509-3. OCLC 10307589. pap.
For newcomers to prayer or occasional pray-ers in need of spiritual deepening, here is guidance, explanation and spiritual direction from a Russian
Orthodox archbishop and former French resistance fighter. The day when
we truly experience God's absence is often the day authentic prayer begins,
Bloom suggests, for in that experience of abandonment we cry out, and the
dynamic process starts. In choosing one's first words of prayer, he advises
choosing what one truly feels comfortable with, can identify with; prayer
is speaking to the inmost self as well as to God; it is important to set
aside time to be still before God as well as to pray verbally. Simply
written and extremely rich, with--in this edition, at least--an introductory
interview between Archbishop Bloom and Timothy Wilson in which Bloom shares
his personal journey from atheism to faith and reflects on the dynamics of
detachment, the importance of a personal encounter with Jesus's presence,
and living as an emigre.

102. Vaswig, William L. At your word, Lord: how prayer releases the power
     of God in your life. Minneapolis, MN: Augsburg, 1982. 128p. LC
     81-52272. ISBN 0-8066-1904-X. OCLC 8352574. pap.
An introduction to the dynamics of prayer for those just starting or wishing to overcome hindrances. Vaswig discusses the faith relationship, use
of visualization, and--in detail--praying for healing: inner healing of
the memories, physical healing for a vast array of ailments like heart
disease, hypertension, cancer, allergies, and emotional healing for anorexia nervosa, depression, neuroses, schizophrenia, homosexuality, etc.
Discusses also the mystery of suffering, questions about unanswered prayer,
praise/meditation, and spirituality. Touches many bases in a rather superficial fashion.

103. Griffin, Emilie. Clinging: the experience of prayer. San Francisco:
     Harper, 1984. xiii, 72p. notes. LC 83-48989. ISBN 0-06-063461-8.
     OCLC 10375067.
Sharing her understanding of the dynamics of prayer, the author of Turning
(Doubleday, 1980) draws on the metaphor of a jewel that radiates light
from its several facets, and her brief book, crafted with the poetic compression of a disciplined intelligence, is itself a small gem. The dimensions of prayer life Griffin describes here, such as yielding, darkness,
transparency, and clinging, are drawn from her own experience but fully
transcend the particular; much richer than a mere "how-to," this will be
supremely useful to all who struggle seriously with the challenge of
prayer.

104. Gallagher, Maureen and others. Praying with Scripture. New York:
     Paulist, 1983. 120p. illus. LC 82-62923. ISBN 0-8091-2544-7. OCLC
     10565072. pap. (also leader's manual).
Gallagher's imaginative, multi-faceted guide to prayer integrates scriptural study with exploration of personal experience. She first discusses
the call to prayer, then looks at meditation, journaling, praying through
biblical verses, and the psychodynamics of the faith journey, offering
various resources/exercises as aids to reflection: pictures, open-ended
fill-ins examining feelings, reprints of essays by others, passages from
Scripture, etc. Emphasis on depth spirituality rather than specific
Catholic theology.

105. Helleberg, Marilyn. Beyond TM: a practical guide to the lost tradi-
     tion of Christian meditation. New York: Paulist, 1981. x, 129p. LC
     80-82811. ISBN 0-8091-2325-8. OCLC 7423265. pap.
Helleberg's excellent and readable book is based on the premise that far
from being un-Christian (as many believe), meditation can be a useful
means of experiencing God's presence as well as a source of beneficial
side effects like emotional control, reduced anxiety, heightened creativity, etc. Chapters are organized around these benefits and include general
discussion together with specific "guided meditations." Helleberg shares
personal experience and concludes with thoughts on keeping a spiritual
journal and group meditation. For public, church and seminary libraries.

106. Gill, Jean. Images of myself: meditation and self-exploration through
     the imagery of the Gospels. New York: Paulist, 1982. 88p. LC 82-81188.
     ISBN 0-8091-2463-7. OCLC 9142624. pap.
Gill's style of biblical meditation involves the traditional four stages--
a look at the scriptural background of each tale, re-creation of the
event, reflection on the story's inner meaning, and the meditative process

itself--but emphasis here is on the last two as she guides the reader into
dialogue with his/her own "inner Pharisee" or "inner child." Approaches
Scripture as a Gestalt therapist would approach dream material; a good
choice for popular spirituality collections, with a Jungian perspective.

107. Neill, Mary and others. How shall we find the Father?: meditations
     for mixed voices. New York: Seabury, 1983. 114p. notes. LC 83-4745.
     ISBN 0-8164-2623-6. OCLC 9441912. pap.
A "meditation workbook," the third in a series (see also The woman's
tale, Seabury, 1980, and Bringing the mother with you, Seabury, 1982),
this addresses the quest for the Father, using the petitions of the Lord's
Prayer as a way of focusing on what fathering can mean. The authors'
voices are deliberately kept distinct so their unique struggles can be
affirmed as they explore the psychodynamics involved in addressing God as
Father. Includes discussion of how prior experience can intrude and inhibit.

108. Catoir, John T. Enjoy the Lord: a guide to contemplation. New York:
     Arena Lettres, 1978. xii, 113p. notes. LC 78-62471. ISBN
     0-88479-023-1. OCLC 4562429. pap.
The director of The Christophers, an ecumenical organization promoting
love of one's neighbor, writes this simple, practical guide to contemplative prayer for "household" rather than monastic living. Part One--
the bulk of the book--discusses psychological obstacles to prayer (including theological attitudes fostering distrust), characteristics of
"good prayer," removing guilt and fear, learning to trust, practicing the
presence of God, etc. Part Two, on contemplation itself (enjoying union
with God) is very brief, a simple, joyful culmination.

109. Pennington, M. Basil. Centering prayer: renewing an ancient Christian
     prayer form. Garden City, NY: Image-Doubleday, 1980. 254p. bibliog.
     LC 82-45077. ISBN 0-385-18179-5. OCLC 5499884. pap. (also cloth).
Centering prayer is described in full: its nature, roots in church tradition, the techniques involved, spiritual/psychological dynamics. Orig-
inating with the desert fathers, described in The cloud of unknowing,
it has a new "packaging" today, says Pennington, but still involves going
beyond thought, imagery, senses and the rational mind to tap the center of
being through use of a "prayer word" that deflects distraction. In psychological language, it is getting past the "false self" and its constructs.
A chapter with questions and answers near the end of the book addresses
objections, distinctions between this and other prayer/meditation approaches, guidelines for use, etc.

110. Bloesch, Donald G. The struggle of prayer. San Francisco: Harper,
     1980. 180p. notes. LC 79-3589. ISBN 0-06-060797-1. OCLC 6278158.
Presented as an alternative to meditation and contemplative prayer, this
book by a foremost evangelical spokesman seeks to delineate the "outlines
of an evangelical spirituality." Bloesch stresses what he calls a biblical
personalism with roots in the Protestant Reformation and its tradition of
prayerful (sometimes conflict ridden) dialogue between the believer and
God. Intended as a theology of prayer rather than a purely practical
guide, this is included because of Bloesch's stature in the evangelical
community; designed to counteract what he sees as an overemphasis on "pop
mysticism" and to promote genuine dialogue between the evangelical and
mystical traditions.

111. Brandt, Priscilla. Two-way prayer. Waco, TX: Word, 1979. 151p. illus.
    bibliog. notes. LC 78-65802. ISBN 0-8499-0022-0. OCLC 5707062. (o.p.).
By a registered nurse, based on her personal search in the spiritual, medical and psychological realms (prayers for more receptivity; exploration
in biofeedback and meditative exercises), this is a discussion of discoveries about "two-way prayer" in which one actively listens for God's
response rather than merely praying "to" Him. Brandt examines the power
of the inner world (mind/body interaction, the alpha state), the anatomy
of prayer (on the subconscious level and the "Christ-conscious level")
the visualizing powers of the mind, the power of forgiveness, moving
through turbulence to stillness, and more. A guidebook integrating phys-
iological/spiritual insights with practical advice.

112. Seamands, David A. Healing for damaged emotions. Wheaton, IL: Victor,
    1981. 144p. LC 80-54723. ISBN 0-88207-228-5. OCLC 7934194. pap.
A United Methodist minister and a college/seminary counselor explains that
some areas of need are not subject to ordinary discipline and willpower
but require healing by the Holy Spirit. What individuals can do on the
"human" end to facilitate this healing process is the subject under discussion here. Seamands advocates facing the problem, accepting responsibility, asking if one genuinely wants healing, forgiving anyone involved,
forgiving oneself, then asking the Holy Spirit to show the true nature of
the difficulty and the right way to pray. This is more cognitive in emphasis than some other books on inner healing, with less stress on imaginative reconstruction. A sequel is Putting away childish things (Victor,
1982), which discusses the "hidden child" and how God can reprogram immature behavior patterns.

113. Stapleton, Ruth Carter. Experience of inner healing. Waco, TX: Word,
    1977. 213p. LC 76-56479. ISBN 0-87680-507-1. OCLC 3101042. (also
    pap., large type).
Stapleton's first book, The gift of inner healing (Word, 1976), shared how
she came into her evangelical ministry after psychological difficulties of
her own and how she practiced inner healing with others. This second book
is a fuller exposition of the process, aimed at helping readers learn to
experience their own healings through her technique of "faith imagination,"
which replaces negative memories with positive Christ-centered images,
created with the help of guided fantasy. Stapleton looks in particular
at the spiritual components of healing: love, faith, surrender, forgiveness, confession, self-acceptance, release, and more.

114. Bennett, Rita. Emotionally free. Old Tappan, NJ: Power-Revell, 1982.
    254p. bibliog. index. LC 81-21177. ISBN 0-8007-5083-7. OCLC 8050857.
    pap.
With husband Dennis Bennett, an Episcopal priest, the author has been active in the charismatic renewal. The Bennetts' "soul healing" seems very
similar to Ruth Carter Stapleton's "inner healing"; painful memories are
prayerfully relived, then imaginatively revised under guidance from the
Holy Spirit. Case histories illustrate the technique, and later chapters
discuss the importance of forgiveness, praying for family members, etc.
For popular spirituality collections.

115. Dobson, Theodore. How to pray for spiritual growth. New York: Paulist,
    1982. vi, 216p. bibliogs. LC 81-83182. ISBN 0-8091-2419-X. OCLC
    8351079. pap
Spiritual growth involves shedding the "false self" (St. Paul's "old self"
plus its psychological results) and moving toward the "true self" (St.

Paul's "new self" plus its psychological results). This is facilitated
by inner healing prayer, which Dobson discusses in three main categories:
finding the true self (cleansing the imagination and mind, listening, journaling, and integrating opposites); freeing the true self (forgiveness,
self-deliverance, and experiencing religious imagery); and finally, healing
of memories (seeing Christ in our experiences and ourselves in His, and
working with specific feelings). There is real spiritual richness here.
Self-disclosure complements objective guidance, and sample prayers and
study questions are very helpful.

116. Linn, Dennis and Matthew Linn. Healing life's hurts: healing memories
     through five stages of forgiveness. New York: Paulist, 1978. ix,
     249p. illus. notes. LC 77-14794. ISBN 0-8091-2059-3. OCLC 3830108.
     pap.
Suggesting that healing a memory resembles the process of dying, the authors, two Jesuits active in the healing ministry, show how Elisabeth
Kubler-Ross' five stages in coming to terms with death (denial, anger, bar-
gaining, depression and acceptance) can be integrated with St. Ignatius'
"Spiritual Exercises" and applied to the dynamics of forgiveness. Explores
emotional and physical healing, spiritual predispositions for the dying/
forgiveness process, the Eucharist as symbol, and how to get started.
Appendix includes prayer questions, detailed steps and exercises, and discussion of Jesus' Seven Last Words and the Stations of the Cross.

117. Faricy, Robert. Praying for inner healing. New York: Paulist, 1979.
     vii, 86p. notes. LC 79-92857. ISBN 0-8091-2250-2. OCLC 6447457. pap.
This is designed to help readers pray for their own inner healing, so
while the theological context is clearly spelled out, the stress is on
practicality. Chapter One suggests steps to use in praying for healing
(ask, repent, focus on a specific area, forgive everyone involved, imagine
the Lord in the situation, and request healing). Subsequent chapters
discuss the dynamics, the role of the Cross, healing through praise, and
the gifts of the Spirit, all within the context of a charismatic theology.

118. Shlemon, Barbara Leahy. Healing the hidden self. Notre Dame, IN: Ave
     Maria, 1982. 127p. notes. LC 81-70022. ISBN 0-87793-244-1. OCLC
     8539768. pap.
The author is a Roman Catholic nurse who has spent many years in a healing
ministry. She stresses that healing is a process, not a matter of techniques, and that inner healing begins when a person admits his or her ultimate powerlessness and enters a relationship with Christ. Within this
context, Shlemon looks at six stages of human development (conception and
foetal development, birth, infancy, childhood, adolescence, young adulthood
and adulthood), typical problems encountered during each stage, illustrative cases, and healing prayers.

119. Savary, Louis M. and Patricia H. Berne. Prayerways. San Francisco:
     Harper, 1980. xiv, 161p. notes. LC 80-7737. ISBN 0-06-067068-1.
     OCLC 6250208.
Here are a variety of "prayerful strategies" intended to help burned-out
people whose usual modes of coping have failed them. Reflecting the authors' involvements in spirituality and counseling, the techniques (which
include centering and relaxing; owning, drawing, or dialoguing with one's
feelings; writing letters; touching; keeping a journal; dancing; groaning,
crying, or screaming) are all emotionally expressive acts that can be
performed in a spiritually open fashion regardless of religious affiliation

or lack of it. At times the mix of pop psych and New Age jargon degener-
ates into cliche ("This energy center enables you to ... say to others,
'I'm OK--You're OK'"), yet beneath the surface gimmickry are useful suggestions and insights that could help readers who are not put off by
the tone.

120. O'Connor, Elizabeth. Search for silence. Waco, TX: Word, 1972. 186p.
     bibliog. notes. LC 74-188067. ISBN 0-87680-808-9. OCLC 334281. pap.
The final volume in a trilogy beginning with Our many selves and continuing
in Eighth day of creation (see annotations), this offers various meditational readings, reprinted from a range of philosophical, psychological
and spiritual writings, as reflective "exercises" for inner growth. The
focus is on the process of confessing our humanity (acknowledging and
accepting the dark and light sides) and then on moving into deep prayer
in a contemplative mode.

121. Thornton, Edward E. Being transformed: an inner way of spiritual
     growth. Philadelphia: Westminster (Potentials: Guides for Pro-
     ductive Living), 1984. 114p. LC 83-27331. ISBN 0-664-24523-4. OCLC
     10301043. pap.
Many discussions of contemplative prayer and related disciplines come out
of the Catholic tradition. Here is one by a Protestant--immersed for
many years in the behavioral sciences after being alienated from the rote
quality of his childhood faith--which describes disciplines of relaxation,
centering, and contemplation, encouraging the reader to discover his or
her true self and ultimately to reach a "prayer-of-the-heart" communion
with God. Bible study exercises from this perspective are offered, together with physical/imaginative activities and--from the "other side of
silence"--a look at the primacy of obedience and spontaneity harmonized
through a genuine discernment.

122. Marshall, Catherine and Leonard LeSourd. My personal prayer diary.
     New expanded ed. New York: Epiphany-Ballantine, 1983. 400p. index.
     LC 79-16773. ISBN 0-345-30612-0. OCLC 9191218. (originally published
     in 1979 by Chosen Books). pap.
Here are 365 prayer meditations on obedience, trust, guidance, depression,
etc. with related scriptural passages plus, at the end of each month, a
page to log specific prayer requests and the ways God answered. The book
opens with two introductory statements in which the authors (husband and
wife) share how they have experienced and learned from a daily prayer time
over the years. Includes topical index.

123. Carroll, Frances L. The Christian's diary: a personal journal for
     Bible study, prayer, and spiritual growth. Englewood Cliffs, NJ:
     Prentice-Hall (Steeple Books), 1984. 304p. LC 83-27075. ISBN 0-13-
     133793-9. OCLC 10273287. pap. (also cloth).
The purpose here is to draw the reader into a closer relationship with
Jesus Christ based on "heart knowledge" rather than mere "head knowledge."
The method is to integrate journaling with scriptural study and prayer, so
the bulk of the book is devoted to triads of Scripture passages (with discussions, "thought questions" and room for notes), spaces for journaling
on attitudes, feelings, needs, and fill-in's for specific prayer requests
and answers. Sequences are grouped thematically from "First steps" to "The
Lord is over all."

F. INNER EXPLORATION AND WHOLENESS

124. Kelsey, Morton T. Adventure inward: Christian growth through personal
     journal writing. Minneapolis, MN: Augsburg, 1980. 216p. bibliog. LC
     80-65551. ISBN 0-8066-1796-9. OCLC 7088509. pap.
Believing that Christianity provides a rich context for journaling, this
is a practical, specific guide for keeping a spiritual journal. Kelsey
considers reasons for beginning, the mechanics of journaling, getting
started, the journal as symbol of one's unique value, the process of
spiritual growth, certain dangers, ideas for dream interpretation, depth
journaling, the creative powers of the imagination, and common benefits.
Christian depth psychology in a "do-it-yourself" format.

125. Klug, Ronald. How to keep a spiritual journal. Nashville, TN: Thomas
     Nelson, 1982. 142p. bibliog. LC 82-14383. ISBN 0-8407-5815-4. OCLC
     8763732. pap.
An introduction to the purpose and process of "spiritual journaling,"
this discusses spiritual development vis-a-vis self development, the "nuts-
and-bolts" of starting (when, how often, what sort of notebook), types of
entries, and ways journal writing can help in goal setting, time management, sticking to a devotional program, or learning from the past. Begin-
ners (especially those a bit shy about the whole idea) will be the ideal
audience here, but veterans may find useful tips too. For public, church
libraries.

126. Cargas, Harry J. and Roger J. Radley. Keeping a spiritual journal.
     Garden City, NY: Nazareth-Doubleday, 1981. 128p. LC 80-2072. ISBN
     0-385-17439-X. OCLC 6815204. pap. (1980 Collins ed.).
After an initial look at basic guidelines (be honest, don't adopt con-
straining rules, keep it entirely private), this concentrates on techniques
and exercises for journal writers, especially teenagers, to help identify
behavior and response patterns, relive past events related to the present,
and learn to dialogue with self and others. Includes reflections on God's
forgiveness, prayers/meditations, and an occasional far-out technique
like the "automatic writing" exercise in which readers are advised to pray
for vision, write anything and everything, then touch all parts of their
bodies while praying "Amen."

127. Vaughn, Ruth. Write to discover yourself. Garden City, NY: Galilee-
     Doubleday, 1980. viii, 230p. LC 79-6748. ISBN 0-385-15912-9. OCLC
     6424329. pap.
Creative writing, says Vaughn, is important for its own sake, for the self-
discovery it facilitates, rather than just in order to produce a "product"
or to get published. It is wonderful, too, as a way of worshipping God
(sorting out experiences to come to integrity/gratitude) and for sharing with others. Vaughn looks at various styles/elements/formats in writing (journaling, letters, meditations, poetry, the use of compression,
prayer, figures of speech) and, with real joy and reassuring exuberance,
urges readers to take the plunge. She presents her guidance in a comfortable, chatty style, and this tone, coupled with her many concrete and helpful suggestions, should do much to relax readers who feel shy about putting
pen to paper.

128. Chilson, Richard. The way to Christianity: in search of spiritual
     growth. Minneapolis, MN: Winston, 1980. 343p. LC 79-64652. ISBN
     0-03-053426-7. OCLC 6569732. pap.
By the author of I can pray, you can pray (McKay, 1978) this once again
integrates Christianity with Eastern traditions, offering in workbook format (guided meditations, Scripture readings, journal activities, imaginative exercises) a "pilgrimage" for encountering Jesus as He lives in the
Gospels rather than as church doctrine has traditionally presented Him.
Organized around Gospel themes: Jesus and the Kingdom, the program for
transformation, the path ahead, the gifts of the Spirit.

129. Wicks, Robert J. Christian introspection: self-ministry through
     self-understanding. New York: Crossroad, 1983. 128p. notes. LC
     83-1932. ISBN 0-8245-0583-2. OCLC 9255928. pap.
Wicks presents a self-examination tool based on 75 sentence-completion exercises ("My family...," "I look forward to...," "God tells me...," etc.)
plus discussion on how to evaluate results and understand feelings, role
model attitudes, guilts, etc. The exercises themselves, as evidenced by
the above examples, are very open-ended, designed to stimulate rich, complex responses; Wicks' goal is to help people arrest burn-out through
revitalizing self-awareness.

130. Kemp, Charles F. Thinking and acting biblically. Nashville, TN: Abing-
     don, 1976. 111p. LC 75-43850. ISBN 0-687-41739-2. OCLC 1975279. pap.
     (o.p.).
This is designed to help people identify and work with their own attitudes
toward various scriptural issues. Kemp presents a "Biblical Attitudes
Survey"--selected passages followed by questions exploring how they make
the reader feel--and a manual discussing each item in the survey, giving
background information, typical responses most people have to the passages
in question, and suggested ways of applying the verses' insights. Intended
for encouragement, challenge, and comfort.

131. Strunk, Orlo, Jr. The secret self. Nashville, TN: Abingdon, 1976.
     110p. LC 76-14780. ISBN 0-687-37299-2. OCLC 2189239. (different BIP
     ed.).
Strunk, a minister/counselor/educator, writes primarily for those under-
going some form of transition in their lives; his aim is to help them get
in touch with their innermost selves and to work fruitfully with the private meanings of what they experience. He looks at the importance of tolerating ambiguity, personhood as a "gift" and not a "goal," life as a
"mystery" rather than just a "problem," and the value of befriending oneself in the midst of unfolding reality. Spiritual direction for the re-
flectively inclined.

132. Cooper, John C. Fantasy and the human spirit: finding out who you are
     and what you would like to be. New York: Crossroad-Seabury, 1975.
     178p. notes. LC 74-34567. ISBN 0-8164-0264-7. OCLC 1174727. (o.p.).
Everyone, Cooper believes, not only has an inner life story but is his/her
inner story, and one's "religious posture in the world" is ultimately determined by the kind of story that is. This explores several archetypal
inner identities, some conducive to more shallow styles of living and
others--e.g., the Wounded Healer--facilitating deep spirituality. Because
Cooper feels we can become "twice born" when we learn to live our own stories and break out of those that have been superimposed on us by others,
he spends a good deal of time offering guidance on changing our scenarios.
Imaginative and reflective.

133. Kelsey, Morton. <u>Dreams: a way to listen to God</u>. New York: Paulist, 1978.
     104p. bibliog. LC 77-83583. ISBN 0-8091-2046-1. OCLC 3947409. <u>pap</u>.
Based on lectures given in 1973, this is aimed at the general reader with
little or no background in psychology or theology, who wishes to interpret
his/her dreams from a Christian point of view. Kelsey, Episcopalian
priest/psychologist, opens by stressing that God does speak to people
through dreams in spite of theological views (briefly summarized) that might
deny this. He then looks at the process of dreaming, as well as at visions
and intuition, to show, via discussion and example, how spiritual truths
can break through in this fashion. Types of dreams, guidelines for interpretation, and instances of dreaming in the Bible follow, with a closing
look at some modern dreams and a dream sequence. Like Riffel's book (below), this has a clear Jungian orientation, but has less self-disclosure.

134. Riffel, Herman H. <u>Your dreams: God's neglected gift</u>. Lincoln, VA:
     Chosen-Zondervan, 1982. 160p. index. LC 81-21635. ISBN 0-310-60350-1.
     OCLC 8052191.
In 1964 Riffel was moved by a disturbing dream to embark on a search that
ultimately led him out of his conservative pastorate (his flock felt
threatened), through Jungian training, and into a new dream ministry with
wife Lillie. Dreams, he argues here, are simply one more tool for coming
to know God's will, not a threat to religious faith, and he discusses
scriptural examples, common symbols, animus/anima concepts, and more, in
a simple, readable style. A good book for Christians who are somewhat
anxious about the whole subject; for public, church libraries.

135. Reid, Clyde H. <u>Dreams: discovering your inner teacher</u>. Minneapolis,
     MN: Winston, 1983. 108p. bibliog. LC 82-51158. ISBN 0-86683-703-5.
     OCLC 9906465. <u>pap</u>.
An introductory book for the lay reader by a Jungian therapist which will
probably appeal most to those interested in Catholic spirituality. Reid
discusses basic assumptions of dream work, a few symbols, archetypes, remembering the dream, dreams as a way to the "inner teacher," sharing
groups, journaling, etc. Written in a relaxed, comfortable tone, this
stresses individual respect: ultimately you are the only one who can interpret your dreams authoritatively. Less specific attention to the theological component than Riffel's, say, and less suited to the evangelically
inclined.

136. Savary, Louis M. and others. <u>Dreams and spiritual growth: a Christian
     approach to dreamwork</u>. New York: Paulist, 1984. xi, 241p. illus. bib-
     liog. LC 84-60566. ISBN 0-8091-2629-X. <u>pap</u>.
This differs from other annotated titles on this subject in its emphasis
on specific techniques for personal dreamwork. Savary and co-author
Patricia H. Berne have written extensively in the area of spiritual psychodynamics and inner exploration; here, with Strephon Williams, they divide
their material into three main areas--relating to God, to oneself, and to
the community via dreams and dreamwork--and, after brief discussions of
biblical perspectives and current theory, present 37 specific techniques
for personal use in exploring dreams.

137. Vanderwall, Francis W. <u>Spiritual direction: an invitation to abundant
     life</u>. New York: Paulist, 1981. xi, 99p. LC 81-83185. ISBN 0-8091-2399-1.
     OCLC 8126098. <u>pap</u>.
Here is an introductory volume by a priest and long-time spiritual director
aimed at those seeking personal growth and/or hoping to become directors

themselves. Vanderwall feels all believers can profit from guidance, and
lay people as well as priests and religious can make good directors. With
these assumptions, he discusses the process of direction (listening coupled
with sound discernment of creative versus destructive feeling states) and
what to look for in a spiritual guide; he also shares case material and
personal experiences reflecting his own vulnerability. A useful book for
popular and/or professional collections.

138. Edwards, Tilden H. Spiritual friend: reclaiming the gift of spiritual
     direction. New York: Paulist, 1980. 264p. bibliog. notes. LC 79-91408.
     ISBN 0-8091-2288-X. OCLC 6492351. pap.
Exploring the ancient Roman Catholic/Anglican tradition of spiritual direction and its contemporary usefulness, this is in large part aimed at the
Church and its leaders but is also for the lay reader who may wish to seek
his/her own guide. Edwards uses a mix of "languages" (theological, behav-
ioral/scientific, humanistic) and takes an ecumenical approach, reaching
out to non-Christians while still affirming his own identity as an Episcopalian priest. Very richly textured.

139. English, John. Choosing life: the significance of personal history
     in decision-making. New York: Paulist, 1978. 229p. LC 78-58315.
     ISBN 0-8091-2113-1. OCLC 4458155. pap. (also cloth).
For Christians who want to make spiritually authentic personal decisions,
and also for those who direct them, this is a guide to using one's life
story as the context for spiritual consolation throughout the decision-
making process. Instruction for meditating on one's history, phases of
remembering, searching for pattern, states of wholeness and openness,
meditation exercises (from St. Ignatius), and personal sharing.

140. Hulme, William E. Dealing with double-mindedness. San Francisco:
     Harper, 1982. viii, 112p. notes. LC 82-47745. ISBN 0-06-064079-0.
     OCLC 8473940. pap.
The Epistle of James warns against double-mindedness; pastoral counselor
Hulme has written a clear, readable book exploring this concept. Citing
biblical examples (OT and NT both), case histories, and personal experiences, he looks at the nature of double-mindedness (or ambivalence), its
psychological causes (fear, guilt, divided loyalties), and resolution via
commitment and growth in the direction of God's call.

141. Wilson, Earl D. The undivided self: bringing your whole life in line
     with God's will. Downers Grove, IL: InterVarsity, 1983. 191p. illus.
     notes. LC 83-6189. ISBN 0-87784-842-4. OCLC 9412513. pap.
Wilson's aim is to help readers attain inner wholeness in their faith relationship with God. Stressing that such integrated trust takes time, he
explores how the processes of thinking, feeling, choosing, and doing can
be brought into mutual harmony, eliminating the dualism that results when,
for instance, we think one thing but feel (or choose, or do) another.
This is a practical, clear exposition, fleshed out with many examples
drawn from Wilson's own life and the lives of counselees.

142. O'Connor, Elizabeth. Our many selves. New York: Harper, 1971. xxi,
     201p. bibliog. LC 78-124699. OCLC 113915. pap.
The first book in a trilogy presenting exercises for spiritual reflection
and growth (see also Search for silence and Eighth day of creation, both
annotated), this focuses on the need to identify, observe, and listen to
our contradictory inner voices so as to move from a position where we are

overly prone to judge, into a capacity for empathy, creative suffering,
and--finally--genuine integration. The exercises are actually extended
sequences of readings culled from philosophy, psychology, literature and
the Bible; O'Connor's introductory essays work to facilitate the reader's
ability to use the readings as catalysts for inner transformation.

143. Osborne, Cecil G. The art of becoming a whole person. Waco, TX: Word,
     1978. 187p. notes. LC 77-92465. ISBN 0-8499-0075-1. OCLC 4499307.
A look at factors which make us less than whole and at some approaches/
movements (retreats, Faith-at-Work workshops, Yokefellow groups, secular
therapy styles) that can nurture integration and spiritual-emotional well-
being. Osborne stresses that wholeness does not mean perfection but instead signifies patience and openness to growth; his thoughts on how a
faulty God-concept (excessively legalistic, etc.) can inhibit integration
and on how we need to transcend moralistic thinking should please liberally
inclined readers.

144. Hudnut, Robert K. The bootstrap fallacy: what the self-help books
     don't tell you. Cleveland, OH: Collins, 1978. 146p. notes. LC
     78-69974. ISBN 0-529-05495-7. OCLC 4759237.
The main point in this interesting book is that attempts to achieve by
conscious effort alone can only produce growth up to a point; beyond that,
it is important to make contact with one's "opposites," with "who I am
not," through passive acts of the spirit--dreaming, praying, self-emptying--
since the real goal should be wholeness, not just achievement. Hudnut
also emphasizes that God and biblical parables/imagery are the ultimate
resources for wholeness.

145. Larson, Bruce. Ask me to dance. Waco, TX: Key Word-Word, 1972. 151p.
     bibliog. notes. LC 72-84396. ISBN 0-8499-4107-5. OCLC 482717. pap.
Designed to help Christians attain personal wholeness while simultaneously
serving as creative presence in the lives of others, this explores six
dimensions of the whole life (emotional, physical, volitional, conceptual,
confessional and relational) and offers guidance for growth. Beyond conversion, Larson believes, one's conceptual vision has the power to effect
transformation, and he considers, too, working with feelings of guilt and
anger, listening to one's body, the sexual dimension, and "the Jesus style"
of authentic relationships. Includes questions for personal exploration.

G.   CONVERSION AND PERSONAL SPIRITUALITY

146. Graham, Billy. How to be born again. Waco, TX: Key Word-Word, 1979,
     c. 1977. 222p. notes. LC 77-76057. ISBN 0-8499-4119-9. OCLC 3140468.
     pap.
A direct, basic statement on how to embrace Christian faith. After acknow-
ledgment of the theological differences over fine points, evangelist Graham
proceeds to discuss the "new birth" from a practical angle, to help readers
enter in personally. The discussion is in three parts: "Man's problem"
(alienation from God as a result of sin), "God's answer" (Jesus' saving
death and Resurrection), and "Man's response" (the "new birth" as a present
reality growing into the future). In the style of Graham's sermons,
filled with examples from contemporary culture and everyday life, presented in direct, familiar language with evangelical appeal.

147. Miller, Keith and Bruce Larson. The edge of adventure: an experiment
     in faith. Waco, TX: Word, 1974. 226p. notes. LC 74-79955. ISBN
     0-87680-979-4. pap.
Described as "an itinerary of first steps" for the new Christian, this
shares reflections and experiences on the themes of becoming committed
and taking the risk of faith, praying, reading the Bible, experiencing
changes in relationships (both happy and frightening), relating to family
members, work/school associates, and the church fellowship, etc. Excerpts
are drawn from previous books by Miller and Larson, identified at the end;
some of the material has been originally written for the present title.
A sequel, Living the adventure: faith and "hidden" difficulties (Word,
1975) presents guidance in a similar format on loneliness, rejection, fantasy, sexual and material needs/desires, and other topics.

148. Carothers, Merlin. Prison to praise. Escondido, CA: Foundation of
     Praise, 1970. 106p. ISBN 0-943026-02-4. OCLC 10843099. pap.
Carothers' "praise" books are well known (Power in praise, Answers to praise
Praise works, etc.). This is his personal story of how he first came into
the ministry from the background of an AWOL sentence, his years as a military chaplain (including duty in Korea and Vietnam) and his unfolding discoveries: first, of the power of the Spirit when he received the gift of
tongues on retreat after an abortive search for resources via the "Spiritual Frontiers" movement; next, of the principle of giving thanks in all
circumstances. Extremely informal in style with many conversations back
and forth between Carothers and the Lord as lessons sink in, and numerous
instances of dramatic answers to prayer.

149. Parry, David. This promise is for you: spiritual renewal and the cha-
     rismatic movement. New York: Paulist, 1978. 147p. LC 77-99305. ISBN
     0-8091-2098-4. OCLC 3892624. pap.
Firstly, an introduction to the nature of charismatic experience, and secondly, guidance on receiving Baptism in the Spirit and opening to gifts.
For those who are impeded from attending prayer meetings or seminars where
these topics are covered, this is intended as personal instruction. Parry
draws from topics covered in "Life in the Spirit" seminars as he discusses
the process of Baptism in the Spirit and cultivation of new life in the
Spirit, some impediments (doubts, failure to forgive, etc.), the ongoing
dynamic (prayer habits, obedience), and perseverance. In the form of a
seven week presentation, with meditations for daily reflection. Mainly
for Catholic readers but potentially useful for others, too.

150. Bennett, Dennis and Rita Bennett. The Holy Spirit and you: a study-guid
     to the Spirit-filled life. New rev. ed. Plainfield, NJ: Logos, 1971.
     232p. bibliog. notes. index. LC 71-140673. ISBN 0-912106-34-4. OCLC
     226380. pap. (available through Bridge).
The Bennetts are both Episcopalians (he is a priest) and have been active
over a decade in the charismatic renewal. Nine o'clock in the morning told
their personal story (Logos, 1970); this is a theological and psychological
handbook on the process of receiving Baptism in the Holy Spirit. Starting
with orthodox doctrine on the new birth, it proceeds to discuss how "filling
with the Spirit facilitates Christian growth, then looks at gifts (examined
separately) and their interplay with fruits, the nature of the "narrow
way" (avoiding extremes), and the importance of prayer/praise in the believer's response to God and His works. Some thoughts, too, on the value of
fellowship and mutual submission as criteria by which to assess a church
family, and on the need to cooperate with God and the Holy Spirit over time

151. Byrne, James E. Living in the Spirit: a handbook on Catholic charis-
    matic Christianity. New York: Paulist, 1975. 184p. bibliog. notes.
    LC 75-28628. ISBN 0-8091-1902-1. OCLC 1857703. (o.p.).
A clear, useful mix of doctrine and practical guidelines designed to help
lay Catholics incorporate the charismatic experience into their daily living. Discusses the process of "receiving the Spirit," characteristics of
authentic spirituality, nurturing the inner life, opening to guidance,
source/purpose/classification of gifts (with particular attention to tongues,
prophecy and healing), and--in conclusion--steps toward true community in
the Church. Includes cautionary words re. abusing gifts, placing undue
emphasis on tongues, etc.

152. Whitehead, Evelyn Eaton and James D. Whitehead. Christian life pat-
    terns: the psychological challenges and religious invitations of
    adult life. Garden City, NY: Image-Doubleday, 1982. 256p. bibliog.
    index. LC 81-43442. ISBN 0-385-15131-4. pap. (also cloth).
Acknowledging that "holiness" has traditionally been seen as dangerous,
destructive, reserved for the atypical person, the Whiteheads explore
whether it cannot really be understood as wholeness, with nature and grace
in partnership rather than at odds. Integrating an Eriksonian approach to
adult development with insights in the Christian theological tradition,
they look at the phenomenon of change (as opposed to stability), adult
crises in terms of psychological structure and spiritual meaning, intimacy's challenges (and its relationship to religious growth), midlife
issues (and religious generativity), and growing old faithfully. Hefty--
too substantive, really, to be considered "self-help" in any standard
sense--but extremely graceful and stimulating.

153. Oates, Wayne E. Nurturing silence in a noisy heart. Garden City, NY:
    Galilee-Doubleday, 1979. 134p. bibliog. index. LC 78-20089. ISBN
    0-385-14787-2. OCLC 4835217.
Pastoral counselor Oates defines "noise" as any sound you do not want or
that comes between you and something you care to listen to--including "between folks" noise as well as impersonal distraction. The quest for silence involves discovering privacy, down-to-earth centering, and con-
sciously silencing noise one finds within. Some discussion, too, of destructive silences, or signs something is seriously wrong--with spouses,
say, or with children. Christian spirituality (the ultimate quest is
always for God) in a simple, reflective mode.

154. Ryan, Thomas. Fasting rediscovered: a guide to health and wholeness
    for your body-spirit. New York: Paulist, 1981. 160p. bibliog. LC
    80-81581. ISBN 0-8091-2323-1. OCLC 7439074. pap.
A Paulist priest looks at Old and New Testament references to fasting,
plus Catholic traditions, in an effort to bring together informational,
theological, experiential, historical, and practical dimensions. Ryan sees
fasting as an act of worship, ministry, spiritual joy, faith, love, prayer,
and meditation, and he offers advice on medical issues (don't fast if you
are pregnant, underweight, on medication, etc.), and side effects, together
with general guidelines.

155. Edwards, Tilden. Living simply through the day. New York: Paulist,
    1978. 225p. illus. notes. LC 77-14855. ISBN 0-8091-2045-3. OCLC
    3650933. pap. (also cloth).
Edwards is director of Shalem, a spiritual development group in Washington,
D.C., and an Episcopalian priest. He starts by sharing his own journey,--

he traveled to the West Coast to explore spiritual movements of an Eastern
orientation and integrate them with Christianity--then offers reflections
on grounding, waking, praying, relating, eating, serving, aching, etc.,
showing how everyday activities can be the context of a deeper spiritual
awareness. Lovely drawings in clear, graceful lines (of open hands, an
uplifted face, a candle) complement the narrative.

156. May, Gerald G. Simply sane: the spirituality of mental health. New
     York: Crossroad, 1982. 130p. LC 81-70379. ISBN 0-8245-0448-8. OCLC
     2947425. pap. (1977 Paulist ed. examined).
A psychiatrist who is also active in the Shalem Institute for Spiritual
Development in Washington, D.C. argues that people are not objects to be
fixed, built or improved upon, and urges readers to let themselves be who
they are, finding their way to growth in the process and rejecting a manipulative "fix-me-up" religious stance. A loose, unspecified, eclectic
theological sense underlies these thoughts on spiritual consciousness;
May values faith and authentic prayer but believes that God is beyond concepts or "labeling" and that as the experience of God deepens, there is
less need for theological concepts.

157. Nouwen, Henri J. M. Making all things new: an invitation to the spir-
     itual life. San Francisco: Harper, 1981. 96p. LC 80-8897. ISBN
     0-06-066326-X. OCLC 7197150.
Nouwen intends this book to be both enticement and guide for the general
reader--Christian or non-Christian--who is drawn to but possibly confused
about the spiritual life. For the sake of brevity he focuses his discussion on the theme of worrying: first, exploring its destructive effects;
next, looking at Jesus' response to man's anxieties; finally, examining
particular disciplines used in spiritual communities. Simply and artfully
written, this would be a good choice for spirituality collections in public, church, or seminary libraries.

158. Van Kaam, Adrian and Susan Annette Muto. Am I living a spiritual life?
     questions and answers on formative spirituality. Denville, NJ:
     Dimension Books, 1978. 184p. LC 78-61428. ISBN 0-87193-065-X. OCLC
     4305057. pap.
Van Kaam, founder of the Institute of Formative Spirituality at Duquesne
University, and Muto, the present director, team up here to address three
major issues in spiritual living: developing a spiritual life, integrating
prayer and participation, and living in Christian community. The text is
organized around catalytic questions which the authors answer in clear,
accessible terms, touching on subjects like useful reflective aids, the
creative tension between the inner and outer worlds, ways of resolving
conflict, and more. In the book's Foreword Fr. Van Kaam explains the essential concepts underlying the theory of formative spirituality: that
God calls each person to discover his/her unique form of life in Christ
and to develop it over time through concrete life experiences.

159. Calian, Carnegie Samuel. For all your seasons: biblical direction
     through life's passages. Atlanta, GA: John Knox, 1979. 135p. LC
     78-71050. ISBN 0-8042-2084-0. OCLC 4859137. (o.p.).
Focusing on five broad developmental issues (the process of doubting, the
search for relationships, mid-life exploration, challenges of aging, encounters with stress), this presents related scriptural passages in each
case, plus reflections/guidance of a pastoral nature. Specific topics
which arise in the discussions include self-acceptance, strengthening a marriage, making friends, facing death, overcoming boredom, career change, etc

160. Wittman, E. C. and C. R. Bollman. Bible therapy: how the Bible solves
     your problems; a guide to God's Word. New York: Simon and Schuster,
     1977. 267p. indexes. LC 77-24678. ISBN 0-671-22860-9. OCLC 3186440.
     (o.p.).
For thirty-one alphabetically arranged subject headings (aging, alcoholism/
addiction, anger, bereavement, failure, fear, greed, poverty, stress, etc.)
the authors provide reassuring pastoral advice with scriptural verses. Intended as on-the-spot comfort rather than in-depth analysis; subjects tend
to be somewhat general and not as specifically developmental as in Calian
(see preceding entry); there are, for instance, no citations for "child-
rearing" or "divorce."

161. Smith, M. Blaine. Knowing God's will: biblical principles of guidance.
     Downers Grove, IL: InterVarsity, 1979. 141p. notes. LC 78-24756.
     ISBN 0-87784-610-3. OCLC 5675311. pap.
Smith sees a continuum between questions for which there are clear-cut moral answers in the Bible and more complex, non-moral ones for which there
are no such definite responses and which we must personally assess in deciding how to proceed. Essentially this is a plea to exercise adult responsibility when it comes to decision-making and not to fall back on magical, superstitious modes of seeking God's will (waiting for visions, putting out "fleeces," etc.). Includes appendix on authority relationships,
stressing common sense over rigid hierarchical assumptions.

162. Elliot, Elisabeth. A slow and certain light: some thoughts on the
     guidance of God. Waco, TX: Word, 1973. 122p. notes. LC 73-76252.
     ISBN 0-87680-864-X. OCLC 700996. pap.
Here are thoughts on discerning and living by God's guidance--first, by
understanding what has been promised in the way of guidance, what the conditions of these promises are (that we recognize God, believe, obey, begin
wherever we can, pray) and what His objectives are (to lead us to Him, to
enable us to help others). Only then, once a context has been established,
is it really time to seek God's will in particular situations: through
"supernatural means" (visible signs, audible signs, angels, dreams/visions,
prophets) and through "natural means" (duty, timing, experiences of being
"called by name," human agents, gifts/abilities, desires, advice from
friends, etc.). Includes biblical examples and personal sharing.

163. Marshall, Catherine. Something more: in search of a deeper faith.
     New York: Avon, 1976. 276p. notes. LC 74-4235. ISBN 0-380-51045-6.
     OCLC 2770125. pap. (other eds. available).
Since A man called Peter, the best-selling biography of her first husband,
Senate Chaplain Peter Marshall, Catherine Marshall has become a dominant
figure in inspirational writing. Later books (To live again; Beyond ourselves) established her style of how-it-was-with-me sharing, coupled with
clear, effective guidance for the reader and discerning exploration of
biblical/theological concepts. Something more, the first of her books
published within the time period covered by this bibliography, draws on
a wealth of biblical study and personal experience (in her second marriage
to Leonard LeSourd) as well as on the insights of numerous friends and
associates. She discusses a wealth of material: on praise, forgiveness,
obedience, the psychodynamics of dreaming, new controversies breaking in
on the Christian community, Satanism, and much more. Substantive, helpful,
and very effectively written. A major contribution to inspirational literature and spiritual self-help.

164. Truman, Ruth. How to be a liberated Christian. Nashville, TN: Abing-
     don, 1981. 158p. bibliogs. LC 80-27302. ISBN 0-687-17710-3. OCLC
     6943027.
Here is a practical guidebook for readers wishing to explore a Christ-centered faith while remaining free from the control of rigid theologies or
authoritarian churches. Truman discusses such topics as how to form Christian relationships, different modes of prayer, various Bible translations,
challenges for married and single people, and the importance of getting in
touch with feelings. While stressing the desirability of fellowship in a
"yes church," she also underlines the need for individual exploration. A
fine book, appropriate for larger public and church collections.

165. Jackson, Catherine. The Christian's secret of a happy life for today:
     a paraphrase of Hannah Whitall Smith's classic. Old Tappan, NJ:
     Power-Revell, 1979. 223p. LC 78-9896. ISBN 0-8007-5061-6. OCLC 4211331.
     pap.
Quaker Hannah Whitall Smith's classic of spiritual guidance, The Christian's
secret of a happy life, still available in various editions, was first published in 1870. Here is a paraphrase--an abridgement, actually--that takes
the original, chapter by chapter, simplifying the prose from its nineteenth
century style and compressing the insights for the average reader. The
design of the original--on the "Life," the "Difficulties," and the "Results"--is lost somewhat by eliminating the three-part division and string-
ing all twenty chapters into one sequence, but the substance is still
here, easily accessible.

166. Thielicke, Helmut. Being a Christian when the chips are down. Phila-
     delphia: Fortress, 1979. 125p. LC 78-54562. ISBN 0-8006-0541-1.
     OCLC 4492125. pap.
Down to earth spiritual guidance for the general reader by a writer considered to be one of the most significant contemporary evangelical theologians. Thielicke first looks at basic questions regarding identity,
fear, purposelessness, the difficulty of forgiving, one's relationships
to neighbors, starting afresh, authentic faith, etc. Then, in conclusion,
he explores some underlying spiritual meanings of Christmas, Good Friday,
Easter and Pentecost. Emphasizes the difference between a full Christian
faith and mere lip service to ethical ideals.

167. Miller, Calvin. The taste of joy. Downers Grove, IL: InterVarsity,
     1983. 138p. notes. LC 83-7839. ISBN 0-87784-831-9. pap.
The first joy that comes with conversion cannot be expected to last, Miller
explains; thereafter, real happiness comes over time, the result of one's
walk with Christ in faith and loyalty; it is always a consequence, and
should never be viewed as an end in itself. This is a sensitive, intelligent discussion by a popular author (a Doctor of Ministry and Baptist
pastor) that explores love as a covenant, transcending inner divisions and
sins of "attitude," loving God, one's mate, and the world, and moving into
Christian ministry.

2.
FAMILY AND
DEVELOPMENTAL ISSUES

A. PRE-TEENS, ADOLESCENTS, AND COLLEGE AGE YOUTH

168. Jones, Chris. Lord, I want to tell you something: prayers for boys.
    Minneapolis, MN: Augsburg, 1973. 96p. illus. LC 73-78266. ISBN
    0-8066-1330-0. OCLC 802905. pap.
Informal, conversational free-verse prayers for boys from the ages eight
to twelve. Under the general headings, "God, you're great," "I'm sorry,
Lord," "Thank you, Jesus," and "Hear me, Lord," these deal with feelings
and responses to daily experience: wonder, sadness, shame, guilt, joy,
laughter, puzzlement, etc. Line drawings by David Koechel.

169. Johnson, Lois. Just a minute, Lord: prayers for girls. Minneapolis,
    MN: Augsburg, 1973. 96p. illus. LC 73-78265. ISBN 0-8066-1329-7.
    OCLC 762693. pap.
Analogous to the preceding title, but aimed, this time, at girls, eight
to twelve. Focused around the themes of "looking in " (feelings and conflicts), "looking out" (friendships, relationships), "looking around"
(trying to make sense of the world), and "looking up" (centering on God).
Again, line drawings by David Koechel.

170. Dobson, James. Preparing for adolescence. Santa Ana, CA: Vision House,
    1978. 192p. LC 78-57673. ISBN 0-88449-034-3. OCLC 4290640. pap.
Written for young people entering their teens by the popular evangelical
counselor, this is a solidly grounded, comfortably empathic book that
stresses what to expect in the way of psychological changes (feelings of
inferiority are discussed at length) and offers advice on how to cope in
fruitful ways: compensating for weakness by developing strengths, concentrating on building genuine friendships rather than getting swept up
by pressures to conform, learning to see past the intensities of the moment and to develop perspective. Less detailed advice on dating than many
such books and emphasizing, instead, psychological foundations.

171. Mueller, Charles and Donald R. Bardill. Thank God I'm a teenager.
    Minneapolis, MN: Augsburg, 1976. 125p. LC 76-3854. ISBN 0-8066-1536-2.
    OCLC 2523164. pap.
The authors--a pastor and a social worker--stress the importance of feeling good about oneself as the "unique you" God made in this book of coun-

sel for young people in their early teens. Much of the advice consists
of general guidelines on communication, living with one's family, and forming relationships. Sensible and middle-of-the-road.

172. Richards, Larry. How I can be real. Rev. ed. Grand Rapids, MI: Zon-
     dervan (Answers for Youth), 1979. 125p. illus. notes. LC 79-20735.
     ISBN 0-310-38971-2. OCLC 5353075. pap.
One of the "Answers for Youth" series that explores issues of developmental tasks for teens, this discusses self-acceptance and confidence,
pressures to conform to the expectations of others, and dynamics of choosin
to stand up for one's own sense of values. Especially good in its efforts
to distinguish between faithful living that results in genuine desire to
grow in God's will vs. a more legalistic stance in which principles are
seen as rigid rules. Occasional cartoons.

173. Hartley, Fred. Growing pains: first aid for teenagers. Old Tappan,
     N J: Power-Revell, 1981. 159p. illus. LC 81-11952. ISBN 0-8007-5067-5
     OCLC 7672111. pap.
Hartley is a youth minister who had his own transforming experience when
he was forced to give up football after a concussion and thereafter gave
his life over to God on a deeper level. Here he looks at various problems
teens encounter--re self-image, parents, dating, matters of conscience,
pain, the future--stressing the importance of Jesus as anchor/resource.
A look, too, at different kinds of negative relationships--overcommitted,
undercommitted, ingrown, possessive--and how they can be healed. A conservative evangelical position on issues of dating and sex.

174. McDowell, Josh and Paul Lewis. Givers, takers and other kinds of
     lovers. Wheaton, IL: Tyndale, 1980. 119p. LC 79-91985. ISBN
     0-8423-1033-9. OCLC 7635547. pap.
McDowell is best known for his formidable Christian apologetics, debating-
style, with Campus Crusade and in several books (e.g., Evidence that demands a verdict, Campus Crusade, 1979). Here he offers advice to teens on
dating and sex, giving a witty presentation of standard, conservative
guidelines. In addition to the moral pep talk, this includes some observations on kinds of love ("if" love, "because of" love, and "love, period")
ways one can program thinking, how to start afresh after an unfortunate
or sinful involvement, and "fun" things to do on a date.

175. Vaughn, Ruth. To be a girl, to be a woman. Old Tappan, NJ: Revell,
     1983. 160p. LC 82-12263. ISBN 0-8007-1328-1. OCLC 8588377.
A minister's wife and author/playwright shares thoughts for maturing teenage girls as they deal with identity issues in the present and anticipate
future roles as women. Stressed throughout is the importance of being the
unique person God intended you to be, and not getting sidetracked with
comparisons or concern over others' expectations. Vaughn discusses the need
for discipline, women as givers, homemaking as the noblest profession (but
the exciting potential, too, in positive aspects of the women's movement),
sex in marriage, etc. A blend of conservative standards and real exuberance.

176. Trobisch, Walter. Living with unfulfilled desires. Downers Grove, IL:
     InterVarsity, 1979. 130p. LC 79-2718. ISBN 0-87784-736-3. OCLC
     6177658. pap.
Trobisch had an extensive counseling ministry through the mail with young
people before his death. Here are representative letters from teens toge-

ther with his responses, touching on a wide range of problems pertaining to sexuality and relationships. Combining a strict conservative stand with an ability to become intensely involved with young people's feelings, Trobisch's letters exhibit deep empathy and concern as long as his counselees seem to accept his values, but can turn quite hard (perhaps unconsciously) when he detects defiance or rebellious challenge. Set against a European or African background (he lived in Austria), Trobisch's books are considered very highly in conservative evangelical circles.

177. Stafford, Tim. A love story: questions and answers on sex. Grand
     Rapids, MI: Zondervan/Campus Life, 1977. 160p. LC 77-2136. ISBN
     0-310-32971-X. OCLC 2818323. pap.
A thoroughly orthodox but sensitive and comfortable book of guidance for teens by the author of Campus Life magazine's column on sex. Stafford discusses why sex belongs only in marriage, how far to go, masturbation, singleness, homosexuality, dating, etc. He is good about keeping things in perspective (he is much more low-key on masturbation, say, than many authors), and he stresses honesty and communication rather than emphasizing legalistic sounding pronouncements. An excellent choice for conservative Christians.

178. Trobisch, Walter and Ingrid Trobisch. My beautiful feeling: corre-
     spondence with Ilona. Downers Grove, IL: InterVarsity, 1976. 123p.
     notes. LC 76-21459. ISBN 0-87784-577-8. OCLC 2694896. pap.
In collaboration with his wife, counselor Trobisch shares the correspondence they had with a seventeen year old girl on the subject of masturbation. The importance that the Trobisches attach to the issue can be ascertained by the fact that an entire book is devoted to it; some intelligent, sensitive points are raised here, and husband and wife feel free to express divergent views at times, which adds to the interest.

179. Lynn. Youth ask Lynn. Nashville, TN: Broadman, 1978. ix, 119p. LC 77-
     91075. ISBN 0-8054-5328-8. OCLC 4499445. pap.
The author of the "Lynn" column offering guidance to young people, published first in Upward and then in Event, sponsored by the Sunday School Board of the Southern Baptist Convention, brings together a number of letters she has received and responses she has given. While explicitly Christian, Lynn's suggestions are less evangelical than in some other books, and her orientation will probably please main-line Christians more than very conservative ones (e.g., she tells a boy who is worried about homosexuality that "God accepts all of us just as we are" in the event that counseling fails to facilitate a heterosexual orientation.

180. Hulme, William E. When I don't like myself. New York: Thomas Nelson
     (Youth Forum Books), 1971. v, 83p. notes. LC 79-169034. ISBN
     0-8407-5318-7. OCLC 216412. pap. (o.p.).
The "Youth Forum" books are jointly published by the Youth Research Center, Inc., of Minneapolis and Nelson; they deal with concerns the center's surveys have found to be especially pertinent to young people, and they assume the importance of religious faith. This title is for those overcome with a sense of guilt or paralysis. It is essentially an exploration of the Gospel message that God loves people unconditionally, where they are, and through this love renders them able to experience creative tension between the "is" and the "should," and hence to grow into freedom and fruitfulness. An extremely reassuring, well-written book.

181. Stafford, Tim. Do you sometimes feel like a nobody? Grand Rapids, MI:
     Zondervan/Campus Life, 1980. 139p. photogs. LC 79-25556. ISBN
     0-310-32951-5. OCLC 5799895. pap.
Here are reflective thoughts, with photos, for teens who are struggling with
a low self-image. Stafford writes on cycles of self-hate, learning to
think more fruitfully, life's meaning, God's forgiveness (and ours), being
loved, etc. He draws on articles from Campus Life magazine and on other
books and periodicals as well; he himself is the author of reflections for
which no by-line appears.

182. Wilkerson, David. Have you felt like giving up lately? Old Tappan,
     NJ: Power-Revell, 1980. 157p. LC 80-10402. ISBN 0-8007-1118-1. OCLC
     5992567.
The founder of Teen Challenge ministries and author of The cross and the
switchblade offers thoughts on coping with dry spells and discouragement.
His main message is that we can't make it alone, but are all dependent on
Jesus' strength; within this context, he discusses victory over trouble-
some sins and temptations, laying down your guilt once you have sought forgiveness, ways God can use people in spite of weakness, Jesus and healing,
etc.

183. Collins, Gary. Give me a break! Old Tappan, NJ: Power-Revell, 1982.
     160p. illus. bibliog. LC 82-538. ISBN 0-8007-5093-4. OCLC 8195131.
     pap.
Advice for teens on coping with ten different kinds of stress--in relations
with others, peer pressure, drugs/alcohol temptations, parental conflicts,
family difficulties, poor self-image, difficulty with feelings, sexual turbulence, religious doubt, and future uncertainties. Collins, a psychologist, opens with a look at various modes of coping with stress (complaining
avoidance, etc.) and urges the benefits of the "believer reaction": turning
to God for guidance and allowing a new awareness of Him to emerge through
adolescent struggles.

184. Nystrom, Carolyn. Lord, I want to have a quiet time: thoughtful studie
     for teens. Chappaqua, NY: Christian Herald, 1981. 163p. illus. LC
     80-69305. ISBN 0-915684-77-2. OCLC 6982360. pap.
Really a guided Bible study from a conservative perspective, this deals
with such major areas as prayer, worship, living "in the world," etc. by
presenting hypothetical life situations a young person might encounter toge
ther with Bible passages, and then asking open-ended questions that stimulate reflection on how one might apply Scripture to the imaginary problem.
Includes space for notes, plans, and responses.

185. Lohmann, Hartwig. I can tell you anything, God. Philadelphia:
     Fortress, 1978. 63p. LC 77-15237. ISBN 0-8006-1324-4. OCLC 3609031.
     pap.
More conversational free-verse prayers for young people. Thematic categories are "prayers for home and family" (including reflections on divorce,
death, dissension), "prayers for understanding" (on being a loner and wondering whether the military really serves the cause of peace), "prayers for
love and friendship" (including romance and the loss of love), "prayers for
students," "prayers for jobs," "prayers for faith," and "lead me on the
right path." Translated by Ingalill H. Hjelm.

186. Lawhead, Steve, ed. After you graduate: a guide to life after high
     school. Grand Rapids, MI: Zondervan/Campus Life, 1978. 121p. illus.
     LC 77-26649. ISBN 0-310-36960-6. OCLC 3516566. (also pap.).
Aimed at high school grads, this deals with four general subject areas--
decisions, changes, jobs, and college--offering advice from the staff of
Campus Life magazine on seeking God's will, dealing with transitions, exploring options, etc. A new edition (not seen by reviewer) was released
in the spring of 1984.

187. Wayne, David J. and Nancy N. Rue. Home: love it and leave it. Grand
     Rapids, MI: Baker Book House, 1983. 101p. ISBN 0-8010-9662-6. OCLC
     10925707. pap.
A marriage/family counselor and a high school teacher team up on a book
for young people who have not yet left home physically but are in the psychological throes of preparing--perhaps unconsciously--to do so. To enable
readers to strengthen the self-concept, to understand the way others influence them in decision making, and to learn to communicate more effectively, they offer guidance in these three areas with some low-key reference to biblical concepts, a series of self-evaluation exercises, and much
colloquial reassurance. Avoids biblical "shoulds" and concentrates more
on psychodynamics.

188. Lawhead, Steve, ed. Welcome to the family: how to find a home with
     other believers. Grand Rapids, MI: Zondervan/Campus Life, 1982. 127p.
     photogs. LC 81-23173. ISBN 0-310-35491-9. OCLC 8170431. pap.
Aimed at the recently converted college age student, these essays/reflec-
tions are centered in the theme of finding a new home, a new family and
identity, and celebrating this identity as it unfolds one step at a time.
Various well known Christian writers--Charlie Shedd, Tim Stafford--have
pieces reprinted here in addition to Lawhead's own thoughts. Large photos
capturing a variety of moods and highlighting basic themes are included.

189. Toohey, William. Life after birth: spirituality for college students.
     New York: Seabury, 1980. x, 133p. LC 80-17268. ISBN 0-8164-2290-7.
     OCLC 6446560. pap.
Toohey, who is director of Notre Dame's campus ministry, writes specifically for undergraduates in this very readable book. The chapters (brief
essays) relate the Gospel message to the daily concerns of students:
forming relationships, preparing for jobs, deciding about sex, etc. The
dominant theme is the nature of Christ's love and the importance of learning to trust and to make ourselves vulnerable. Some attention is also paid
to social and political issues (the bomb, poverty).

190. Hollaway, Stephen and Bill Junker. Working things out. Nashville,
     TN: Broadman, 1974. 128p. LC 74-76913. ISBN 0-8054-5219-2. OCLC
     1093783. pap. (o.p.).
For biblical evangelicals, this exploration of issues arising in college
life is written as a dialogue between Hollaway (a recent college grad) and
Junker, who has been active in student ministries over two decades. The
age difference lends an added dimension to the narrative, and the dialogue
has an authentic, lively ring as the two grapple with issues from their
own perspectives. Touches on ethical and spiritual concerns (dating and
drinking, studies, prayer life, witnessing, politics, etc.).

191. Lawhead, Alice and Steve Lawhead. The ultimate student handbook. West-
      chester, IL: Crossway-Good News, 1984. 233p. illus. LC 83-71749. ISBN
      0-89107-297-7. OCLC 10713286. pap.
A number of evangelical guides for college students approach the secular
campus as hostile territory. This is a much friendlier book, covering all
phases of college life (academics, dealing with the administration, room-
mates, managing time, on vs. off-campus living, etc.). The Lawheads offer
a mix of cutesy lifts (what professors' words really mean), thoughtful counsel (on establishing identity) and nitty-gritty information. This is aimed
at Christians, but save for a few sections--e.g., on the importance of spiritual fellowship--non-Christian readers could use it just as well.

192. White, Jerry. The Christian student's how to study guide. Colorado
      Springs, CO: Navpress, 1980. 107p. illus. bibliog. LC 80-81905. ISBN
      0-89109-446-6. OCLC 7279334. pap.
In his first chapter, White shares the basic Christian assumptions of the
book and suggests readers first straighten out any problems in their relationship with Christ in order for the rest to make sense. Thereafter he
discusses general principles of studying (be responsible, don't cut, start
projects early), questions of scheduling, balancing academics and spiritual
growth via Christian activities, attitudes toward achievement (aim at doing
your best given a 40-50 hour study week), analyzing attitudes, and facing
major problems re grades, preparation, or lack of money.

193. Conway, Jim. Your family: a love and maintenance manual for people
      with parents and other relatives: a His reader. Downers Grove, IL:
      InterVarsity, 1982. 129p. bibliog. LC 81-20809. ISBN 0-87784-370-8.
      OCLC 8034540. pap.
An anthology of evangelical essays/articles sponsored by His magazine on
forming better relationships and sharing one's faith with family members,
this is aimed at a college age audience. Includes contributions from a
counseling perspective (e.g. Walter Trobisch's correspondence with a girl
living in Africa) as well as thoughts from young people themselves, exploring their struggles and insights. Topics covered include parental divorce,
a father's drinking, ways of loving one's parents, and preparing for marriage.

194. Rusbuldt, Richard E. Planning your life: understanding yourself and
      the person you want to become. Valley Forge, PA: Judson, 1978. 88p.
      illus. LC 78-8767. ISBN 0-8170-0817-9. OCLC 4004727. pap.
A twelve session course to help young people discover a sense of personal
purpose and plan for the future, this workbook is intended to be used in
a group context but could conceivably be useful, as well, on an individual
basis. Exercises, open-ended fill-ins, etc., help readers explore questions
of identity, values, the meaning of life, attitudes, objectives, planning,
and so forth. Not evangelical, though scriptural references and faith issues are integrated in a low-key sort of way.

195. Campolo, Tony. You can make a difference. Waco, TX: Word, 1984. 154p.
      LC 83-26024. ISBN 0-8499-2979-2. OCLC 10277375. pap. (study guide by
      Denny Rydberg included).
A book adaptation of a film series by the same name, this tell-it-like-it-
is challenge to young people by sociologist/minister Campolo is grounded
in the premise that God doesn't save people primarily so they can go to
heaven later on, but rather so they will be able to make a difference now:

to suffer and be angry at injustice (Satan's work) and help create a better world. Discusses commitment, vocation, dating, and discipleship.
Done with real flair.

B. BEING A MAN, BEING A WOMAN

196. Getz, Gene A. The measure of a man. Glendale, CA: Regal, 1974, 219p.
    LC 74-175983. ISBN 0-8307-0291-1. OCLC 1010339. pap.
Each of these self-contained chapters presents one trait of Christian manhood, derived from a scriptural passage, together with a "personal project"
to help the reader work at developing the particular characteristic. The
brief essays explore ramifications of the introductory biblical passages
and relate the qualities under discussion to our contemporary situation.

197. Schmidt, Jerry and Raymond Brock. Emotions of a man: what men are
    discovering... what women need to know. Eugene, OR: Harvest House,
    1983. 206p. notes. LC 82-84080. ISBN 0-89081-330-2. OCLC 9750709. pap.
The counselors reflect on men's dilemma today and on how the biblical
Christian view of masculinity offers an alternative. Looking mainly at
Titus and I Timothy (with a smattering of such "secular" types as Erik
Erikson or Herb Goldberg), they endorse developing relationships, authenticity and forgiveness as opposed to the loneliness, perfectionism and
competition society often nurtures. Next they discuss expressing emotions,
and the man as husband, father, worker, and aging human being. A look,
finally, at Jesus as the perfect man.

198. Smith, David W. The friendless American male. Ventura, CA: Regal,
    1983. 194p. notes. LC 82-21518. ISBN 0-8307-0803-4. OCLC 3052488. pap.
Men, says the author, are conditioned to project invulnerability and to
hide their emotions, which inhibits true friendship. Here he looks at
the differences between the sexes, biblical principles of friendship like
respect and self-discipline, qualities men look for in friends, stages of
a developing friendship, understanding oneself, and confronting American
culture. Emphasizes that a covenant relationship with God is the ideal
context for the candor, involvement, and respect that make for true
friendship.

199. Kilgore, James E. The intimate man: intimacy and masculinity in the
    80's. Nashville, TN: Abingdon, 1984. 144p. LC 83-15908. ISBN
    0-687-19128-9. OCLC 9893973. pap.
By a marriage and family counselor, this explores "intimacy in the mascu-
line world" (fear of it in spite of its desirability, developmental aspects),
"masculinity in the feminine world" (the son's relationship with mother
and challenges of creating intimacy with a wife), "intimacy in the changing world" over the life-cycle, including mid-life crisis, and "intimacy
and reality" (issues of aging and spirituality). Assumes that true intimacy requires a relationship with God as father.

200. Benson, Dan. The total man. Wheaton, IL: Tyndale, 1977. 272p. illus.
    notes. LC 76-58134. ISBN 0-8423-7290-3. OCLC 3030384. (also pap.).
Attempting to redress the imbalance that often leaves men solely concerned
with career/success to the exclusion of a genuine personal life, Benson
tackles his subject in two ways. Section One discusses self assessment,
setting priorities, physical fitness, ways of using failures productively,

and the importance of "wisdom, stature and favor with God and man" as a
foundation for right living. Section Two looks at husbandly leadership
(authority within a context of loving mutual submission), communication,
fathering, money, and sex (a relaxed, down-to-earth discussion). Basic
guidance from a conservative evangelical perspective.

201. Holmes, Marjorie. Who am I, God? Garden City, NY: Doubleday, 1971.
     x, 176p. illus. LC 77-139035. ISBN 0-385-00240-8. OCLC 128076. (also
     Bantam ed., pap.).
Prayer reflections in the author's characteristic mode (personal, traditionally feminine in concern and style, occasionally sentimental) dealing
with various dimensions of womanhood: relationships with children, with
other women, with work, with men and with the world, plus feminine awareness, growth, inner identity, suffering, loneliness, and faith in God. An
awareness of psychological and cultural realities beyond her own milieu is
occasionally present (e.g., "My black sister"), but mainly this is grounded
in and crying for traditional values ("Oh, Lord, have mercy upon all your
liberated women").

202. Schlafly, Phyllis. The power of the Christian woman. Cincinnati, OH:
     Standard, 1981. 272p. photogs. notes. index. LC 81-50352. ISBN
     0-87239-457-3. OCLC 7460722. pap.
Schlafly first published this as The power of the positive woman. There
is some conservative biblical rhetoric on God's plan for marriage, the
differences between the sexes, glorification of motherhood, "spinning the
fabric of civilization," etc., but political views ultimately predominate
here as Schlafly discusses the woman's right to financial support and
horrors lurking beneath the seemingly benign language of the ERA. An appendix contains photos taken during a 1976 ERA rally.

203. Hunt, Gladys. Ms.means myself. Grand Rapids, MI: Zondervan, 1975. 145p.
     LC 72-85566. ISBN 0-310-26392-1. OCLC 578150. pap.
True femininity, says Hunt, means being centered in a committed relationship
to God which frees us to be whole people. Stressing that the Genesis account shows male and female created together in God's image, she looks at
some thorny Pauline passages in terms of their cultural setting and explores
implications of women's whole personhood for marriage (the husband is leader, but the wife can be truly creative), for single living (love is the
real need, not sex), and for creative expression in the world (women do
teach in various scriptural contexts, for instance). An emphasis on finding identity in who one is, not just what one does.

204. Briscoe, Jill. Queen of hearts: the role of today's woman based on
     Proverbs 31. Old Tappan, NJ: Revell, 1984. 189p. LC 83-21253. ISBN
     0-8007-1387-7. OCLC 10045954.
Another study of womanhood--i.e., practical guidelines for today's woman--
based on Proverbs 31. Where Gundry (see next annotation) comes from an
explicitly liberationist stance, this is more traditional and low-key
with a chatty style, and Briscoe's characteristically "cute" headings
("Limp loins" for a section on fitness). It starts with the importance
of being "queen of your own heart" (accepting yourself where you are, with
a healthy sense of humor, as a prelude to future growth), then moves on to
discuss being queen in the hearts of one's children, husband, and servants,
as well as in the hearts of the poor, of merchants, and of the Lord. Beneath the somewhat gimmicky surface, there are genuine insights on the importance of an expanding awareness and of functioning in the wider world
while retaining femininity.

205. Gundry, Patricia. The complete woman. Garden City, NY: Galilee-Double-
     day, 1981. 237p. bibliog. LC 79-8928. ISBN 0-385-15521-2. OCLC
     6915902.
Squaring off against Marabel Morgan, Gundry argues that a woman can (and
should) work to develop her own strengths regardless of whether or not she
happens to be married. As a biblical role model she focuses on the ideal
woman described in Proverbs 31, devoting successive chapters to the various
traits this woman embodies: her trustworthiness, her skills as investor,
manufacturer, etc. Anecdotes from Gundry's own life add to this useful
book which Christian feminists should appreciate.

206. Follis, Anne Bowen. I'm not a women's libber, but.... Nashville, TN:
     Abingdon, 1981. 128p. LC 81-1241. ISBN 0-687-18687-0. OCLC 7283659.
     (also Avon ed., pap.).
Follis is a mother, a minister's wife, a born-again Christian, and founder
of the Homemakers' Equal Rights Association, an outgrowth of Housewives for
ERA. In this warm, honest book she shares her personal struggles in moving
from initial defensiveness over ERA to a position of full-fledged support
and explains how she reconciled apparent contradictions between the Bible
and the women's movement by searching for the deeper scriptural message
instead of focusing on glib catch-phrases.

207. Scanzoni, Letha and Nancy Hardesty. All we're meant to be: a biblical
     approach to women's liberation. Waco, TX: Word, 1974. 233p. notes.
     index. LC 74-78041. ISBN 0-87680-897-6. OCLC 1093808. pap.
The first two chapters of Genesis, say the authors, show that God planned
for man and woman to be partners, and that now, thanks to Christ's redeeming power, it is possible to go back to the ideals of Paradise. What follows is a biblically centered, liberally interpreted discussion of a range
of issues related to women's self-fulfillment and male/female partnership.
Not a straight self-help guide, but containing numerous practical implications. New edition has twenty-page study guide.

208. Barnhouse, Ruth T. Identity. Philadelphia: Westminster (Choices:
     Guides for Today's Woman), 1984. 120p. bibliog. LC 84-3664. ISBN
     0-664-24545-5. OCLC 10507729. pap.
Barnhouse is a lay Episcopal theologian and Jungian therapist; here she
looks at women's identity in a Christian context. Taking a moderately
liberal approach to Scripture and stressing Jung's concepts, she argues
that it is women's--and men's--task to integrate their male/female qualities to incarnate God's rich, androgynous nature more completely, while
balancing individual fulfillment against needs of the community. Intelligent and low-key, done with real grace and simplicity.

209. Berry, Jo. Can you love yourself?: self-esteem for today's woman.
     Glendale, CA: Regal, 1978. 159p. LC 77-89395. ISBN 0-8307-0579-1.
     OCLC 4747218. pap.
Stressing the importance of a realistic (not a perfect) self-image as a
basis for fruitful living, Berry offers practical guidelines and a variety
of exercises that women can use in learning to see themselves more clearly,
to identify and develop gifts, etc. Especially useful is the chapter on
how to "agape" yourself, e.g. sacrificially develop true self-worth by
choosing to be centered in God's will rather than being distracted by
temporary expediencies. Includes thoughts on spiritual self-examination
and closes with a look at the self-image of biblical characters.

210. Landorf, Joyce. The fragrance of beauty. Wheaton, IL: Victor, 1973.
     143p. LC 73-76813. ISBN 0-88207-231-5. OCLC 750004. pap.
A popular guide to inner/outer beauty, this discusses key psychological
enemies of beauty (fear, worry, anger, inferiority feelings) and how to
transform them with faith, prayer, self-acceptance and forgiveness. Common
sense advice on the above is interspersed with thoughts on grooming, attractive make-up, physical health, and the importance of cleanliness.
Anecdotes from the lives of family and friends.

211. Ortlund, Anne. Disciplines of the beautiful woman. Waco, TX: Word,
     1977. 132p. notes. LC 77-76347. ISBN 0-8499-0000-X. OCLC 3294384.
A pastor's wife writes on the disciplines involved in growing to Christian
maturity and developing a holistic beauty. Ortlund discusses priorities
(God first, the whole Christian family second, one's individual family
third), goals (she favors setting precise yearly goals and daily schedules,
based on her priorities), spiritual growth (good books, programmed Bible
reading, daily quiet time), close relationships (covenant and fellowship
groups can be very valuable), as well as issues of exercise, grooming, sim-
plification for the sake of serenity, etc. The public and private spheres
are naturally interwoven in Ortlund's thinking; i.e., in writing on building a wardrobe, she places her advice in the context of the gap between
American affluence and poverty in primitive lands. This is much warmer and
more relaxed than, perhaps, it sounds; a hysterectomy and the emotions surrounding it were important as instigating factors in clarifying Ortlund's
thinking.

C.   FROM LONELINESS TO INTIMACY

212. Ripple, Paula. Walking with loneliness. Notre Dame, IN: Ave Maria,
     1982. 159p. notes. LC 82-73048. ISBN 0-87793-259-X. OCLC 9031753. pap.
The theme here is the value of befriending one's own loneliness so that it
becomes a kind of companion, challenging us to risk encounter with others.
Ripple is very much concerned with both inner and outer journeys: dreaming
dreams and "naming our days" (being in charge of one's life), as well as
moving faithfully into the risks of a deep prayer life while embracing the
human condition. Starting with the condition of loneliness, then, this
moves into discussion of the whole spiritual journey.

213. Carter, W. Leslie and others. Why be lonely?: a guide to meaningful
     relationships. Grand Rapids, MI: Baker Book House, 1983. 169p. LC
     82-71425. ISBN 0-8010-2475-7. OCLC 8757223. pap. (also cloth).
Psychiatric colleagues in the Minirth-Meier-Goodin Psychiatric Clinic in
Dallas offer a very practical self-help guide on the causes and cures of
loneliness. They open with an overview of its nature (ways of avoiding
intimacy, a 65-item T-F inventory, discussion of clinical personality
types), look at psychodynamics and sociological/theological dimensions of
the problem, and conclude with positive advice: be active, learn to think
realistically, practice involvement with God in prayer and with others in
your life. Conservative and evangelical,--a discussion of Adam and Eve and
the Fall is included as one cause--but mainly practical, down-to-earth advice.

214. Rohrer, Norman B. and S. Philip Sutherland. Why am I shy?: turning
     shyness into confidence. Minneapolis, MN: Augsburg, 1978. 128p. LC
     78-52182. ISBN 0-8066-1656-3. OCLC 4193370. pap.
A Christian writer who conquered a bad case of shyness and a psychotherapist
who has counseled many shy people team up here to discuss various dimensions
of the problem. Included is a look at different types of shyness, ways of
helping shy children, plus being single and shy, married and shy, and turning shyness into an asset. The book takes a very practical approach--exer-
cises, sample cases, description of a shyness clinic--without too much concentration on the Christian dimension, though the authors do explore briefly
how theological distortions can hurt and a right understanding of God's unconditional love can help.

215. Osborne, Cecil G. The art of getting along with people. Grand Rapids,
     MI: Zondervan, 1980. 200p. notes. LC 80-12832. ISBN 0-310-30612-4.
     OCLC 10043210. pap.
Osborne offers general guidelines on effective communication: the importance of grace and tact; working through differences; getting along with
children, neurotics and "difficult people"; when and how to confront; how
inferiority feelings inhibit relationships; and types of reactions/responses.
The introductory chapter with its look at Jesus' style in human relations
sets the tone for the genuinely Christian but non-doctrinaire advice Osborne
offers, and for his emphasis on the importance of recognizing our own imperfections and refraining from judging others.

216. Walters, Richard Paul. How to be a friend people want to be friends
     with. Ventura, CA: Regal, 1981. 176p. notes. LC 81-52163. ISBN
     0-8307-0746-8. OCLC 7875295. pap.
A "servant friend" is one who cares to notice and respond to another's genuine need--discerning, affirming, sharing, giving and receiving trust. The
best way to get such friends, psychologist Walters advises, is to be one,
and in this comfortable, accessible book he tells how, combining insights
from counseling psychology with real-life examples as he discusses listening skills, trust, confrontation, self-disclosure, forgiving, etc. It is
to Walters' credit that besides exploring how Christian faith can help, he
acknowledges that nonbelievers sometimes may prove better friends than
believers. For public and church libraries.

217. McGinnis, Alan Loy. The friendship factor: how to get closer to the
     people you care for. Minneapolis, MN: Augsburg, 1979. 192p. LC
     79-50076. ISBN 0-8066-1711-X. OCLC 5010744. pap. (Spanish ed. only
     in BIP).
Here are ways to deepen friendships via self-disclosure, warmth, manifes-
ting caring in action, handling negative emotions constructively, etc.
McGinnis emphasizes the value of letting oneself be openly vulnerable
through touch, tears, honest conversation; he stresses, too, ways of sal-
vaging hurting relationships (forgiveness, loyalty) and the dynamics of
different sex friendships, e.g., keeping eros under control while still
letting feelings deepen. This closes with reassurance that no one succeeds
all the time and that in order to grow, one must have some space to fail, ab-
sorbing occasional rejection but still reaching out anew with others. Gospel passages are used illustratively rather than as pre-programmed "blueprints" for living, and a study guide is available also.

218. Howard, J. Grant. The trauma of transparency: a biblical approach to
    interpersonal communication. Portland, OR: Multnomah (Critical Con-
    cern Books), 1979. 235p. illus. bibliogs. indexes. LC 79-87716. ISBN
    0-930014-28-6. OCLC 5944437. (also pap. and study guide).
This is a guide for biblically centered interpersonal communication which
starts with the premise that one's relationship with God is the context
for effective communication with oneself and others. Howard first looks at
how to talk with and listen to God, then proceeds to other modes of communication. We tend, he says, to "hide" or "hurl" when in tricky or upset-
ting situations and must learn to grow beyond these patterns, since they
throw up barriers and prevent the sort of open communication God desires.

219. Swindoll, Charles R. Dropping your guard. Waco, TX: Word, 1983. 213p.
    notes. LC 83-17021. ISBN 0-8499-0352-1. OCLC 9853600. pap.
Swindoll is thinking mainly of building the body of Christ when he speaks
about the importance of open, vulnerable relationships and a caring fellowship; however, his words are certainly applicable to forming relationships in personal living, too, apart from the context of a congregation.
Here he discusses principles for honest friendship, including risk-taking,
authentic love, tolerance and compassion, rising above legalism, etc. Pastor of an Evangelical Free Church and known through his "Insight for Living"
radio program in addition to a number of books, Swindoll cites the Bible
frequently as he offers counsel.

220. Miller, Keith. The becomers. Waco, TX: Word, 1973. 185p. illus. bibliog
    LC 72-96363. ISBN 0-87680-321-4. OCLC 672029.
Miller, one of the leaders of the "relational Christianity" movement, explores the value of living an open, vulnerable lifestyle and the implications of such a style for one's faith. He looks at some internal psychodynamics, at how we usually hide from revealing ourselves to others, and
at how the conversion process (by which the struggle toward growth is set
in motion) leads us continually to surrender security props as they are
revealed to us over time. Includes personal sharing and examples from
others' lives.

221. Cerling, Charles E. Holy boldness. Chappaqua, NY: Christian Herald,
    1980. 162p. LC 80-65435. ISBN 0-915684-67-5. OCLC 6790586. pap.
Written by a pastor and counselor, this book argues that assertiveness (as
contrasted to aggressiveness) is a valid Christian style. Much of the material can be found in standard self-help manuals (how to send "I-messages,"
how to practice "active listening," why to avoid manipulation), but Cerling
does make a unique contribution in explicitly integrating these techniques
with scriptural values and in stressing the importance of assertiveness in
witnessing as well as in personal relationships. The chapters on anger are
especially useful. Includes exercises, references to Scripture, assignments for practicing techniques.

222. Augsburger, David and John Faul. Beyond assertiveness. Waco, TX: Cal-
    ibre Books-Word, 1980. 235p. illus. bibliog. LC 80-51450. ISBN
    0-8499-2925-3. OCLC 7000854. pap. (o.p.).
The point of this book is to integrate assertiveness and loving behavior;
assertiveness training which doesn't also focus on the need for affirmation, say the authors, is one-sided and incomplete. The first section emphasizes this need for power and love to be joined in wholeness; thereafter
comes a discussion on how behavior patterns are learned and how feelings

are formed; finally there are instructions and exercises on becoming affirmative and assertive, becoming observant, becoming impactful, and creating
community. Many exercises; not very much scriptural discussion.

223. Augsburger, David. Caring enough to confront. Rev. ed. Ventura, CA:
      Regal, 1980. 142p. notes. LC 80-123568. ISBN 0-8307-0733-6. OCLC
      844256. pap. (other eds. available).
Augsburger, a Mennonite professor of pastoral care, has written a series
of "Caring Enough" books (Caring enough to hear and be heard, When caring
is not enough: resolving conflict through fair fighting, and Caring enough
to forgive/caring enough to not forgive). Caring enough to confront was
originally published in 1973 as The love fight (Herald) and here, in a
revised edition, explores integrating one's own needs and wants with those
of others, using conflict for creative growth, owning anger, and balancing
truth with love in a style that involves "care-fronting" and ultimately
leads to eliminating blame and letting go of the conflict entirely.

224. Krebs, Richard L. Creative conflict. Minneapolis, MN: Augsburg, 1982.
      111p. LC 82-70945. ISBN 0-8066-1920-1. OCLC 8636948. pap.
Krebs, a Christian psychologist, sets forth four principles--commitment,
caring, firmness and protection--which, when applied, can make conflict
creative rather than destructive. Citing Jesus' "creative conflicts" with
his mother, his disciples and his opponents, he offers advice on using the
four principles in conflicts with spouse, boss and church colleagues as well
as with oneself (conflict "inside your head"). Examples from his own and
others' experiences are included.

225. Buckingham, Jamie. Coping with criticism. Plainfield, NJ: Haven-Logos,
      1978. 158p. LC 78-60994. ISBN 0-88270-327-7. OCLC 4884251. pap. (avail-
      able through Bridge).
Critics and criticism, Buckingham says, can be good for us in helping us
grow into Jesus' image; whether justified or unjustified, another's negative comments can always be used in fruitful ways. In preparing oneself
to be the sort who can use criticism well, he suggests an honest attitude,
clear goals so we won't be lost in defensiveness, an empathic attitude, and
a secure Christian identity. Discusses the dynamics of getting past the
"point of reaction" to the "point of recovery" and how to work constructively with what one has been told.

226. Sanford, John. Between people: communicating one-to-one. New York:
      Paulist, 1982. 96p. LC 81-84350. ISBN 0-8091-2440-8. OCLC 8365070. pap.
Starting with some standard ideas on topics like creative listening and
working through agendas, this moves on to employ Jungian theory in some
very interesting ways, using animus/anima and typological concepts to describe styles of inter-personal psychodynamics. Includes discussion of
"gigantic emotions" which can potentially overwhelm, and how to handle them
effectively. With implications for a variety of close relationships, this
offers some interesting psychological insights as well as theological exploration. By an Episcopalian priest and Jungian analyst.

227. Kinzer, Mark. Taming the tongue. Ann Arbor, MI: Servant (Living as a
      Christian), 1982. 143p. ISBN 0-89283-165-0. OCLC 9513537. pap.
Kinzer stresses that speech has a real life-and-death power, so it is important Christians learn to control what they say. He looks first at the
"dark side" of speech--ways people can cause damage through fighting, whis-
pering slander, "slapping with a smile," etc.--and then at ways to use

speech to build one another up, e.g., correcting gracefully, praising God, and so on. The stress is on changing ways of listening, thinking, and responding.

228. Keating, Charles J. Dealing with difficult people. New York: Paulist, 1984. 212p. bibliog. index. LC 83-82018. ISBN 0-8091-2596-X. OCLC 11051771. pap.
The author, who is a personal counselor and business management consultant, offers guidance on working through personality conflicts with difficult relatives, work associates, group members, etc. Drawing on Transactional Analysis techniques and Jungian typological theory as reconstructed by Isabel Briggs Myer, he explains ways of working through "games" people play with one another and of dealing successfully with others in "one to one" situations. An emphasis on the psychology of conflict resolution and the role of feelings, with theological exploration kept to a minimum.

229. Landorf, Joyce. Irregular people. Waco, TX: Word, 1982. 155p. bibliog. LC 82-50842. ISBN 0-8499-0291-6. OCLC 8765560.
"Irregular people" are those to whom one is related in some close way-- parents, siblings, spouses, in-laws--who seem to cause endless frustration and pain by their cramped, unloving attitudes. There is much sharing here re Landorf's agony at the hands of her own "irregular person" (familial role hinted at rather than openly identified); her breakthrough apparently came via advice from psychologist James Dobson, who encouraged her to regard the "irregularity" as a handicap analogous to being blind or deaf, and to try and accept the difficult person as he is, leaving him in God's hands.

230. Wilson, Ken. How to repair the wrong you've done: steps to restoring relationships. Ann Arbor, MI: Servant (Living as a Christian), 1982. 87p. ISBN 0-89283-116-2. OCLC 9183365. pap.
A brief additional title in the "Living as a Christian" series, this dis- cusses the various steps involved in reconciliation: admitting one's wrongs, renouncing them, being reconciled, making restitution, and begin- ning to assess damages and make repairs. Like others in the series, this stresses practical, specific kinds of behavior growing out of orthodox Christian attitudes.

231. Kraybill, Ronald S. Repairing the breach: ministering in community conflict. Scottdale, PA: Herald, 1981. 95p. notes. LC 82-80586. ISBN 0-8361-3302-1. OCLC 8917477. pap.
Though primarily intended for church leaders, this nonetheless contains advice that could be very useful for others in resolving disputes between friends, family, or community members. Kraybill, who is director of the Conciliation Service of the Mennonite Central Committee, takes a case study approach to conflict resolution and looks in concrete, practical ways at mediation strategies for disagreements between groups, between individuals, and within groups. A "how to" book for the "peacemaker/mediator."

232. Towner, Jason. Forgiveness is for giving. Nashville, TN: Impact, 1982. 165p. LC 81-84923. ISBN 0-914850-56-3. OCLC 8283884. pap. (also Zon- dervan ed.).
Forgiveness, says the author of Jason loves Jane but they got a divorce (Impact, 1978), is a definite promise of God and operates according to specific principles: it is not negotiable, it is not earned, it must be demonstrated, it is an investment in future potential, etc. Sprinkled with

biblical references, this explores in extremely colloquial language forgiving one's ex, the church, one's parents, one's children, oneself, and
life itself.

233. Smedes, Lewis B. Forgive and forget: healing the hurts we don't de-
     serve. San Francisco: Harper, 1984. 152p. LC 84-47736. ISBN
     0-06-067408-3. OCLC 10751255.
By the author of How can it be all right when everything is all wrong?
(Harper, 1982), here is a first-rate self-help book. It is clear and readable in its discussion of the four stages of forgiveness, people who are
hard to forgive, how the process works, and why it is so important. Then
too, Smedes does a masterful job of conveying the emotional dimensions
involved, both resistances and that mysterious bedrock of faith and trust
in spite of suffering which, in the end, carries us through. Finally, the
honest self-disclosure adds enormously.

234. Donnelly, Doris. Learning to forgive. New York: Macmillan, 1979. xiv,
     127p. notes. index. LC 79-15964. ISBN 0-02-532140-4. OCLC 5101214.
     (Abingdon ed. in BIP).
Recognizing that true forgiveness cannot be rushed and presupposes confrontation with our own wounds, Donnelly first discusses why it is neither easy
nor "natural" to forgive and what happens when we don't, then moves on to
explore the forgiveness process itself and its redemptive value, concluding
with a look at modes of forgiveness manifested in Jesus' life. Donnelly
is a theologian, and her faith permeates her writing. Her style, however,
is not evangelical. She cites Arendt, Jung, and May along with the Bible.
Her prose itself is so lucid and graceful that this is ideal for the general
reader.

235. Augsburger, David. Caring enough to forgive: true forgiveness and
     Caring enough to not forgive: false forgiveness. 2 vols. in 1. Scott-
     dale, PA: Herald, 1981. 98, 75p. illus. LC 81-80913. ISBN 0-8361-1965-7.
     OCLC 8129190. pap.
Another in Augsburger's excellent "Caring Enough" series, this is an off-
beat, effective book. Open it from one side to find a discussion of "true
forgiveness" based on "the mutual recognition that repentance is genuine,
and right (righteous) relationships are now achieved"; then turn it over
for a look at "false forgiveness" which, under the guise of benevolence,
actually plays games of one-upmanship as it denies and distorts feelings.
Augsburger, a Mennonite professor of pastoral care, writes simply and clearly with useful charts, exercises, biblical guides. Moreover, he makes some
very fine points.

236. Montgomery, Dan. Courage to love. Glendale, CA: Regal, 1980. 125p.
     illus. LC 79-65421. ISBN 0-8307-0720-4. OCLC 6173985. pap. (o.p.).
God, says counselor Montgomery, wants us to experience more of ourselves,
to open up in vulnerability so we can truly love. He offers some exercises
designed to help readers experience feelings they often cover up, plus
discussion questions to help them get past inhibitions and realize all their
mixed feelings toward God, anger as well as gratitude.

237. Fosmire, Bea. Growing pains: the risks and rewards of love. Grand
     Rapids, MI: Zondervan, 1983. 127p. notes. LC 83-7008. ISBN
     0-310-29331-6. OCLC 9413158. pap.
Not a straight "how to" book, this explores through the author's own experiences and those of people she knows the many ways love works for growth

even in the midst of conflict and pain. Even when we lose people and relationships seem to be utterly destroyed, Fosmire stresses, God's love is
still eternal. There are some very deep feelings that are touched on here—
e.g., in the case of a father who rejected his drug-addicted teen-age
daughter, then later lost her to suicide. Essentially an impassioned plea
urging people to take all the risks involved in opening themselves to genuine caring.

238. Powell, John. Unconditional love. Niles, IL: Argus, 1978. 118p. illus.
     LC 78-74154. ISBN 0-89505-029-3. OCLC 5102935. pap.
Asserting that everyone has a dominant "life principle" which will one day
possess him or her, Powell suggests that Jesus' dominant principle was
orientation to the Kingdom of God as a reality of unconditional love for
others, and he offers this as the best approach to living for people today.
Such unconditional love, Powell says, is best suited to meet our contemporary crisis, the loss of fidelity in love; then he discusses the dynamics
of giving oneself as a full person in truly loving relationships. Spirituality by a popular priest/psychologist.

D. SINGLES, SEXUALITY, AND FORMING COMMITMENTS

239. Collins, Gary R., ed. It's O.K. to be single: a guidebook for singles
     and the church. Waco, TX: Word, 1976. 165p. notes. LC 76-2857. ISBN
     0-87680-858-5. OCLC 2507280. pap.
Containing essays by various Christian writers and leaders who spoke at a
1975 conference on the family, this deals both with what singles want from
the church and how they can most fruitfully approach the church (e.g., by
offering their gifts rather than just looking to have their own needs met).
Includes reflections pertinent to the divorced, bereaved, and never-married,
as well as to college students and young people generally. Closes with a
"Christian life-style for singles."

240. Clarkson, Margaret. So you're single. Wheaton, IL: Shaw, 1978. 166p.
     LC 78-53012. ISBN 0-87788-772-1. OCLC 4747098. pap.
This is more a biblically based spiritual guide to the single experience
than a practical "how to" book, and if the reader is sympathetic to Clarkson's very conservative Christian stance, he or she will find much that
is quite profound here. Singleness, Clarkson says, is one of the results
of sin in the world rather than a state originally intended by God, but He
meets us all where we are in His sovereignty. Singles can be free in
Christ to be fully themselves, as whole sexual beings (though there is to
be no sexual activity per se outside marriage). God's gifts to help sus-
tain single people through loneliness can be the roots of job or home,
friendships with others (including married couples), and church fellowships, with a stress on areas of interest and modes of service, not marital
status. A very empathic tone.

241. Fix, Janet with Zola Levitt. For singles only. Old Tappan, NJ: Power-
     Revell, 1978. 126p. LC 78-9754. ISBN 0-8007-0946-2. OCLC 3912595. pap.
By the director of a California singles ministry for Christians, this evangelical guide offers counsel with an emphasis on complete surrender to
Christ in the "now" as a context for fulfillment. Fix advises singles to
make a conscious choice to put aside forbidden "natural" desires as she
writes on emotions, liberation, love, and heartbreak. The underlying yearn-

ing to be part of a couple is clear; single living, in this book, is obviously considered an unwelcome state that requires acceptance rather than
a condition, or calling, embraced with genuine happiness.

242. McAllaster, Elva. Free to be single. Chappaqua, NY: Christian Herald,
     1979. 279p. notes. LC 78-64838. ISBN 0-915684-45-4. OCLC 4834624.
     (also pap.).
McAllaster, an English professor, engages in a kind of conversational dialogue with the reader here, reflecting on her own experiences as a single
and encouraging others to take a more positive view of the single life.
She stresses the opportunities--for deep self-giving with a variety of
friends, say--and encourages married couples in the church to enter imaginatively into the singles' situation and to be open to what unmarried
persons can contribute. Orthodox on questions of sexuality; written with
great humor and style.

243. Miller, Keith and Andrea Wells Miller. The single experience. Waco,
     TX: Word, 1981. 262p. LC 80-54551. ISBN 0-8499-0286-X. OCLC 8081159.
Miller and his second wife share personal experiences as "single again"
Christians after their own divorces and before their remarriage to one
another. Chapter topics are introduced by their notes to one another suggesting discussion on this or that theme: beginning again as a single;
loneliness; the psychodynamics of identity development; breaking depend-
encies on your parents (or helping your children to do so); money; friendships; single parenting; dating and the dynamics of intimacy; sex; faith
in God. Keith Miller is well known as a spokesman for the "relational
Christianity" movement, and the discussions here on the psychodynamics and
role of sex, say, are more open than in many other books. Still, the biblical ideal is clearly affirmed.

244. Payne, Dorothy. Singleness. Philadelphia: Westminster (Choices:
     Guides for Today's Woman), 1983. 112p. bibliog. LC 83-10174. ISBN
     0-664-24541-2. OCLC 9643749. pap.
The author is a Presbyterian minister who directs a woman's center; here
she looks at the phenomenon of singleness among women, stereotypes and
discrimination, coping with problems like low self-esteem and loneliness,
meeting needs for relationship, home, and economic security, opportunities
for single women to grow in self-determination, and God's special gifts to
singles such as resources for rootedness, community, celibacy, belonging,
and fulfillment. At the liberal end of the spectrum (Payne considers
certain sexual relationships outside marriage as possibilities), this is
a clear, sensitive presentation of issues/options.

245. Muto, Susan Annette. Celebrating the single life: a spirituality for
     single persons in today's world. Garden City, NY: Doubleday, 1982.
     191p. bibliogs. LC 81-43770. ISBN 0-385-18102-7. OCLC 8306750.
Unlike the how-to books for singles which assume marriage as an eventual
goal, this stresses the possibility of a true vocation of singleness for
lay people. Muto, herself a committed single and Director of the Institute
of Formative Spirituality, emphasizes contributions singles can make as,
for instance, models of human uniqueness adept at balancing opposite modes
like detachment and involvement. Unfortunately, the theoretical framework
("the science of foundational formation") is never fully explained, so its
jargon may confuse the uninitiated. Still, this will be very useful for
reflective readers.

246. Scanzoni, Letha Dawson. Sexuality. Philadelphia: Westminster
     (Choices: Guides for Today's Woman), 1984. 113p. bibliog. LC 83-27375.
     ISBN 0-664-24548-X. OCLC 10301164. pap.
Scanzoni has previously written on sex from an evangelical perspective and
co-authored Is the homosexual my neighbor? (see annotation). In this
title she sensitively explores diverse aspects of female sexuality: experiencing and understanding it, expressing it, hurts that can occur (rape,
incest), and sex over the life span. While gently reinforcing the biblical
view of sex in "covenant," she still quotes from sources like The Hite
Report. Singles are encouraged to express sexualityin ways other than
through intercourse.

247. Wilson, Earl D. Sexual sanity: breaking free from uncontrolled habits.
     Downers Grove, IL: InterVarsity, 1984. 144p. notes. LC 83-22753. ISBN
     0-87784-919-6. OCLC 10162666. pap.
A clinical psychologist affiliated with Western Conservative Baptist Seminary offers thoughts on breaking free of "sexual insanity" (reflected in
obsessions, promiscuity, voyeurism, homosexuality, etc.) and attaining
"sexual sanity" by learning to re-program thinking patterns. Wilson clearly believes that the cognitive component is crucial in sexual behavior,
and his advice is almost entirely on this level; e.g., he calls homosexuality a "learned behavior" (that can be unlearned). For some genuinely
motivated readers, this may be of help. Those not already committed to
Wilson's perspective, however, may protest.

248. Ohanneson, Joan. And they felt no shame: Christians reclaim their
     sexuality. Minneapolis, MN: Winston, 1983. 352p. notes. LC 82-70488.
     ISBN 0-86683-676-4. OCLC 9405822. pap.
The general context for this book is the Catholic Church's emerging awareness of the need for young adult ministries, and for drawing younger and
older people into dialogue; specifically, Ohanneson is working with what
she observed at a YA conference on ministry in Los Angeles and on her own
contacts with YA's. The assortment of first person accounts here, sharing painful struggles to integrate spirituality and embodied sexuality,
testify to the unresolved questions and real anguish many are experiencing
in this area, as well as to feelings of liberation and joy. Consciousness
raising rather than supportive of traditional doctrine.

249. Gustafson, Janie. Celibate passion. San Francisco: Harper, 1978.
     x, 133p. notes. LC 77-20439. ISBN 0-06-063536-3. OCLC 3771929.
The title is apt, for this is a genuinely passionate book. Gustafson, a
young Catholic sister, explores how it feels to her to live a celibate life
while being simultaneously involved in a whole range of human emotions and
relationships. She discusses the dynamics of her relationship with God--
alternations between a fervent sense of mystical presence and the dry, darker time--and how such intimacy with God helps keep the expression of intimacy with other people within limits; she explores as well the alternations between involvement with others and withdrawal into temporary solitude
The portrait of a journey, eloquently shared.

250. Payne, Leanne. The broken image: restoring personal wholeness through
     healing prayer. Westchester, IL: Crossway-Good News, 1981. 187p. notes.
     LC 81-65468. ISBN 0-89107-215-2. OCLC 7668537. pap.
With numerous case histories explored in depth--both in terms of the psychodynamics involved and the experience of healing prayer--this testifies
to the author's faith that homosexuals and lesbians can be brought to a

new sexual identity. Payne wrote this as a research fellow at Yale Divinity School and while she points to the desirability, and hope, of a reorientation in sexuality for homosexuals, she avoids a legalistic mentality and stresses the experience of spiritual journey rather than simply laying down a set of normative standards.

251. Evans, Barbara. Joy!: correspondence with Pat Boone. Carol Stream, IL: Creation House, 1973. 144p. notes. LC 72-94923. ISBN 0-88419-060-9. OCLC 704694. (o.p.).
Evans, then a lesbian of ten years' duration, wrote Pat Boone when she read his book, A new song, sharing her anguish and desire to change. He answered the letter, and a correspondence ensued, reprinted here. Evans' letters pour out her feelings and report on progress; his offer biblical counsel. The correspondence charts a course into progressively more "normal" feelings and behavior: her release from sexual desire for her former lover; tentative, emerging fantasies about a possible marriage some day with a Christian husband; growth in the faith; a deepening ability to forgive her parents. A postscript by Boone tells, from his perspective, how he came to be involved and offers thoughts on the homosexual scene.

252. Linehan, Kevin. Such were some of you. Scottdale, PA: Herald, 1979. 231p. LC 79-12178. ISBN 0-8361-1890-1. OCLC 4857461. pap.
An intimate and heartfelt personal narrative that will please conservatives on this issue and, no doubt, disturb liberals. Linehan was reared Catholic and struggled abortively to enter monastic life. When he discovered his homosexual orientation he was horrified (his story includes suicide attempts, parental rejection, efforts to change through therapy), but he lived as a homosexual for some years before being "saved" while reading the Gospel of Matthew after a drug trip. Today he believes that he is no longer a homosexual in God's eyes, and he pastors a house church affiliated with an evangelical Protestant fellowship. This is his plea for compassion, grounded in a conservative biblical stance.

253. Woods, Richard. Another kind of love: homosexuality and spirituality. Garden City, NY: Image-Doubleday, 1978. 155p. bibliog. LC 77-27729. ISBN 0-385-14312-5. OCLC 4265044. pap. (o.p.).
Woods is a Dominican priest who has ministered extensively to gays. Here he offers a discussion on the church's position (constitutional homosexuality, he believes, has never been adequately addressed in Church writings) and words of spiritual counsel for gays themselves. Theologically liberal, he believes that homosexuality is a natural, not a sinful, condition, but that in order to grow spiritually gays need to act responsibly and with integrity, rejecting promiscuity. More theoretical than self-help.

254. Fortunato, John E. Embracing the exile: healing journeys of gay Christians. New York: Seabury, 1982. 137p. bibliog. LC 81-21253. ISBN 0-8164-0506-9. OCLC 7998081.
Written by an ex-Carmelite, now therapist—and a homosexual—this is intended primarily for other counselors and spiritual directors but has as a secondary audience gays themselves, together with their family and friends. There is much deep self-disclosure here as Fortunato explains, from his own experiences and those of clients, how it feels to be Christian and gay in America. At the book's core is the conviction that all kinds of love come from God, and that gays have gifts to offer the church whether or not the church is willing to accept them. An intimate look at one man's journey in moving from denial, through anguish and grieving, to eventual peace.

255. Schaffer, Ulrich. Love reaches out: meditations for people in love.
     New York: Harper, 1980. 127p. photogs. LC 79-3757. ISBN 0-06-067080-0.
     OCLC 5892136. pap.
Here are beautiful, truly discerning free verse reflections on the basic
themes of "daring to get to know" and "changing and growing." Issues
Schaffer deals with in these pieces include the inevitable ups and downs,
the stifling nature of possessiveness, the need to reach out to Jesus to
renew one's resources for loving, the dynamics of intimacy and communication. Extremely well done.

256. Shedd, Charlie. How to know if you're really in love. Kansas City, KS:
     Sheed, Andrews and McMeel, 1978. 155p. LC 78-9965. ISBN 0-8362-2803-0.
     OCLC 4211320.
Organized according to ten categorical areas (transparency, unselfishness,
sexuality, money, fun, holiness, etc.), this presents typical letters Shedd
has received in his capacity as pastoral columnist for teenagers, together
with his responses. The counsel on self-assessment (and assessment of
one's friend) is supplemented by two sets of questionnaires (one for each
party), exploring attitudes on the above topics. As always, Shedd's writing
is comfortable and acceptant while endorsing traditional standards.

257. Coleman, William L. Engaged: when love takes root. Wheaton, IL: Tyn-
     dale, 1980. 153p. LC 79-55644. ISBN 0-8423-0693-5. OCLC 7551417. pap.
Eighteen chapters of simple, practical, biblical advice mixed with common
sense, blended nicely. Some of the themes covered are as follows: you can
control love; ups and downs are inevitable; good people make good marriages;
relationships grow and change; low self-esteem can turn out later to be a
bad problem; it's good to be aware of problem areas without dwelling on
the negative; marriage with a non-believer is forbidden biblically; and
couples should be comfortable discussing sexuality.

258. Roberts, Wes and H. Norman Wright. Before you say "I do": a marriage
     preparation manual for couples. Irvine, CA: Harvest House, 1978. 76p.
     photogs. LC 77-94133. ISBN 0-89081-119-9. OCLC 4660032. pap.
In large workbook format with photos and exercises, this is primarily a
guided Bible study exploring scriptural passages on the nature of marriage,
each partner's uniqueness, biblical views on love, expectations, stages,
goals, and needs in marriage, roles, responsibilities, decision-making,
and so on. The intent is to facilitate dialogue on the concepts discussed
with agree/disagree questionnaires. Middle-of-the-road theologically
(explanation of the scriptural passages stresses that the husband submits,
too), this should be useful to a variety of readers.

E. MARRIAGE AND MARRIAGE DYNAMICS

259. The encyclopedia of Christian marriage. Old Tappan, NJ: Revell, 1984.
     414p. bibliogs. index. LC 83-13780. ISBN 0-8007-1376-1. OCLC 9784137.
Similar in format to Revell's Encyclopedia of Christian parenting (see annotation), this brings together articles and excerpts from books by a
variety of Christian writers (e.g., John Powell, Charlie Shedd, Dwight
Hervey Small, Evelyn and James Whitehead, Gordon MacDonald, etc.) as well
as a smattering of miscellaneous "secular" contributors (e.g., Elizabeth
Post on wedding etiquette, or Lederer and Jackson, authors of The mirages
of marriage). Seven main sections deal with premarriage and the engagement

period, the wedding, husband and wife, sex and reproduction, family life
and parenting, finances, and divorce, while a multitude of subdivisions
fine-tune the organizational format. Primarily evangelical in thrust.

260. Hart, Thomas and Kathleen Fischer Hart. The first two years of mar-
     riage: foundations for a life together. New York: Paulist, 1983. v,
     132p. bibliog. LC 83-60375. ISBN 0-8091-2553-6. OCLC 10365499. pap.
This differs from most marriage guides in its focus on the foundational
early period. The Harts, who are active counselors/enrichment facilitators,
offer practical, sensitive advice on expectations, communication, intimacy/
autonomy, sex, in-laws, the first child, etc. Their theology is gently
liberal (they favor a "mutuality" model over a "hierarchical" one), and
their approach to scriptural issues is sufficiently ecumenical for Protestants as well as Catholics to find this very useful.

261. Yancey, Philip. After the wedding. Waco, TX: Word, 1976. 160p. notes.
     LC 76-19537. ISBN 0-87680-456-3. OCLC 3017233. pap.
Intended to reassure partners encountering problems in the difficult early
years of marriage, this shares the stories of nine couples whom the author
and his wife knew in the context of "young marrieds" groups. Each story
is told in the form of a dialogue between husband and wife; next comes a
discussion in which Yancey explores biblical principles that are applicable to the case in point. Appendix shares stories of two well known
older Christian couples, the Shedds and the Tourniers.

262. Sanford, Ruth. The first years together: encouragement and advice for
     the newly married woman. Ann Arbor, MI: Servant, 1983. 123p. ISBN
     0-89283-134-0. OCLC 10444605. pap.
An extremely useful book that discusses a number of surprises, ambivalences
and anxieties that can occur early in marriage. Sanford explores feelings
that one has married a stranger and that sex is not what one was expecting,
as well as adjustments vis-a-vis families and friends, making new women
friends, handling the workload, becoming pregnant, and giving birth.
Faith is brought into the discussion in a sensitive sort of way, and a
number of difficult areas are wisely handled: e.g., feelings of guilt if
one has had prior lovers, learning to anticipate an unplanned pregnancy
happily, jealousy among old friends, handling in-laws, etc.

263. LaHaye, Tim and Beverly LaHaye. The act of marriage: the beauty of
     sexual love. Grand Rapids, MI: Zondervan, 1976. 315p. illus. bibliog.
     LC 75-37742. ISBN 0-310-27062-6. OCLC 1859880. pap.
The LaHayes, founders of Family Life Seminars and conservative evangelical
leaders, offer a wide range of information on male and female sexuality
here, including physiological details, with the goal of helping partners
overcome inhibitions about sharing their needs so as to find a more fulfilling sexual relationship. Separate sections deal with men's and women's
needs and responses, respectively; the assumption is made that women may
need to be taught physical passion over a period of time, and that they
will probably become more open in this area as other needs--e.g., for companionship, affection, romance, compassion--are met. Near the end of the
book the LaHayes deal explicitly with an evangelical message, presenting
steps involved in receiving Christ and urging this as the best foundation
for an integral spiritual/physical relationship. Throughout--and especially in the Question and Answer section on such issues as oral sex and mas-
turbation--they cite scriptural mandates (if applicable) together with
opinions of Christian doctors and pastors. Very conservative.

264. Wheat, Ed and Gaye Wheat. Intended for pleasure. Rev. ed. Old Tappan, NJ: Revell, 1981. 256p. illus. bibliog. index. LC 81-10528. ISBN 0-8007-1253-6. OCLC 7573199.
An evangelical guide to sexual intimacy in marriage, this begins with dis- cussion of marriage/sex/love in God's design (sex is intended for pleasure; agape love can revitalize waning eros) and some general principles and guidelines on marriage itself (stay out of debt; keep independent of in- laws; never go to bed with unresolved conflicts; seek outside counsel when needed). Thereafter the Wheats move to the topic of sex per se: questions of anatomy, technique, infertility, impotence, birth control, elderly sex, sex after illness. The stress is on the dynamics of intimacy, letting go of anger, being thoughtful, and enjoying affectionate touching apart from sex itself. Very helpful.

265. Trobisch, Ingrid. The joy of being a woman... and what a man can do. New York: Harper, 1975. xvi, 136p. illus. bibliog. LC 75-9324. ISBN 0-06-068453-4. OCLC 1527454. pap.
A guide to sexuality for married women. Trobisch stresses self-acceptance as a foundational key, discussing also fertility, pregnancy, childbirth, breast feeding, menopause, maturing. She indicates her hope that men will read the book too, and that couples will share it. Developmentally orien- ted (she explores sexual issues in the order they are likely to surface in marriage), this has more information on childbirth than in most sex guides, with some good words for the sympto-thermal method when it comes to the question of birth control.

266. Leman, Kevin. Sex begins in the kitchen. Ventura, CA: Regal, 1981. 157p. notes. LC 80-54004. ISBN 0-8307-0787-5. OCLC 7769287.
Leman, a popular Christian psychologist active on the TV and lecture cir- cuits, has written an eminently sensible and witty book that should be of real value. His thesis: a couple's marriage should be their number one priority (before both children and careers); love in the scriptural sense consists of "action, not words"; and "sex begins in the kitchen," in that acts of mutual thoughtfulness (doing the dishes for one's mate, say) create feelings of gratitude and affection that are sure to find their way back to the bedroom. Leman seems devoid of inhibitions, and his humor and ease will help others enormously.

267. Hulme, William E. When two become one: reflections for the newly mar- ried. Minneapolis, MN: Augsburg, 1972. 96p. LC 76-176481. ISBN 0-8066-1212-6. OCLC 315327. pap. (1974 ed. in BIP).
This deals with developmental marital issues (the process of commitment, caring for feelings, sexuality, parenting, work/play balance, in-law relations, and reaching out to the larger community) but emphasizes a de- votional approach: i.e., meditational readings on the above topics explore ways a couple can build a deeper spiritual sharing over time, and each sec- tion concludes with a scriptural passage and a prayer. Sensitive and thoughtful.

268. Schaffer, Ulrich. A growing love: meditations on marriage and commit- ment. New York: Harper, 1977. 127p. photogs. LC 76-62951. ISBN 0-06-067079-7. OCLC 5892137. pap.
By the same author and in the same format as Love reaches out (see anno- tation), this explores the dynamics of love's maturation once the initial commitment has been made. Basic themes are "The dialogue of joy and pain," "Alone together," "What's really happening?" and "Thank you for...". In

Schaffer's view, marriage does not involve pre-established roles, but rather, a process of deepening honesty and mutual exploration. A lovely
book that captures and catalyzes many feelings.

269. Brandt, Leslie and Edith Brandt. Growing together: prayers for married
     people. Minneapolis, MN: Augsburg, 1975. 96p. LC 75-2830. ISBN
     0-8066-1476-5. OCLC 1365064. pap.
These prayers, in the form of free verse poems, cover all stages of the
marriage relationship and its predictable problems/joys/challenges: early
ecstatic times, ambivalence over having children, depression on the part
of a spouse, blocks in intimacy, discrepancies in growth, etc. Broadly
divided into such categories as "Maturing," "Struggling," "Celebrating,"
and "Wondering," they are sensitively written from the perspectives of
both husband and wife, and often contain insights which could be of real
use to people grappling with the situations depicted.

270. Osborne, Cecil G. The art of understanding your mate. Grand Rapids,
     MI: Zondervan, 1970. 192p. LC 74-95047. ISBN 0-310-30602-7. OCLC
     58828. pap.
A counselor/author looks at problems and possibilities of marriage in a
low-key Christian style with references, as well, to current psychological
concepts ("inner child," etc.). Osborne examines male-female differences,
areas of vulnerability, how to avoid destructive behavior and increase
one's tolerance for frustration, the value of fellowship groups, and other
topics. A nice light touch ("Ten commandments" for husbands and wives,
eight types of neurotic husbands and wives) with a stress on Christ-like
compassion.

271. Fairfield, James G. T. When you don't agree: a guide to resolving
     marriage and family conflicts. Scottdale, PA: Herald, 1977. 243p.
     bibliog. LC 77-3133. ISBN 0-8361-1819-7. OCLC 3415368. pap.
Here is an attempt from the Mennonite perspective to operationalize Jesus'
behavioral principles into a style for resolving conflicts in marriage,
family, community and work relationships. Fairfield discusses how messages
get sent, perceived, and scrambled; he includes exercises and discussion
questions for evaluating one's own patterns/progress; and he concludes
with a look at characteristics of "creative conflict" which facilitate
the reconciling action of Christ's love. Emphasizing that Jesus neither
"withdrew" nor "yielded" in conflict situations, this is a thoughtful effort toward a biblical style of conflict resolution.

272. Mace, David. Love and anger in marriage. Grand Rapids, MI: Zondervan,
     1982. 135p. bibliog. LC 82-4776. ISBN 0-310-45290-2. OCLC 8306433.
     (trade pap. ed., Jan. 1984).
Any marriage will inevitably generate some anger, Mace says; the aim is
to use it as raw material in developing deeper intimacy. Here he discusses
skills for using anger creatively to foster love rather than alienation,
drawing on the perspective of 49 years of marriage and knowledge as a counselor. Part One discusses the nature of anger, with a look at body language (the physical dimension), aggression (the social dimension), love/
anger (the relational dimension) and questions of sin (the ethical/spiritual
dimension). Part Two is on managing anger: patterns and processes, with
a program for relational growth. Includes some interesting comments on
the whole question of "headship"; Mace explains Paul's words about wifely
submission as evidence he merely accepted the hierarchical pattern of the

day as appropriate, also, for Christian families--not that he intended to
lay down hard and fast rules that would hold forever.

273. Gallagher, Chuck. Love is a couple. New York: Sadlier, 1976. 143p.
     illus. LC 76-4329. ISBN 0-8215-6464-1. OCLC 3031412. pap.
For husbands and wives whose marriages are basically good but who desire
to improve them even more, this is a sort of workbook/discussion resource
based on the method used in Fr. Gallagher's Marriage Encounter weekends.
Organized around four basic themes--listening, decision making, fighting
and healing--this offers questions encouraging readers to explore their
personal styles in these areas, plus discussions focusing on explanation/
guidance regarding processes involved. Not theological in approach, with
no preconceptions regarding male or female role expectations. For a description of the Marriage Encounter experience itself, see Antoinette
Bosco's Marriage Encounter: the rediscovery of love (Abbey, 1972) or Fr.
Gallagher's The marriage encounter (Doubleday, 1975).

274. Christenson, Larry and Nordis Christenson. The Christian couple.
     Minneapolis, MN: Bethany House, 1977. 183p. notes. LC 77-24085.
     ISBN 0-87123-053-4. OCLC 3089645. pap.
Larry Christenson previously wrote The Christian family (see annotation).
This present book is an evangelical marriage guide with an emphasis on
traditional views and roles. The Christensons organize their presentation
according to several basic dimensions of the marital relationship: the
couple are to be pioneers (facing a challenging call together), lovers
(with sensitivity, enjoyment, and obedience that releases the flow of
faith), friends (different but equal) and saints (moving on with the
call). Includes an interesting discussion of natural birth control methods
from a Protestant perspective. Husbandly authority and wifely submission
are upheld, though sensitivity is stressed.

275. Swindoll, Charles R. Strike the original match. Portland, OR: Multno-
     mah, 1980. 196p. LC 80-15639. ISBN 0-930014-37-5. OCLC 6331122. pap.
     (study guide also).
Well known through his "Insight for Living" radio program and various books
Swindoll places a heavy emphasis on biblical "blueprints" in the marital
counsel contained here. Wives are advised to use the "bricks" of appear-
ance, behavior, attitude and responses as they build the structure of their
partnership; husbands are given "bricks" of truly living with, knowing,
and honoring their wives. Looks, too, at fighting fruitfully, handling
money, stages of marriage, and the theology of divorce from a conservative
perspective.

276. Timmons, Tim. Maximum marriage. Old Tappan, NJ: Power-Revell, 1976.
     128p. illus. LC 76-10746. ISBN 0-8007-0801-6. OCLC 2188965. pap.
     (rev. updated ed. in BIP).
The founder of "Maximum Marriage Seminars" explains that marriages often
fail because they are based on competition and comparison. Instead he
offers a "game plan" for total fulfillment of the husband and wife as
individuals within the relationship based on the concept of "completion"--
husband head, wife helpmate, each in dynamic relationship with one another
and with God. There is a lengthy discussion of what real headship on the
part of the husband and submission on the part of the wife should mean,
plus a look at communication patterns and at God's design for marriage as
expounded in Genesis. Done with a light touch, numerous anecdotes, cartoons to illustrate points, etc.

277. Morgan, Marabel. The total woman. Old Tappan, NJ: Spire-Revell, 1973.
     192p. illus. bibliog. LC 73-11474. ISBN 0-8007-0608-0. OCLC 677348.
     (later eds.--Revell and Pocket Books--in BIP).
In this, her original book, Morgan shares how she salvaged her dying marriage through research in marriage manuals and Scripture after which she
came up with the concept of the four "A's" (accept, admire, adapt, appreciate) and the now-famous techniques to revive sexual interest (even women
with toddlers requiring a 6:07 feeding are told to take a bubble bath and
be "squeaky clean" before their man's arrival home). Some thoughts, too,
on communication--e.g., listen, forgive, forget, and shut your mouth. At
the end she tells the story of her own born-again experience. See also
Total joy, a sequel (Revell, 1977).

278. Elliot, Elisabeth. Let me be a woman: notes on womanhood for Valerie.
     Wheaton, IL: Tyndale, 1976. 190p. LC 76-1324. ISBN 0-8423-2160-8.
     OCLC 2590522. (also pap.).
Here are 49 brief reflections Elliot wrote on the eve of her daughter's
marriage, ranging over a variety of topics within a conservative evangelical context. She suggests phrasing identity questions not in terms of
"Who am I?" but "Whose am I?" and stresses that freedom is found within
discipline, every choice sets limits, women should accept God's divine
order of authority (the husband is head), and marriage is a union of opposites, not equals. A look, too, at single living to which some woman
may be called and where, as within marriage, the need is to give totally
of oneself.

279. Dillow, Linda. Creative counterpart. Nashville, TN: Thomas Nelson,
     1977. 170p. notes. LC 76-30387. ISBN 0-8407-5617-8. OCLC 2645510. pap.
God's plan for marriage involves a "spiritual head" (the husband) and a
"creative counterpart" (the wife), says Dillow, who directs a marriage
seminar ministry together with her husband. The context for making it all
happen is a vital relationship with God; priorities are (1) God, (2) husband,
(3) children, (4) home, (5) yourself, and (6) activities outside the home.
Wives are counseled to be their husbands' best fans, and to win change by
their own beautifully submissive behavior. Standard conservative evangelical guidance, then, but a bit more lively in its style than some, with
some light, fun-loving suggestions on spicing up the sex life.

280. Cook, Jerry and Barbara Cook. Choosing to love. Ventura, CA: Regal,
     1982. 141p. LC 81-84566. ISBN 0-8307-0818-9. OCLC 7999598. (also
     pap.).
A Foursquare Church pastor and his wife share their learnings born of
Bible study and their own experience. Deciding that the "creeping sepa-
rateness" they were coming to feel originated in faulty attitudes absorbed
from the culture, they committed themselves to exploring Christian alternatives and here explain what they came to understand: "agape" love is
the basis; the original plan in Genesis was for a truly equal partnership;
submission does not imply hierarchy but means giving, accepting, encouraging,
acknowledging disagreements, and communicating; sexual love in "agape" is
a continual choice rather than an experience of being overwhelmed. The
authors' poems and letters greatly enrich the discussion, which closes with
thoughts on the process of growing in personhood through Christ, and the
difference this makes in the deepening fellowship of marriage, replacing
misconceptions and false assumptions with a new ability to discern truth,
accept reality, and engage in authentic communication.

281. Evans, Colleen Townsend and Louis H. Evans, Jr. My lover, my friend.
     Old Tappan, NJ: Revell, 1976. 159p. LC 76-22480. ISBN 0-8007-0751-6.
     OCLC 2332285. (o.p.).
There are, say the Evanses, four phases to humanity: created innocence,
the Fall, recreation in Christ, and final glorification. They believe
that the cultural subjugation of women reflected in the Old Testament was
never God's ideal will but rather a result of the Fall; today all Christians, as part of the "new creation," are to make Christ Lord above all,
in which context husbands and wives are to be mutually submitted to one
another, not caught in static hierarchy. A warm, joyful book that encourages respect for each other's identity, friendship between equals, and
a balance between personal interests and shared activities.

282. Gundry, Patricia. Heirs together: mutual submission in marriage. Grand
     Rapids, MI: Zondervan, 1980. 192p. illus. notes. index. LC 79-25500.
     ISBN 0-310-25370-5. OCLC 5799728. (1982 ed. in BIP).
Stressing that a good marriage is one that makes room for people to be fully themselves, Gundry explores historical foundations behind contemporary
hierarchical approaches, argues that such views are not truly biblical,
and shows that the Genesis account as well as Jesus' views, depicted in
the Gospels, favor a "mutuality" model in which the focus is on the relationship rather than on preconceived roles, and the husband's "headship"
is used to lift the wife up and affirm her in equal partnership.

283. Scanzoni, John. Love and negotiate: creative conflict in marriage.
     Waco, TX: Word, 1979. 148p. notes. LC 78-65816. ISBN 0-8499-0100-6.
     OCLC 5318314. pap.
The best approach to marital partnership, Scanzoni argues, lies in mutual
submission rather than in a concept of hierarchy, for the latter inhibits
the development of deep, intimate friendship between husband and wife,
whereas the former nurtures it and also facilitates creative decision-
making. After a look at the biblical bases for his position, Scanzoni
proceeds to a detailed examination of the negotiating process in sample
conflict situations. A look, too, at child-rearing and the situation of
the single adult.

284. Dufresne, Edward R. Partnership: marriage and the committed life. New
     York: Paulist, 1975. xvi, 135p. photogs. LC 74-27423. ISBN
     0-8091-1866-1. OCLC 1340563. pap.
A work of deeply personal spiritual reflections rather than a straight
"how to" guide, with many rich and creative suggestions. Dufresne stresses
what he and his wife have learned about making the marital partnership a
context for on-going growth in ministry rather than a self-contained end
in itself. He explores the double standard and its influence, solitude,
intimacy and community in marriage, the importance of acceptance, sexual
partnership, and issues of time and possessions. Theologically liberal
and spiritually rich, with lovely black and white photos that nurture a
meditative mood.

285. Senter, Ruth. So you're the pastor's wife. Grand Rapids, MI: Zondervan
     1979. 114p. LC 79-9340. ISBN 0-310-38820-1. OCLC 5101768.
Written for other ministers' wives, this is an extremely open, honest book
sharing the author's struggles, failures and successes as she learned to
cope with her role. Deals with inevitable human limitations, the pain of
"pedestal living," the need to acknowledge feelings and work through resent

ments, jealousies over the threat of other women, etc. The most personal of the various guides on living as a pastor's wife which this reviewer has seen.

286. Ross, Charlotte. Who is the minister's wife?: a search for personal
     fulfillment. Philadelphia: Westminster, 1980. 132p. bibliog. LC
     79-24027. ISBN 0-664-24302-9. OCLC 5676366. pap.
Rather than straight advice, this offers a discussion of the results of a survey conducted by one of the United Presbyterian Church in the U.S.A.'s task forces: questionnaires were mailed to clergy wives, clergymen and lay-people, inquiring on ways the role of minister's wife has changed today. Even though this is a report rather than a guidebook, the results are discussed in such a conversational, anecdotal style that it could easily be used for sharing/self-help purposes.

287. Sinclair, Donna. The pastor's wife today. Nashville, TN: Abingdon
     (Creative Leadership Series), 1981. 126p. bibliog. LC 80-26076.
     ISBN 0-687-30269-2. OCLC 6916574. pap.
Drawing on her own experiences and on talks with others, Sinclair sets forth a continuum of options ranging from the helpmate/enabler to the liberated wife and increasingly autonomous career woman. None of these positions are "good" or "bad," she suggests, and whatever a woman chooses, there will be trade-offs and pressures. Still, this seems more aimed at the "liberated" than the "traditional" consciousness.

288. Schiappa, Barbara. Mixing: Catholic-Protestant marriages in the
     1980's. New York: Paulist, 1982. 144p. bibliog. LC 81-84387.
     ISBN 0-8091-2443-2. OCLC 8331528. pap.
A fine exploration of the dynamics involved in interfaith marriages between Catholics and Protestants. Discussing a number of couples who have attained varying degrees of fulfillment, Schiappa posits a triangular model wherein husband and wife, in addition to their relationship together, are both involved as well in a relationship with God. Interestingly, it seems that similarity in the depth of the partners' faith commitments may actually be more important for the marriage than membership in the same denomination. Highly recommended.

289. Luka, Ronald and Bernard Zlotowitz. When a Christian and a Jew marry.
     New York: Paulist, 1973. v, 89p. bibliog. LC 73-77393. ISBN
     0-8091-1748-7. OCLC 673638. pap.
The Catholic University Chaplain issues, first, some standard warnings on the difficulties of such interfaith marriages. Given the decision to under-take them, however, the point should be to minimize the liabilities and stress the assets. The Christian, Luka suggests, is not called to give abstract verbal testimonies about God's nature but to embody His love through his/her own love of God, spouse, children, in-laws, neighbors, friends, and people in need. Neither spouse should work for the conversion of the other but should stand with integrity in his/her personal commitment. Luka does note that if both parties are extremely devout, they will probably feel it is important to marry someone of the same faith. Contains a sample wedding ceremony, and reflections on the Jewish perspective by Rabbi Bernard M. Zlotowitz in which he discusses, very briefly, the traditional Jewish opposition to intermarriage on religious grounds and encourages Jewish families to nurture a strong faith identity in young people so they will be more likely to marry within their own tradition.

290. Berry, Jo. <u>Beloved unbeliever: loving your husband into the faith.</u>
     Grand Rapids, MI: Zondervan, 1981. 169p. LC 81-4518. ISBN
     0-310-42621-9. OCLC 7278390. <u>pap.</u>
The first chapter explores what it means to be "unequally yoked" (married
to a non-believer) and how spiritually disastrous it can be. Having established the importance of avoiding such a situation if possible, Berry then
turns to advising those who are already so yoked. She stresses that biblical principles apply here, too--e.g., the husband is still the "head"--
and recommends standard workshop-style exercises, plus prayer methods
(visualizing Jesus' light flooding over the spouse) and loving influence.

291. Branch, Robert. <u>So your wife came home speaking in tongues? So did</u>
     <u>mine!</u> Old Tappan, NJ: Revell, 1973. 126p. bibliog. LC 73-7521. ISBN
     0-8007-0611-0. OCLC 624116. <u>pap.</u> (o.p.).
A down-to-earth, open sharing of one husband's reactions, and the crisis
that ensued in the marriage, when his wife received the "Baptism in the
Spirit" and became engrossed in the phenomenon of tongues. The Branches
came to a point near divorce before they were able to come together once
more in understanding and reach a new level of mature love. This argues
strongly for humility, putting Christ first, and tolerating stylistic differences among Christians. Bibliography of "pro" and "con" books on the
subject of tongues is included.

292. Wright, H. Norman. <u>Seasons of a marriage.</u> Ventura, CA: Regal, 1982.
     165p. notes. LC 82-80010. ISBN 0-8307-0841-3. OCLC 8346857. (<u>pap.</u> ed.
     in <u>BIP</u>).
Designed to help couples deal with typical stages in a marriage and their
related challenges, this discusses from an evangelical perspective initial
expectations (bound to remain unfulfilled!), early years, mid-life transitions, empty nest syndrome, temptations to infidelity, healing after a
possible affair, parent-child reversals occurring during the aging process, and preparation for death. Biblical principles together with space
to fill in ideas for personal application.

F. FAMILY PLANNING, PREGNANCY, AND CHILDBIRTH

293. Critelli, Ida and Tom Schick. <u>Unmarried and pregnant: what now?</u> Cin-
     cinatti, OH: St. Anthony Messenger Pr., 1977. v, 137p. illus. index.
     ISBN 0-912228-34-2. OCLC 3739445. (o.p.).
Both authors were involved in founding Birthright, a national organization
which counsels in alternatives to abortion. Their book looks at the pregnancy period in terms of immediate needs/options and in its broader context
as part of the total life experience challenging the individual to grow.
Chapters deal with the need to find listeners, arguments against abortion
(gently phrased), the pros and cons of marriage, adoption, keeping the
baby as a single mother, the role of Birthright and other services, and
biological facts about pregnancy and foetal development. Appendix lists
Birthright groups or similar resources in 50 large metropolitan areas of
the United States. Together with Martha Zimmerman's book (see next entry),
this provides guidance aimed at the young pregnant woman herself. For a
title addressing these issues more from the perspective of the family of th
pregnant single woman, see entry 411, Bev O'Brien's <u>Mom, I'm pregnant.</u>

294. Zimmerman, Martha. Should I keep my baby? Minneapolis, MN: Bethany
     House, 1983. 96p. illus. LC 83-6068. ISBN 0-87123-578-1. OCLC
     9393174. pap.
Written to support teenagers as they ask inevitably painful questions, this
is very empathic and refrains from offering pat solutions. Zimmerman openly counsels against abortion, but she does give information on getting to
crisis centers offering it, and she urges readers who do decide on abortion to get simultaneous counseling. For those deciding to have the baby,
she considers the pros and cons of marriage, and single parenting vs. adoption, stressing the importance of seriously asking for God's guidance and
then following through. Looks, too, at dynamics of forgiveness and caring
for oneself physically.

295. Mace, David R. Abortion: the agonizing decision. Nashville, TN: Abing-
     don, 1972. 144p. bibliog. LC 70-187590. ISBN 0-687-00653-8. OCLC
     323712. (also pap.). (o.p.).
Mace wrote this as a guide for the individual woman faced with a problem
pregnancy and the newly won option (at the time of publication) of legal
abortion. It is done in the form of an imaginary abortion conference where
successive sessions explore foetal development, past and present attitudes
to abortion, a world perspective on liberalizing abortion laws, the value
of unborn life, and the need for counseling. While the ostensible position
is that abortion can sometimes be right for an individual, the real thrust
(in an implicit Judeo-Christian context) seems to be toward the conservative position. Includes resource list.

296. Roetzer, Jozef. Family planning the natural way: a complete guide to
     the sympto-thermal method. Old Tappan, NJ: Revell, 1981. 123p. illus.
     LC 81-10568. ISBN 0-8007-1185-8. OCLC 7573321. pap.
Introductory chapters deal with the nature of scriptural love, with an emphasis on the "one flesh" theme; the physical symptoms of ovulation are
seen as part of a series of natural, God-given rhythms and signs. Roetzer
advises being open to God's call regarding the proper size of one's family,
then spends the rest of the book describing the sympto-thermal method in
detail. Includes questionnaires, charts, and technical illustrations.
Foreword by Ingrid Trobisch.

297. Stigger, Judith A. Coping with infertility. Minneapolis, MN: Augsburg
     (Religion and Medicine), 1983. 110p. bibliog. LC 82-72649. ISBN
     0-8066-1956-2. OCLC 9328811. pap.
A trained social worker, drawing on her own experience with infertility
and interviews with others, offers this guidance for infertile (or possibly
infertile) persons, their family and friends, counselors, clergy, physi-
cians. Stigger defines the problem and discusses the onset of awareness,
emotional stages in recognition and acceptance, choosing a doctor, typical
medical work-ups (for both men and women), and reasonable expectations and
options. There is some discussion of moving toward "faith on God's terms"
as one struggles with anger and confusion, and on the role of the Christian
community as support group. An excellent and useful book.

298. Anderson, Ann Kiemel. Taste of tears, touch of God. Nashville, TN: Tho-
     mas Nelson, 1984. 202p. photogs. ISBN 0-8407-9025-2. OCLC 10913821.
Scheduled for publication in Sept., 1984, this was not actually examined.
However, as described in pre-publication ads, it is Ann Kiemel Anderson's
personal story of her struggle for self-identification when faced with a

childless marriage. Because of the author's enormous popularity in the
evangelical community, established by evangelism/sharing books prior to
her marriage (see annotation of I'm out to change my world), and because
of the topic, it seemed worthy of note.

299. Halverson, Kaye with Karen M. Hess. The wedded unmother. Minneapolis,
     MN: Augsburg, 1980. 128p. bibliog. LC 79-54123. ISBN 0-8066-1768-3.
     OCLC 6256511. pap.
Family-oriented, daughter of a Lutheran minister, Halverson was traumatized
on learning of her infertility. She tells here of four years' unsuccessful
struggle to conceive and of concomitant depression, anger against God, etc.
There is little perspective or general discussion, and the reasons for certain medical steps she takes are unclear. Still, her book (which ends with
adoption, a new career, increased self-acceptance) will help others in
this situation feel less alone. Appendix of relevant publications and organizations.

300. Vredevelt, Pam W. Empty arms: emotional support for those who have
     suffered miscarriage or stillbirth. Portland, OR: Multnomah, 1984.
     126p. illus. bibliog. notes. LC 84-2049. ISBN 0-88070-042-4. OCLC
     10404092. pap.
The author, a counselor and pastor's wife, went through the tragedy of
stillbirth and begins by sharing her own experience. She discusses grief
dynamics, dealing with anger and guilt, spiritual battles, responding to
the reactions of others, the pain of the husband, questions from children,
etc., as well as mood swings, the importance of exercise, and the process
of starting over. Includes reflections on biblical comfort, with an epilogue on what she and her husband have learned personally through their
experience.

301. Macmanus, Sheila. The adoption book. New York: Paulist, 1984. vii,
     131p. bibliog. notes. tables. LC 83-62018. ISBN 0-8091-2578-1. OCLC
     10569048. pap.
Here is a practical handbook together with a historical overview of develop
ments vis-a-vis adoption. The theological context, established at the
outset, is one in which God's parenthood over all has profound implications for the adoptive process, so that the blended family is not just the
result of an idiosyncratic whim but reflects God's loving plan. The discussion of specific issues includes a look at baby selling, independent
adoptions, open adoption, sealed records, single parent adoption, trans-
racial and mixed race adoption. Part Two explores resources for special
needs adoption, intercountry adoption, public and licensed private adoption agencies, national and local advocates, support groups, etc. Finally,
Macmanus discusses federal/corporate/state activity, plus laws and policies. The appendix has the text of a U.N. draft declaration, bibliographic
material, address lists, and notes.

302. Musser, Sandra Kay. I would have searched forever. Plainfield, NJ:
     Haven-Logos, 1979. 144p. bibliog. LC 79-64955. ISBN 0-88270-487-7.
     OCLC 5531246. pap. (Jan Pubns. ed. in BIP).
This is a woman's personal story of how, twenty-two years after giving
birth to an illegitimate daughter, she finally managed by dint of great
perseverance to establish contact with the adoptive family and the young
woman herself; it also brings together personal case histories of others
who gave up their children, plus some background information on the adop-

tion system and ways it might be improved. Musser's personal narrative
does not have an entirely happy ending,--her daughter had trouble accepting
the idea of a relationship--but this is still interesting and potentially
useful.

303. Wright, H. Norman and Marvin N. Inmon. Preparing for parenthood. Ven-
       tura, CA: Regal, 1980. 192p. illus. LC 79-92949. ISBN 0-8307-0743-3.
       OCLC 6979809. pap. (also workbook).
The author, a psychology professor and marriage counselor, discusses a
range of questions related to the process of deciding to have, and actually having, a child: expectations and myths, responsibilities of mothers
and fathers, pregnancy and childbirth, apprehensions and fears, etc. Chapters include "What do you think?" and "What's your plan?" sections that
focus on biblical passages and possible applications.

304. Hanes, Mari. The child within: nine months of spiritual preparation
       for the woman in waiting. Wheaton, IL: Tyndale, 1979. 115p. LC
       78-57967. ISBN 0-8423-0232-8. OCLC 6446820. pap. (1983 ed. in BIP).
Hanes offers scriptural passages, reflections and study questions for each
month of pregnancy. The reflections describe foetal/maternal circumstances at that particular stage of development (how the mother may be feeling,
for instance--e.g., tired, burdened, filled with anticipation) and direct
the reader to the insights in the relevant biblical passages, which are
then explored more fully via the study questions.

305. O'Connor, Sarah H. The nine-month journey: a Christian mother's re-
       flections on pregnancy and childbirth. Nashville, TN: Abingdon, 1984.
       128p. LC 84-6485. ISBN 0-687-28017-6. OCLC 10711498. pap.
Scheduled for publication in Sept. 1984, this was not actually examined but
sounds, from the pre-publication ads, as if it might be of special interest.
By a wife, mother, and free-lance writer, it explores the emotional and spiritual growth generated by the pregnancy experience and offers support for
moving through pregnancy into a deepening faith in God. Based on the author's personal journal written during her own first pregnancy.

306. Milburn, Joyce and Lynette Smith. The natural childbirth book. Min-
       neapolis, MN: Bethany House, 1981. 188p. illus. bibliogs. LC 81-4647.
       ISBN 0-87123-399-1. OCLC 7307141. pap.
An extremely comprehensive, practical book by two Lamaze instructors, based
on the concept that God's plan for childbirth, as set forth in Genesis, is
not for pain, necessarily, but rather for toil, jointly shared by husband
and wife as "one flesh." Explores diet, exercise, responsibilities, home
vs. hospital birth, the process of labor, bonding with the baby after birth,
maternal/child health care, and much more. Discussion questions throughout stimulate husband and wife to compare feelings and attitudes. Charts,
diagrams, illustrative photos, resources/books for additional information,
etc.

307. Randall, Cher. Total preparation for childbirth. Plainfield, NJ: Logos,
       1979. ix, 165p. bibliog. LC 78-73574. ISBN 0-88270-331-5. OCLC
       5981637. pap. (available through Bridge).
Intended as a supplement to other books on natural childbirth, this focuses
on the pregnancy period month by month, including a discussion of foetal
development (and modern techniques like amniocentesis), preparation for
breast feeding, and assorted thoughts on God's power. There is a section
presenting lessons on the birth process itself and techniques to use

("pray...pant...relax"), though Randall stresses the book should not be viewed as a substitute for attending classes. Concludes with a look at giving birth in the home.

308. Heil, Ruth. My child within. Westchester, IL: Crossway-Good News, 1983. 122p. LC 82-83901. ISBN 0-89107-268-3. OCLC 10083103. pap.
These are journal entries of a young wife and mother beginning at the time of her first pregnancy and continuing through the birth of her fifth child. She reflects on pregnancy itself and feelings associated with it (ambivalence as well as joy), changing attitudes today, what she views as the tragedy of abortion, joy in the Christian relationship, Jesus as an unwanted child, and the process of growth that occurs when one meets children on their own level.

G. BEING A PARENT

309. Hertz, Jacky. The Christian mother: a Mary-Martha balance. New York: Hawthorn, 1976. xii, 162p. LC 76-15427. ISBN 0-801-51280-8. OCLC 2620085. (o.p.).
The "Mary-Martha balance" involves an integrated wholeness whereby mothers are aware of who they are and are able to offer themselves to their families as complete people, yet feel no need to flee from parental responsibilities to establish self-identity. Some subject areas covered include learning from special children, prejudice vs. love, family councils, God and the nervous mother, keeping perspective via humor, and family prayer.

310. Hunter, Brenda. Where have all the mothers gone? Grand Rapids, MI: Zondervan, 1982. 178p. notes. LC 82-13707. ISBN 0-310-45550-2. OCLC 8667049.
Mothers today are in a terrible bind, says Hunter; told by society both to work for status in careers and to have children, they are prey to guilt if they go overboard in either direction. She briefly shares experiences from her own childhood (as a "latch-key" daughter), and tells of the years after her first husband left when she struggled to make it alone and then discovered the resources of Christian faith/fellowship in a L'Abri community in England. She is now convinced that mothers need to be more deeply affirmed and unhooked from guilt, and this book is an effort in that direction. Though traditional in its views, this does not emphasize rigid role definitions but rather mothers' psychological importance for children.

311. MacDonald, Gordon. The effective father. Wheaton, IL: Tyndale, 1977. 256p. LC 76-58136. ISBN 0-8423-0680-3. OCLC 3328843. pap.
An evangelical pastor offers six basic principles for being an effective father: stimulating children to full growth, modeling human experience, practicing foresightful leadership, educating children in wise perspectives/patterns, accepting them for who they are, and turning to God for guidance. Written in a down-to-earth style with many personal anecdotes and frequent illustrations; individual chapters look at concrete applications of the general principles and consider significant distinctions to be drawn like, for example, the distinction between corrective and judicial punishment. The bulk of MacDonald's book is devoted to his second principle--the importance of setting a good example and serving as a model of human experience--and stresses the value of developing listening skills, being approachable, using the raw materials of daily living to nurture children's abilities, and so on.

312. Dobson, James C. <u>Straight talk to men and their wives</u>. Waco, TX: Word, 1980. 222p. illus. notes. LC 80-51595. ISBN 0-8499-0260-6. OCLC 6670287.
Largely a personal tribute to Dobson's own father, this was written soon after the latter's death and shares guidelines for living gleaned from watching the elder Dobson over a lifetime. Women are already motivated to work for better family relations, Dobson says, but what is really needed now are committed husbands and fathers. This, then, is a sort of Christian call-to-arms for a redefinition of manhood (in relationship with children, wife, work, emotions, and God). Also included, however, are words for the wives, and reflections on some contemporary trends (the "children's rights" movement, for instance) that Dobson finds seriously misguided. As always, done with wit and style; conservative evangelical in perspective.

313. Iatesta, Robert R. <u>Fathers: a fresh start for the Christian family</u>. Ann Arbor, MI: Servant, 1980. 228p. index. LC 80-122946. ISBN 0-89283-083-2. OCLC 6735703. <u>pap</u>.
The author, a father of six, became convinced from his involvement with Cursillo, the charismatic renewal, and family enrichment groups that God wants to change men's hearts so they will focus more on family/faith relationships and less on personal achievement. Biblical in its assumptions, this is distinguished by an emphasis on the processes of and resources for transformation rather than doctrinaire blueprints for behavior. Discusses establishing priorities, maturing in Christ, and learning to lead the family.

314. Singer, Wenda Goodhart. <u>Real men enjoy their kids: how to spend quality time with the children in your life</u>. Nashville, TN: Abingdon, 1983. 175p. illus. LC 82-24317. ISBN 0-687-35598-2. OCLC 9111745. <u>pap</u>.
Noting the importance of fathers and other male figures in children's lives and the need men often have for special encouragement in this area, Singer discusses a range of possible activities with children of various ages: household projects, visits to the "work world," leisure time fun, etc. Included are ways of relating to children at times of life crises (separation/divorce, birth, death) and sample activities for social, emotional, cognitive, physical and spiritual development.

315. Drescher, John M. <u>If I were starting my family again</u>. Nashville, TN: Abingdon, 1979. 62p. illus. LC 78-13278. ISBN 0-687-18675-7. OCLC 4194080. (also <u>pap</u>.).
This brief book by a pastor/educator began as a magazine article and radio talk, and was so popular that Drescher expanded it to book form. It is a simple, very moving statement on what he now understands, in retrospect, to be most important about fathering: being free to show affection in front of children, laughing more, praying for his own growth and not just for his family's improvement , sharing God more intimately. An ideal gift book.

316. Ketterman, Grace H. and Herbert L. Ketterman. <u>The complete book of baby and child care for Christian parents</u>. Old Tappan, NJ: Revell, 1982. 559p. bibliog. index. LC 81-17871. ISBN 0-8007-1280-3. OCLC 7922991.
By a husband and wife team, both MD's, this is clearly grounded in a Christian perspective yet avoids imposing a host of predefined expectations. The Kettermans discuss preparing to have a child (including issues of infertility, adoption, and controversial methods like in-vitro fertilization), nurturing newborns and toddlers, treating sick children, rearing

confident children, and helping troubled children. There is much information here on the physical, emotional and spiritual dimensions; special topics include healthy sexual development, "loving correction," teen-age rebellion, runaways, homosexuality, children and divorce, and more. Intended
for an evangelical audience, but potentially useful for a range of Christian readers.

317. The encyclopedia of Christian parenting. Old Tappan, NJ: Revell, 1982.
     464p. bibliogs. index. LC 82-562. ISBN 0-8007-1276-5. OCLC 8222249.
Here is a compilation of articles by assorted Christian leaders/writers,
mainly of a conservative evangelical viewpoint. The subject areas covered
are quite broad,--the book deals with emotional and physical health, learning, behavior, spiritual training, personality, family relationships and
activities--and while a number of the pieces are reprinted from other
sources, some have been originally written. The format is alphabetical for
the 150 or so entries (examples: abortion, anger, God, handicapped child,
inferiority feelings, masturbation, shy, spanking, TV, VD, etc.). Contributors include Francis Schaeffer, Bruce Narramore, and Grace Ketterman.

318. Campbell, Ross. How to really love your child. Wheaton, IL: Victor,
     1977. 132p. LC 77-89470. ISBN 0-88207-751-1. OCLC 3563850. pap.
     (NAL ed. in BIP).
By a Christian psychiatrist specializing in problems of children and adolescents, this discusses focused listening, eye/physical contact, and the
importance of unconditional love. Much attention, also, to the marital
relationship itself (handling ambivalence, etc.), and a lengthy look at
loving discipline with understanding. The discussion of spiritual nurture emphasizes the need for unconditional love, plus the importance of
the parents' own relationship with God.

319. Orr, Bill and Erwin Lutzer. If I could change my mom and dad. Chicago:
     Moody, 1983. 142p. facsimiles. LC 82-18848. ISBN 0-8024-0174-0.
     OCLC 8846740. pap.
Orr holds "Booster rallies" in which he asks children to express their
needs by completing the open-ended sentence, "If I could change my mom and
dad, I would ..."; Lutzer is senior pastor at the Moody Church in Chicago.
The illustrative responses reprinted here from the children's questionnaires reveal the deep need they feel for love and for people to listen
to their true feelings.

320. Dobson, James. Dare to discipline. Wheaton, IL: Tyndale, 1970. 228p.
     illus. LC 75-123283. ISBN 0-8423-0635-8. OCLC 139829. pap. (also other
     eds.).
A general overview of the psychology of discipline rather than a detailed
look at specific circumstances, this stresses the importance of combining
love with discipline. Children, says Dobson, crave firm control plus mutual respect in their relationships with parents; he advocates stability
and consistency, and suggests avoiding excessive materialism. A look, too,
at discipline in the classroom, teaching morality, the problem of drugs,
and techniques of behavioral reinforcement. Dobson is extremely popular a-
mong conservative evangelical readers; within the constraints of his theological context, he writes with real wit and shows much practical common
sense. A related title is The strong-willed child (see entry 365), in which
he addresses the problem of rearing and disciplining assertive youngsters.

321. Tomczak, Larry. God, the rod, and your child's bod: the art of loving
     correction for Christian parents. Old Tappan, NJ: Power-Revell, 1982.
     124p. bibliog. LC 81-23507. ISBN 0-8007-5082-9. OCLC 8133255. pap.
Tomczak's thoughts on discipline spring from and point toward an evangelical motive: with the family crumbling all around, he believes Christians
should model biblical childrearing. One component of this is "loving correction": appropriate spankings for disobedience, consistently applied,
and with friendly relations quickly restored afterwards. Chatty and informal, with discussion questions and a bibliography for suggested reading.

322. Leman, Kevin. Making children mind without losing yours. Old Tappan,
     NJ: Revell, 1984. 191p. LC 83-11233. ISBN 0-8007-1373-7. OCLC
     9643237.
Psychologist Leman begins by discussing the principles of "reality discipline," an "action-oriented" approach that steers a middle course between
authoritarianism and permissiveness (both destructive) and allows children
opportunities within the home (not in public) to learn the consequences of
wrong behavior and, in the process, to become accountable for their own
actions. Reward and punishment no longer work, Leman says, though he
favors spanking on occasion if done out of love and followed by a time of
explanation/reconciliation. The second half of the book applies basic
principles to a variety of specific situations (forgetting, mistakes, sibling rivalry, etc.). Witty and concrete. Evangelical, but a minimum of
Bible quotations.

323. Wagemaker, Herbert J., Jr. Parents and discipline. Philadelphia:
     Westminster (Christian Care Books), 1980. 119p. bibliog. LC 80-14624.
     ISBN 0-664-24328-2. OCLC 6251455. pap.
One of the "Christian Care Books," this takes a developmental approach to
the subject. With young children, rules and limits are important, but as
children grow and enter adolescence, the process of identity formation becomes uppermost, and they need to begin learning how to solve their own
problems; hence negotiating, communication and mutually developed covenants
regarding guidelines are appropriate. The context is explicitly Christian,--Wagemaker is concerned with forming a Christian identity in young-
sters--but this is much more liberal than some other books on the subject.

324. Narramore, Bruce. Help! I'm a parent. Grand Rapids, MI: Zondervan,
     1972. 174p. illus. LC 76-189583. OCLC 403104.
Psychologist Narramore organizes his discussion in four parts: first, he
lays the groundwork with an integration of biblical/psychological insights
on discipline which, he believes, is to be administered for purposes of
training (not to enforce abstract "justice") and without destructive power
struggles; second, he discusses shaping a child's behavior and when to
spank; third, he explores a child's "inner life" and the importance of a
good self-image; fourth, he looks at how parents can keep their own equi-
librium and avoid being manipulated via guilt. Narramore's emphasis is on
disciplining in "positive" ways (via natural consequences of misbehavior,
say) and avoiding parental power trips. See also his Guide to child rearing: a manual for parents to accompany Help! I'm a parent (Zondervan, 1972)
which seeks to make the principles described above more easily applicable
with exercises and discussion questions, and Parenting with love and limits
(Zondervan, 1979) which explores a biblical model of parent-child interaction by looking at God's parental qualities.

325. Leman, Kevin. Smart girls don't and guys don't either. Ventura, CA:
     Regal, 1982. 152p. notes. LC 82-7686. ISBN 0-8307-0824-3. OCLC
     8452445.
By the relaxed, humorous author of Making children mind without losing
yours (see annotation). Leman writes here for parents of adolescents,
aiming to help them establish good relationships with their teen-age children via sharing, honesty and respect, so that they can be effective influences as the young people encounter peer pressure. Including some
statistics and stories on the subject of drugs, sex and alcohol among
youth, this emphasizes the importance of self-esteem. Closes with an open
letter to the adolescent and with sample questions and answers from a
column Leman writes.

326. Oraker, James R. with Char Meredith. Almost grown: a Christian guide
     for parents of teenagers. San Francisco: Harper, 1980. xii, 178p.
     notes. index. LC 78-20585. ISBN 0-06-066393-6. OCLC 5172514. (also
     pap).
A staff psychologist for "Young Life," an outreach ministry with teens,
has written this guide for all families with adolescents, including single
parent and blended families. Oraker looks at stages of adolescence, the
family as community, ways parents can nurture growth, and signs of troubled
families. He explores, too, a range of sexual issues (biological, psychological, social) and shares assorted real-life cases to illustrate general
points. A good blend of biblical discussion and concrete contemporary
concerns.

327. Di Giacomo, James J. and Edward Wakin. Understanding teenagers: a
     guide for parents. Allen, TX: Argus, 1983. 148p. illus. notes. LC
     83-70289. ISBN 0-89505-129-X. OCLC 10484109. pap.
A successor to the authors' earlier We were never their age (Holt, 1972),
this draws on new material (research, interviews) to help parents prepare
their adolescent children to meet the future. Examines the turbulence and
pressures of the teen years, youth's quest for meaning and a place in society, parental conflicts rooted in personal hopes/expectations for their
children, issues of drugs and sex, and religious faith. The stress is on
communication, integrity and faith dynamics, and on helping parents accept
differences between their own theological styles and those of young people
today. Catholic in perspective.

328. Ridenour, Fritz. What teenagers wish their parents knew about kids.
     Waco, TX: Word, 1982. 201p. illus. notes. LC 82-50516. ISBN
     0-8499-0308-4. OCLC 8764602.
Ridenour is the author of several popular spiritual advice-cum-Bible study
titles, often written in a lighthearted vein (e.g., How to be a Christian
without being religious, Regal, 1967). Here he departs from that genre
and offers parents a look at young peoples' major needs, as he sees them:
for identity and self-esteem, for honest, open communication; for a style
of discipline that is based on mutual respect. With an emphasis on attitudes and relationship dynamics, this draws from Ridenour's own talks with
teens plus biblical and psychological insights.

329. Beardsley, Lou. Mothers-in-law can be fun. Eugene, OR: Harvest House,
     1981. 142p. LC 80-84763. ISBN 0-89081-281-0. OCLC 9241132. pap.
This is based on personal experience, Bible study, and a survey taken by
a number of married persons of all ages (reprinted at the back of the book)
that reflects positive and negative behavior qualities among in-laws.

Deals with the engagement, the wedding, the first year of marriage; offers
chapters on being a mother-in-law, a son-in-law, a daughter-in-law, on
dealing with out-of-town children, on being a divorced or widowed mother-
in-law, on relating to grandchildren and to couples who are living together without being married, etc.   In other words, a range of issues.

330. Wright, H. Norman. How to be a better-than-average in-law. Wheaton,
      IL: Victor, 1981. 120p. LC 80-54722. ISBN 0-88207-342-7. OCLC
      7854296. pap.
For mothers-in-law, fathers-in-law, sons and daughters-in-law, this is
advice from a marriage and family counselor, psychology professor, and
director of Christian Family Enrichment seminars.   Wright offers a mix of
inventories and exercises, plus Scripture; (the latter is restricted to
general religious guidelines, since the Bible says nothing specific on the
subject).   Includes concrete advice on nitty-gritty issues like handling
visits, coping with criticism, and psychodynamic conflicts; includes
useful sample dialogues, self-assessment tools, etc.

H.   THE GROWING CHILD

331. Meier, Paul D. Christian child rearing and personality development.
      Grand Rapids, MI: Baker Book House, 1977. xii, 222p. bibliog. LC
      76-57501. ISBN 0-8010-6016-8. OCLC 3129353. pap.
Billed as a "Christian family's survival kit," this covers, from a conservative evangelical perspective, all phases of child development from
the prenatal period through adolescence.   Meier discusses physical, mental,
emotional, spiritual and sexual growth, integrating biblical principles
and psychiatric research, organizing the material into general categories
of "budding self-concept," "from conception to six years," and "six years
to eighteen years."   Some humor (e.g., "ten easy steps for developing your
normal, healthy baby into a drug addict or alcoholic"), but mainly a strict,
straight-and-narrow approach, especially to issues of dating and sex.

332. Krebs, Richard L. It's hard to tell you how I feel: helping children
      express and understand their feelings. Minneapolis, MN: Augsburg,
      1981. 127p. illus. LC 81-65646. ISBN 0-8066-1882-5. OCLC 7738920. pap.
A "feeling," says counselor Krebs, is something inside, which involves the
whole of us, and needs to get outside.   He looks at the developmental pro-
gression whereby children are first only able to express feelings, then
(school age) learn to describe them, later (in adolescence) are able to
explain them, and eventually (in young adulthood) can understand them.
Maturation involves an increasing distancing from feelings so that, with
time, people can learn to control them rather than being overwhelmed.   In
addition to exploring ways to help children with feelings at various developmental stages, this deals with religious feelings and their place in
spirituality.

333. Tengbom, Mildred. Does anyone care how I feel? Minneapolis, MN: Betha-
      ny House, 1981. 122p. illus. LC 81-3808. ISBN 0-87123-142-5. OCLC
      7461830. pap.
A book of family devotionals to help all members appreciate the children's
feelings and grow in understanding of themselves and others.   This is
designed so that children can read the reflective pieces aloud and take
an active part in the discussion; format consists of brief stories, or

reflections, followed by exploratory questions ("Let's talk") and relevant
Bible verses. Themes include the following: wanting to be alone sometimes; when parents argue; when someone cries; when a friend is sick; neighbors getting a divorce; going to the hospital; resentment against parents,
etc. The aim is to facilitate honest expression of a range of feelings,
the bad as well as the good; for grades four and up.

334. Coleman, William L. Today I feel loved! Minneapolis, MN: Bethany
     House, 1982. 128p. illus. LC 82-4187. ISBN 0-87123-566-8. OCLC
     8283622. pap.
Free verse reflections followed by Bible passages on a variety of situations and exploration of feelings that can be read aloud to encourage
children to talk about what they are experiencing. Friendship, anger,
kindness, sorrow, shyness, affection, relationships between brothers and
sisters, are just a few of the many topics covered. For pre-school through
fourth grade.

335. Milburn, Joyce. Helping your children love each other. Minneapolis,
     MN: Bethany House, 1983. 154p. notes. LC 83-15505. ISBN 0-87123-307-X.
     OCLC 9828245. pap.
On the basis of interviews with parents, teachers and child specialists,
together with her own experience, Milburn has come to the conclusion that
while sibling rivalry is natural, it can, to a certain extent, be controlled. Here she discusses God as the model of the perfect parent, and
using the metaphor of a growing plant, looks at preventive measures parents can take with young children to nurture self-esteem and a sense of
acceptance, set a good example, provide spiritual nurture and psychological reinforcement, set limits, and prepare for a sibling's birth ahead of
time. Some thoughts, too, on possible measures to use with older children when problems have already developed. Reflection questions included,
as well as suggestions for "family time" activities.

336. Coleman, William L. Getting ready for my first day of school. Min-
     neapolis, MN: Bethany House, 1983. 123p. photogs. LC 83-3809. ISBN
     0-87123-274-X. OCLC 9324765. pap.
Designed for parents to read aloud to children, here are brief chapters in
free verse format, enhanced by large black and white photos of boys and
girls of various racial/ethnic backgrounds sharing experiences and feelings
associated with starting school. One of Coleman's methods is to build
bridges between home and the school situation with suggestions, for instance, that children tell parents how it went, or ask about what their own
schools days were like; included, too, is miscellaneous practical advice
(send your parents home; know your own name and address).

337. Lockerbie, D. Bruce. Who educates your child? Grand Rapids, MI: Zon-
     dervan, 1981. xvii, 190p. bibliog. LC 80-39962. ISBN 0-310-44001-7.
     OCLC 7172893. pap.
A professional educator (Dean of the Faculty at Stony Brook School on Long
Island) discusses problems in today's public schools, some of their causes,
and various options available to Christian parents. Lockerbie believes
that different children need different environments, and that while some
may do very well in the public school settings, others will not. He emphasizes, too, the importance of family living as a model of spiritual
values and key qualities to look for in a good Christian school, should
parents wish to take that route.

338. Barnette, Helen P. Your child's mind: making the most of public
     schools. Philadelphia: Westminster (Potentials: Guides for Productive
     Living), 1984. 111p. bibliog. LC 83-26109. ISBN 0-664-24519-6. OCLC
     10299319. pap.
Westminster's "Potentials" series (Wayne E. Oates, general editor) addresses today's social issues from the perspective of the individual who must
find personal ways to cope but can, in the process, be a creative influence
on the wider group. The author of the present book is a classroom teacher
in the public school system. She believes that Christian parents who are
putting their energies into campaigns for mass change (re school prayer,
or the content of textbooks, say) might better concentrate on improving
their child's local education: visiting the school (she discusses what to
look for), participating creatively in educational projects at home (suggestions are offered), becoming advocates for disadvantaged youngsters who
have no parental support, mobilizing community resources, etc.

339. Moore, Raymond and Dorothy Moore. Home-spun schools: teaching children
     at home--what parents are doing and how they are doing it. Waco, TX:
     Word, 1982. 181p. bibliog. notes. LC 82-50843. ISBN 0-8499-0326-2. OCLC
     8944880.
The authors, who are both professional educators, advocate parental teaching in the home as a re-assertion of authority. They offer a cross-section
of personal stories from many who have taught their own children and, in
the appendix, look briefly at legal issues involved. Includes summaries
of cases where parents refused to send children to school, a bibliography
of home-study resources, and a table of required ages for school entrance,
state by state.

340. Ketterman, Grace H. How to teach your child about sex. Old Tappan,
     NJ: Revell, 1981. 188p. bibliog. LC 81-1742. ISBN 0-8007-1256-0.
     OCLC 7274088. (also pap).
Ketterman, a child psychiatrist, posits that adults must have healthy attitudes toward sex before they can effectively instruct children. Part
One of her book, then, besides reviewing basic information about sexuality,
aims to help parents achieve a good physical self-image, learn to express
emotions naturally, and understand the social implications of different
views. Part Two explores teaching methods for babies, preschoolers, and
adolescents within a perspective that is sensible, biblical, and compassionate, taking full account of the realities of VD, abortion, homosexuality. Highly recommended.

341. Howell, John C. Teaching your children about sex. Nashville, TN:
     Broadman (Sexuality in Christian Living Series), 1973. 118p. notes.
     LC 72-90038. ISBN 0-8054-5607-4. OCLC 584115. pap.
One of Broadman's sex education series, this is aimed at parents and is
intended to complement other titles which are written specifically for the
children themselves. Howell offers a look at the place of sex education
in the Christian family and tries to place attitudes toward sex in perspective; then he discusses patterns of growth and parental preparation,
plus guidelines for sex education with young children, pre-puberty children, junior high age children, and teens. A glossary is included which offers scientifically accurate terms for concepts, parts of the body, etc.,
that young people may often discuss only in very colloquial language. (See
also entry 345 for another title in this series, aimed specifically at pre-
puberty children.)

342. Buth, Lenore. Sexuality: God's precious gift to parents and children.
    St. Louis, MO: Concordia (New Concordia Sex Education Series), 1982.
    142p. illus. index. LC 82-8097. ISBN 0-570-08480-6. OCLC 8475261.
Volume Six of Concordia's new sex education series, this is aimed at parents
and other adults who will be discussing sex with children or teenagers
and seeks to make them more comfortable with their feelings and attitudes.
The stress is on sexuality within the context of a loving marriage in which
each partner puts the other before him or herself out of a common love for
Christ, thereby transcending obsession with superficial issues like sex-
role stereotypes. A chapter on the single parent emphasizes that celibacy
(required) is not damaging and encourages church singles groups. After
thus exploring adult situations, Buth turns to the children--their interest in sex at different stages, questions they may ask--and anatomical
facts the adults should understand clearly.   Other titles in the series
are Each one specially (ages 3-5), I wonder why (ages 6-8), How you got
to be you (ages 8-11), The new you (ages 11-14) and Lord of life, Lord
of me (ages 14 and up; see entry 346).

343. Nixon, Joan Lowery. Before you were born. Huntington, IN: Our Sunday
    Visitor, 1980. 30p. illus. LC 79-91741. ISBN 0-87973-343-8. OCLC
    6208156. pap.
A read-aloud book for very young children, with large, colorful, abstract
illustrations capturing a mood of beauty and vitality. Not a standard sex
education book, this stresses instead issues of foetal development, communicating the message that at every stage of the process God knows exactly
what the child will be like and loves it (in the text, "you") into being,
up to and through the moment of birth.

344. Alex, Marlee and Benny Alex. You and me and our new little baby. Grand
    Rapids, MI: Zondervan, 1982. 44p. illus. photogs. ISBN 0-310-44981-2.
    OCLC 10892464. pap.
For use with children between four and eight years old in families where
the mother is pregnant, this is a specialized sort of sex education title,
aimed at helping prepare boys and girls for the birth of a sibling. Guidance and discussion on pregnancy, birth, and the new infant's arrival are
presented in the form of a story about a young brother and sister whose
mother is having a third child; photos show the children playing together
(the girl pretending to be pregnant herself, etc.), and illustrations are
offered depicting conception and foetal development.

345. Edens, David. The changing me. Nashville, TN: Broadman (Sexuality in
    Christian Living Series), 1973. 46p. illus. ISBN 0-8054-4411-4. OCLC
    1088055. pap.
One of Broadman's "Sexuality in Christian Living Series," this is aimed
at children nine to eleven years of age who are about to enter puberty.
A look at the creation story is followed by some discussion on the nature
of the family (not all families are alike; some have only one parent, but
whatever the structure, people need each other); thereafter Edens discusses
the body and sex organs, intercourse (a very low-key presentation), foetal
development, birth and care of the newborn, adolescence, puberty and masturbation (perhaps the greatest harm is in guilt). Emphasizes changing
feelings and self-acceptance in their midst. Includes glossary, color
illustrations. (See also entry 341.)

346. Ameiss, Bill and Jane Graver. <u>Lord of life, Lord of me</u>. St. Louis,
     MO: Concordia (New Concordia Sex Education Series), 1982. 120p. illus.
     LC 82-8108. ISBN 0-570-08479-2. OCLC 8475293.
Volume Five of Concordia's sex education series, this is aimed at teenagers fourteen and older. Very clear on forbidding all sex outside of
marriage (heavy petting is described as a sin), it stresses biblical passages, the body as God's temple, and the importance of a personal relationship with Jesus. It is a bit more liberal in acknowledging increased
flexibility in male/female roles today and speaking out against sexual
stereotypes. In question and answer format, it moves beyond basic facts
to examine some complex issues: VD, abortion, birth control, dating, ways
of testing a developing love, communication, etc. (See also entry 342.)

347. Rekers, George Alan. <u>Shaping your child's sexual identity</u>. Grand
     Rapids, MI: Baker Book House, 1982. xii, 170p. notes. index. LC
     82-70461. ISBN 0-8010-7713-3. OCLC 8657108. <u>pap</u>.
By a clinical psychologist, this goes into a fair amount of technical detail as it counsels parents on the importance of encouraging normal sexual
identities in their children by observing distinctive roles for mother and
father within the family and reinforcing appropriate behavior. Rekers
allows for some cross-sex role play among children (e.g., it is OK to let
a boy wear an apron, or a girl play tom-boy, as long as the behavior is
merely occasional and not constant), but on the whole, he seems to be
remarkably concerned about the dangers of potentially androgynous development and eventual homosexuality. Includes detailed discussion of cases
of sexual confusion among children he has counseled.

348. Cully, Iris V. <u>Christian child development</u>. San Francisco: Harper,
     1979. x, 166p. notes. index. LC 78-19507. ISBN 0-06-061648-2. OCLC
     4495713. (1983 ed. in <u>BIP</u>).
This attempts to relate contemporary research findings in learning theory
to the process of children's religious development. Intended for parents,
teachers and clergy, it describes processes by which a child forms a relationship with God in the developmental stages of thinking, feeling and
learning. Covers the beginnings of prayer, learning in a church, and ways
of understanding faith, followed by growth in moral development and making
commitments. Includes a look at the "born again" experience and whether
it can happen to children, as well as a comparison between evangelical and
Catholic attitudes on sin. Draws on Erikson, Piaget, Kohlberg, Fowler,
etc.

349. Thompson, Andrew D. <u>When your child learns to choose</u>. St. Meinrad, IN:
     Abbey (When Books), 1978. 95p. photogs. bibliog. LC 78-73018. ISBN
     0-87029-145-9. OCLC 4884027. <u>pap</u>.
Intended for parents, this describes the moral development of children.
Thompson draws on research findings to identify factors that influence
moral growth and helps parents work in the context of family living to
promote Christian values. Looks separately at the developmental situations of preschoolers, nine year olds, junior high age children, and high
school students, stressing ways of giving children the ability to weigh
various value tensions in society against each other and to see hidden
commonalities beneath seemingly different views. By a professor of religious development at Catholic University.

350. Curran, Dolores. Who, me teach my child religion? Minneapolis, MN: Winston, 1981. xii, 129p. LC 82-131439. ISBN 0-86683-619-5. OCLC 8451295. pap. (1974 ed. examined).
Specifically for Roman Catholic parents, this was first published in 1970. Extremely clear and reassuring, with much "we have been there" style sharing, it considers ways of addressing children's questions "on the spot," linking them up with daily experience and using ordinary examples/resources (newspapers, TV, etc.). Includes a look at parental anxieties (is my child losing the faith?), bridging the gap between newer and more traditional styles of Catholicism.

351. Cranor, Phoebe. Why did God let Grandpa die? Minneapolis, MN: Bethany House, 1976. 128p. LC 76-17737. ISBN 0-87123-603-6. OCLC 2644773. pap.
Here is a book dealing with various questions similar to those commonly asked by children on death, suffering, heaven, hell, prayer, meanness in the world, Jesus' role, etc. For each one, Cranor first shares her own reflections, confusions, and general thought processes as she works her way through to an answer. Thereafter, she offers the answer itself in brief essay form suitable for parents to read aloud to their own children. Scripture readings conclude each section. Cranor's orientation is a conservative evangelical one, and her responses are sensitively phrased with children's developmental experiences in mind.

352. Evans, Colleen Townsend. Teaching your child to pray. Garden City, NY: Galilee-Doubleday, 1982. 64p. photogs. LC 82-1434. ISBN 0-385-15045-8. OCLC 8171657. pap.
Specially designed for parents to use with their young children, this is set up so that read-aloud text is presented in large print, while material for the parents themselves appears in small type. Evans discusses varieties of prayer, emphasizing the importance of honesty and of trusting that we can ask God's help even with difficult feelings (not wanting to pray, among other things). Covers, too, ways God communicates with us—not in words, but via our feelings and ideas. A word by word, phrase by phrase exploration of the Lord's prayer concludes the book, with implications for children. Very simply and sensitively done.

353. Scheihing, Theresa, and Louis M. Savary. Our treasured heritage: teaching Christian meditation to children. New York: Crossroad, 1981. 155p. LC 81-7818. ISBN 0-8245-0078-4. OCLC 7555112.
In consultation with Savary, a counselor and mother suggests ways parents and teachers can introduce children to meditation as a natural means for developing a one-to-one relationship with God. Drawing on Ignatius Loyola's method ("getting ready," "meditating," and "reviewing"), she presents meditative sequences for different seasons of the liturgical year and discusses the general dynamics of meditation (centering, the role of imagination) as well as practical questions (Can children meditate in groups? What about meditation and hyperactive children?). An interesting amalgam of Catholic tradition and humanistic psychology.

354. McCarroll, Tolbert. Guiding God's children: a foundation for spiritual growth in the home. New York: Paulist, 1983. 192p. illus. notes. index. LC 83-60376. ISBN 0-8091-2547-1. OCLC 10467774. pap.
Primarily for parents, whether members of the institutional church or not, but also for pastors, teachers, etc., this stresses the need to work with pre-adolescent children on "spiritual" (as opposed to "religious") education. By a Catholic monk and spiritual director who considers himself a

"Christian humanist," the theoretical framework (explored at length in the first part of the book) unites humanistic/developmental psychology and Eastern approaches with that of Christianity. The "Practical program of twelve steps" (Part III) is short on orthodox doctrine, long on experiential/psychological activities. Closes with a look at future styles of spiritual community and theoretical reflections.

355. Schomp, Gerald. Parent/child/God: bringing you closer together. Cincinnati, OH: St. Anthony Messenger Pr., 1977. 184p. illus. ISBN 0-912228-49-0. OCLC 4822816. pap. (o.p.).
A communications specialist with seven children offers thoughts on integrating religious education with over-all child-rearing. Aside from a few Catholic points of focus, this is generally applicable to all Christians, discussing developmental stages and capacities for understanding, the importance of starting on the pre-school level, integrating love and discipline, helping children internalize values and favorable images of God, using daily events for spiritual education and prayer, "livening up" the Liturgy, telling Bible stories, preparing for first Communion, etc. Discussion questions and practical suggestions for activities; steers a middle way between traditional and progressive approaches, with an accent on parental creativity.

356. Alexander, Olive J. Developing spiritually sensitive children. Minneapolis, MN: Bethany House, 1980. 131p. index. LC 80-23603. ISBN 0-87123-111-5. OCLC 6709060. pap.
Because many books on Christian child-rearing already examine ways of disciplining children--spanking, etc.--Alexander concentrates here on ways parents can work with their own personalities to nurture more effectively. Often, she says, parents focus on defects in their children which, if they only realized it, are also glaring in their own lives, and working actively with one's own shortcomings can be a great aid to more effective child-rearing. With an emphasis, too, on refreshing ways children can demonstrate spiritual sensitivity, reflected in entertaining anecdotes, this makes a positive, useful statement.

357. Westerhoff, John H. III. Bringing up children in the Christian faith. Minneapolis, MN: Winston, 1980. 108p. LC 79-67034. ISBN 0-03-056203-1. OCLC 6916238. pap.
A professor of religion and education stresses that faith--and its communication--is essentially a journey. We can never know that we are right in everything, but we can do the best that we see at any given time, be open to letting our faith deepen, and share our errors as we revise our thinking along the way. The important thing in sharing faith with one's children, then, is to be Christian in one's relationship with them, to pray together, to talk and listen, modeling an adult pilgrimage and nurturing the children's own ways of seeking, according to their developmental stages. Extremely intelligent, thoughtful, and well written.

358. Hunt, Gladys. Honey for a child's heart. Grand Rapids, MI: Zondervan, 1978. 182p. bibliog. LC 78-3488. ISBN 0-310-26380-8. OCLC 3913520. pap.
A new edition of an excellent and unusual book, first published in 1969. Christians, Hunt says, believing in a Creator God, should be leaders in nurturing creativity among children, yet often they are inhibited because they think only reading with a Christian "label" is safe. Here she urges the use of all good books in building spiritually alive children, encourages

reading aloud and sharing together (classics as well as the Bible), and offers ideas on how to evaluate worthwhile books. The title is taken from Erich Fromm's statement that children need both milk (care for the person) and honey (the sweetness of life) from their parents. Includes extensive bibliography of recommended titles.

359. LeFever, Marlene. Growing creative children. Wheaton, IL: Tyndale, 1981. 143p. illus. LC 81-50140. ISBN 0-8423-1232-3. OCLC 7914588. pap.
The main point here is that God is Creator, and Christians should therefore encourage creativity in children by nurturing curiosity, perception, and listening, and emphasizing the processes of exploration and growth rather than just a finished product. LeFever has some very imaginative suggestions for activities that link creativity with the Christian message, e.g., "devotional car trips" to explore the country, or encouraging children to listen to the dissonance of "the world's" music and to compare it with the sounds of "God's" music. Each chapter concludes with a "Would this work in your house?" set of suggestions.

360. Hancock, Maxine. Confident, creative children. Chappaqua, NY: Christian Herald, 1981. 192p. notes. index. LC 78-17580. ISBN 0-915684-97-7. OCLC 8031314. pap.
A teacher and mother, Hancock focuses here on what she sees as three key areas of personal development in pre-schoolers--confidence, character, and creativity--with the first two constituting the foundation out of which the third will properly emerge. She stresses ways biblical Christian standards and guidelines undergird the process (faith in Christ as the ultimate source of confidence, say) and suggests concrete ways parents can reinforce a good self-image in children, drawing on Scripture for training the character.   Explores ways of building order and rhythm into experience, nurturing reflective and analytical thinking, developing various skills, etc. Formerly published as People in process.

361. Nye, Loyal. What color am I? Nashville, TN: Abingdon, 1977. 27p. illus. LC 76-55577. ISBN 0-687-44633-3. OCLC 2645929.
A picture book for young children, grades k-3, designed to nurture a consciousness that will not fall prey to racial stereotyping, this emphasizes the subtlety of differences between people, especially differences of color. People, the text suggests, are not really "white," "red," "black," etc., but are, rather, mixtures: a bit of pink, or tan, or brown. Attractive pictures (including truly "red," "black," "white" or "yellow" faces, to show how unrealistic they look) illustrate the theme.

362. Borgman, Paul. TV: friend or foe? Elgin, IL: David C. Cook, 1979. bibliog. notes. LC 78-73003. ISBN 0-89191-072-7. OCLC 5102983. pap.
An English professor, Borgman was inspired to investigate the meaning that TV programs hold for young people when he realized the depth of his son's attachment to TV heroes. With his students, he interviewed a cross-section of elementary and high school age youth about their TV experiences and, in this handbook, draws on their responses to examine which parental concerns seem valid, what is good viewing, and for whom (with specific attention to cartoons, adventure, comedy, sports, news, drama, and TV fantasy vs. biblical truth). Considers specific problems like sex, violence, and stereotyping and suggests some guidelines for action. Balanced, interesting, and very well written.

363. Coleman, William L. Making TV work for your family. Minneapolis, MN:
     Bethany House, 1983. 106p. illus. LC 83-11881. ISBN 0-87123-322-3.
     OCLC 9622354. pap.
Written at a child's level but intended for use in crystallizing discussion
among all family members, this has thirty brief chapters reflecting on a
variety of questions and concerns re TV and its use, ending with related
verses from Scripture and discussion questions. The emphasis is on making
good use of TV rather than undermining it entirely. The chapters encourage
readers to look for good heroes and role models, to enjoy sports, to appreciate some of the Christian shows, to use current events reporting as
a catalyst for involvement, to discuss TV among family members, etc. Other
essays encourage critical thinking about frightening shows, permissive
sex, and violence.

364. MacGregor, Malcolm. Training your children to handle money. Minneapo-
     lis, MN: Bethany House, 1980. 139p. forms. LC 80-17579. ISBN
     0-87123-540-4. OCLC 7276331. pap.
Emphasizing the importance of involving children in the family's financial
planning, this starts with some basic concerns (all children should learn
to tithe; allowance/earnings systems and options; dealing with problems
like losing, hoarding, overspending and stealing; borrowing), then turns
to a look at ways of handling and earning money, geared to specific developmental periods in a child's growth from pre-school through college-age.
Occasional biblical references; practical and down-to-earth, with a sense
of humor.

                    I. SPECIAL SITUATION PARENTING

365. Dobson, James C. The strong-willed child: birth through adolescence.
     Wheaton, IL: Tyndale, 1978. 240p. illus. notes. LC 77-83559.
     ISBN 0-8423-0664-1. OCLC 3812962.
Extremely humorous and well written with a no-nonsense message, this offers advice for dealing with defiantly assertive children during infancy,
childhood, adolescence, examining such problems as sibling rivalry, hyperactivity, self-image complications, and common parental errors. The point,
Dobson counsels, is to shape the will without breaking the spirit, so while
discipline and boundaries must be firm, love openly expressed is absolutely
essential. Authority issues are discussed in a clearly evangelical context;
very down-to-earth with a wealth of witty anecdotes.

366. Evans, James S. An uncommon gift. Philadelphia: Bridgebooks-West-
     minster, 1983. 180p. LC 82-25930. ISBN 0-664-27009-3. OCLC 9194017.
The son of writer Colleen Townsend Evans and minister/author Louis H. Evans,
Jr., now a student at seminary, shares his experiences growing up as a
dyslexic with severe problems of hyperactivity and stuttering. Evans re-
calls the early difficulties, the trauma of diagnosis and preliminary treatment, ways his attempts to learn new controls over behavior partially back-
fired causing later fear of losing any control and consequent terror of
intimacy. Woven throughout the successes and failures are his parents'
loving concern and a developing faith. Concluding comments from family
members add perspective. A primary audience is, obviously, other dys-
lexics; still, this could be very useful for parents as well.

367. Paterson, George W. Helping your handicapped child. Minneapolis, MN: Augsburg (Religion and Medicine), 1975. 104p. bibliog. LC 74-14185. ISBN 0-8066-1467-6. OCLC 1323696. pap.
One of the "Religion and Medicine" series, this begins with a look at cases illustrating different types of handicaps (deafness, CP, Downs syndrome, etc.), then discusses dynamics of resistance/acceptance, the correlation between faith attitudes and modes of dealing with disabilities, physical/ emotional needs of the children and how to meet them, seeking medical help, future planning, and using resources effectively. Some interesting discussion of the implications of one's God-concept (e.g., God as punitive or God as resource for hope); includes lists of organizational resources.

368. Wheeler, Bonnie. Challenged parenting: a practical handbook for parents of children with handicaps. Ventura, CA: Regal, 1982. 221p. LC 82-18144. ISBN 0-8307-0835-9. OCLC 8827472. pap.
The author and her husband have six children, three adopted, with a variety of handicaps (deaf and blind, CP, hyperactive). This is a practical handbook with suggestions drawn from personal experience, designed to help parents deal fruitfully with self-image problems on the part of the child, threats to the marriage, and complications for siblings. Wheeler begins with the dynamics of accepting the situation, prayerfully moving through grief and into the capacity to cope creatively, and then looks at family relations, friendships, professional resources, and special joys/rewards. Most useful.

369. Roberts, Nancy. You and your retarded child. St. Louis, MO: Concordia, 1974. 77p. photogs. bibliog. LC 73-88948. ISBN 0-570-06768-5. OCLC 1323596. (o.p.).
Roberts has a son with Down's syndrome. Here she writes of the pain and challenges in rearing handicapped children, in a concrete style but with a strong emphasis on the spiritual/emotional dimensions. She discusses patterns of response, crises of faith, options for the child's future, impact on family life, possible institutionalization, the role of the church, and issues surrounding the question of God's will. Photos by her husband depict handicapped children living and playing in various settings. Another title by Roberts, Help for parents of a handicapped child (Concordia 1981) was not seen but is currently in print.

370. Crim, Lottie R. Come care with me. Nashville, TN: Broadman, 1983. 118p. LC 82-073369. ISBN 0-8054-5431-4. OCLC 9447394. pap.
The author has had experience as a special education teacher and draws on that, as well as on interviews with parents of handicapped children, in these pages. The book is jointly directed at parents themselves and at concerned relatives/friends who want to know how best to offer support. Organized according to typical feeling-stages of response (grief, shock, anger, guilt, sorrow and acceptance), the narrative explores various dimensions of the feelings and their expression so all involved can understand what is happening and how to help.

371. Perske, Robert. Hope for the families: new directions for parents of persons with retardation or other disabilities. Nashville, TN: Abingdon, 1981. 96p. illus. by Martha Perske. notes. LC 81-5700. ISBN 0-687-17380-9. OCLC 7550653. pap.
A large-format paperback that captures and crystallizes feelings and issues in families with developmentally disabled members. Perske looks at developmental principles, the importance of human dignity and normaliza-

tion, family systems and games that may emerge, the relationship between parents and professionals, ways family members can create strength out of crisis, and much more. Includes reflections on positive and negative theological attitudes, stressing the value of nurturing faith that God is for joy and for the fullest possible development on the part of the handicapped child. Greatly enriched by Martha Perske's expressive line drawings. See also the author's New life in the neighborhood (Abingdon, 1980), focusing on the capacities of the disabled for life in the community.

372. Dennis, Muriel B. Chosen children. Westchester, IL: Good News, 1978.
     150p. illus. LC 80-132264. ISBN 0-89107-154-7. OCLC 4619522.
The prologue of this guide on adoption explores the analogy between children in need of adoptive parents and all of the human family, in need of a spiritual relationship with God. Thereafter we have stories about adoptive and foster parents and their children (many handicapped children with a variety of problems), followed by information about the adoptive process and its institutions and agencies, presented by Executive Director of the Evangelical Child and Family Agency, Doris Wheeler. Contributors include Dale Evans Rogers and Bonnie Wheeler.

373. Barcus, Nancy B. The family takes a child. Valley Forge, PA: Judson,
     1983. 94p. LC 83-282. ISBN 0-8170-0998-1. OCLC 9350446. pap.
The author and her husband brought an older child into their family; here she shares an imaginary situation reflecting issues that arose in their personal experience. With details changed but principles grounded in reality, she presents the experiences of ten-year old Joey and his new family as they confront homesickness, coming to terms with memories, learning to accept new offerings of love, etc. A simple, direct narrative-cum-guide; scriptural verses conclude each chapter.

374. Felker, Evelyn H. Raising other people's kids: successful childrearing
     in the restructured family. Grand Rapids, MI: Eerdmans, 1981. xii,
     164p. LC 80-28227. ISBN 0-8028-1868-4. OCLC 7206275. pap.
Aimed at parents in "restructured families" who are raising children not biologically their own (foster children, step-children, and adoptive children), this seeks to dispel the myth that such families are more likely to fail. Felker looks at the processes of bringing a new child into the family, establishing developmental goals (pre-school age through teenage), disciplining (in the context of a biblical approach that stresses all of Scripture, taken as a whole, rather than isolated verses), maintaining relationships with the biological family, emotional problems, and the parent's own needs. Very practical advice grounded in a genuine spirituality.

375. Bilow, Pat. And now we are four. Plainfield, NJ: Haven-Logos, 1980.
     xi, 163p. LC 80-82577. ISBN 0-88270-448-6. OCLC 7279391. pap. (available through Bridge).
In recent years Bilow, her husband, and their two sons served as temporary family for two girls and two boys. Now, speaking out of these experiences, she shares some of the joys, heartaches, rewards and frustrations of being a foster parent. Having known both "success" (a good relationship with the girls which facilitated their eventual reunion with their natural mother) and "failure" (one of the boys vandalized the Bilows' house), she is in a good position to discuss a wide range of issues, and her Christian perspective together with her knowledge of trends, statistics, etc., adds to the book's value.

376. Nason, Diane with Birdie Etchison. <u>Celebration family</u>. Nashville, TN:
     Thomas Nelson, 1983. 196p. photogs. LC 83-17440. ISBN 0-8407-5849-9.
     OCLC 9895452. <u>pap</u>.
The story of a very large family: Diane and Dennis Nason, their six biological children, and over 20 adopted or foster children, with assorted
handicaps and representing a variety of racial and ethnic backgrounds.
Most of the emphasis here is on how it all came about--the early years of
the marriage, the decision to adopt, and, chapter by chapter, the stories
of the various children and how they were found and "brought home." Particularly affecting is the story of Danny from El Salvador. A deep, simple
faith in God's call to them to carve out this lifestyle underlies the
Nasons' accomplishments; inspiring "miracles" are shared along the way.

J.   STYLES OF FAMILY LIFE

377. LaHaye, Tim and Bev LaHaye. <u>Spirit-controlled family living</u>. Old Tap-
     pan, NJ: Revell, 1978. 221p. illus. bibliog. LC 78-13526. ISBN
     0-8007-0951-9. OCLC 4136277. <u>pap</u>. (later ed. in <u>BIP</u>).
In the introduction Baptist minister/author LaHaye shares his personal testimony about the life-changing effect (a miserable marriage transformed
into a joyous one) of being filled with the Holy Spirit. In the rest of
the book the LaHayes detail principles which they teach at their Family
Life Seminars on "Spirit-controlled" living: re keys to a happy marriage,
six major problems in the husband-wife relationship, roles for each (very
traditional and clearly defined), etc.

378. Christenson, Larry. <u>The Christian family</u>. Minneapolis, MN: Bethany
     House, 1978. 224p. LC 75-324692. ISBN 0-87123-088-7. OCLC 3932359.
     <u>pap</u>. (various eds. in <u>BIP</u>).
A mix of theology and practical guidance from a conservative evangelical
viewpoint. Part One discusses God's order for the family (i.e., proper
relationships between mates, children, etc., within an established hierarchy), while Part Two explores practicing the presence of Jesus as Savior
and Lord of the family, with the parents as priests and the total family
an embodied witness of Kingdom living. Christenson, while extremely traditional in his view of proper roles, tries hard to avoid legalism; for
instance, while he views all women as vulnerable and in need of a man's
protection (a church leader if not a husband), he does stress that living
in Jesus' presence is more important than concentrating on orderly roles
for their own sake. A healthy, light touch where sex is concerned, and a
call for discipline without bitterness.

379. Getz, Gene A. <u>The measure of a family</u>. Glendale, CA: Regal, 1976. 190p.
     notes. LC 76-46872. ISBN 0-8307-0445-0. OCLC 3962448. <u>pap</u>.
The Bible, says Getz, generally emphasizes supra-cultural <u>functions</u> rather
than specific cultural <u>forms</u>, so the biblical guidelines for family living
--re submission, discipline, divorce and remarriage, the husband's leadership, etc.--point a clear direction but leave room for flexibility when it
comes to particular details. An attempt to uphold the husband's headship
and traditional lines of authority while keeping the door open for dialogue, with separate chapters on the home, the wife, the husband, the children, family nurture and discipline, and the conditions of being "unequally
yoked," being a single parent, and facing divorce or remarriage.

380. Blitchington, W. Peter. Sex roles and the Christian family. Wheaton, IL: Tyndale, 1980. 192p. notes. LC 79-67856. ISBN 0-8423-5878-1. OCLC 7063599. pap.
A conservative Christian psychologist discusses what he sees as the process and causes of disintegration in today's family and describes God's "blueprint" for workable family relations based on the law of complementary sex roles. Citing a mix of Scripture, psychological research, and anthropological findings, he argues that males are intrinsically (and by design) prone to be leaders and women to be followers, and that women's primary role in the home reinforces male fidelity in bread-winning, etc. Chapters discuss helping boys and girls to grow up in this mold, how schools aggravate role confusion, homosexuality, managing sex drive, and the hazards of divorce. More conservative psycho-social criticism than a straight "how to."

381. Schaeffer, Edith. What is a family? Old Tappan, NJ: Power-Revell, 1975. 255p. LC 75-29057. ISBN 0-8007-5088-8. OCLC 1638007. pap.
First issued in hardcover (Revell, 1975) and now in paperback, this shows Edith Schaeffer drawing on her experience as wife (of well-known evangelical leader and writer Francis Schaeffer), mother, grandmother, and hostess to innumerable visitors at L'Abri Fellowship in Switzerland over the years. Grounded in a conservative evangelical world-view, Schaeffer possesses a richly imaginative, poetic sensibility which is highly evident as she describes the family as a mobile, an ecologically balanced environment, a center for building human relationships, etc.

382. Swihart, Judson J. How to treat your family as well as you treat your friends. Ventura, CA: Regal, 1982. 159p. LC 82-11234. ISBN 0-8307-0855-3. OCLC 8553124. pap.
Based on scriptural passages in Matthew 5-7, this explores principles for better family living. Swihart starts with a look at the Beatitudes as basis, then explores ways of dealing with anger, being willing to be reconciled, not returning evil, giving what is yours, the Golden Rule, etc. A genuine effort to apply the principles of the Sermon on the Mount to marriage and family living, this makes a very useful alternative to books of family counsel that stress the importance of hierarchical role relationships.

383. Owens, Virginia Stem. A feast of families. Grand Rapids, MI: Zondervan, 1983. 143p. LC 82-21773. ISBN 0-310-45850-1. OCLC 9066722.
Owens, always a writer of immense intelligence and artfulness, demonstrates those same qualities here in personal reflections on her own experiences of family, growing up in Texas, interspersed with musings on biblical meanings and metaphors, centered in the idea of God as Father. Her sensitivity cuts through any simplistic or culturally conditioned notions, and her erudition is gracefully integrated into the narrative as she ponders the treasure of human interconnectedness in our frequently fragile earthen vessels. Not a "how to" book, but a rich storehouse of insight, with many possible applications for daily living.

384. Moore, Louis and Kay Moore. When you both go to work: how two-paycheck families can stay active in the church. Waco, TX: Word, 1982. 204p. notes. LC 81-71499. ISBN 0-8499-0287-8. OCLC 8872199.
Drawing from their own experience as a two-career family (both are journalists) and from in-depth interviews with other church-going families in the same situation, the Moores look at the church as support or impediment

and reasons for making an effort to relate to the church even where there
is hostility to the couple's life-style. Includes some biblical interpretation, learning to set priorities, juggling domestic tasks, making time
for family relationships, the special role of the father, relating fruitfully to friends, etc.

385. Rowatt, G. Wade, Jr. and Mary Jo Rowatt. The two-career marriage.
     Philadelphia: Westminster (Christian Care Books), 1980. 119p. bibliog.
     LC 79-28408. ISBN 0-664-24298-7. OCLC 5887643. pap.
Drawing from research findings and personal experience, a husband and wife
team discuss positive rewards of dual-career marriages, child-rearing ramifications, questions bearing on the division of labor in the home, time-
management, sex-role issues, and ways the church can help (or hinder). The
Rowatts interviewed a number of couples to get a range of perspectives,
and they include some comments on how restrictive attitudes toward male/
female roles on the part of the churches can do real damage.

386. Blackwell, William L. and Muriel F. Blackwell. Working partners,
     working parents. Nashville, TN: Broadman, 1979. 144p. notes. LC
     79-51134. ISBN 0-8054-5637-6. OCLC 5675670. pap.
The background for the Blackwells' advice is over twenty-eight years of
marriage, successful experience with dual careers, and the assumption that
marriage is a partnership of two equally whole persons--plus extensive
discussion with others. Within an explicitly biblical context they look
at Christian personhood, issues of potential rivalry, assigning duties,
financial matters, shared homemaking, sex, building positive discipline,
and family fulfillment. Their aim is not to convince everyone to choose
their lifestyle, but rather to present it as one acceptable Christian option among many.

387. Mattison, Judith. Mom has a second job: prayer thoughts for working
     mothers. Minneapolis, MN: Augsburg, 1980. 96p. photogs. LC 80-65548.
     ISBN 0-8066-1793-4. OCLC 6918229. pap. (o.p.).
These free verse reflections touch on experiences shared by mothers who
work outside the home and stimulate thinking about their dual role. Subjects covered are positive aspects and preconditions for this lifestyle
(children learning independence; the value of good health), negative feelings (guilt, meeting the criticism of others, missing the old leisure),
needs (for exercise or more time), joys (over cooperation from others,
etc.) and aspects of various work situations. The theme might be described
as the struggle to incorporate valuable facets of the women's movement without abandoning positive aspects of a more traditional role.

388. Kilgore, James E. Dollars and sense: making your money work for you
     and your family. Nashville, TN: Abingdon, 1982. 142p. LC 81-20620.
     ISBN 0-687-11050-5. OCLC 8034203. pap.
Our attitudes toward money and relationships are interrelated, says Kilgore; attitudes toward money are a kind of barometer of our attitudes in
other areas, so as families work with money issues the spiritual ramifications spread. He advocates learning better principles of management
and focusing on ways to increase family enjoyment in good relational living rather than just stressing money per se; when we use money to express
love, increase communication, enhance intimacy, and build up one another,
we will automatically find ourselves managing it better. A very useful
book.

389. FoOshee, George, Jr. You can be financially free: practical Christian
     principles for handling your family finances. Old Tappan, NJ: Power-
     Revell, 1976. 127p. illus. LC 76-1025. ISBN 0-8007-5000-4. OCLC
     2005996. pap.
The author, who is president of a credit agency, discusses three basic
processes--sharing, spending, and saving--in terms of biblical guidelines.
Sharing is crucial, for those who give will also get; spending should be
moderate, as one seeks to be content with simple things; saving prudently
is also counseled. This gets very practical and detailed in spots, as
Fooshee discusses how to budget, renting vs. buying a house (somewhat
dated), what kinds of things to borrow for, and the virtue of tithing.

390. Hales, Edward J. and J. Alan Youngren. Your money/their ministry: a
     guide to responsible Christian giving. Grand Rapids, MI: Eerdmans,
     1981. xi, 113p. LC 81-5541. ISBN 0-8028-1894-3. OCLC 7554409. pap.
Traditional stewardship books, the authors explain, explore why and how
much to give; this focuses instead on how to assess the worth of agencies/
organizations as potential recipients of your donation. They analyze some
different kinds of media exploitation, typical abuses of Christian fund
raising, and potentially useful research tools (such as letters of inquiry)
the reader may wish to use.

391. Leckey, Dolores R. The ordinary way: a family spirituality. New York:
     Crossroad, 1982. xii, 156p. notes. index. LC 81-22206. ISBN 0-8245-
     0442-9. OCLC 8169419. pap.
The "ordinary way" is Leckey's term for daily family living, an enterprise
that can, she suggests, be spiritualized by reflecting on and applying nine
Benedictine rules: for intimacy, equality, authority, prayer, solitude
and silence, play, study, stability, and hospitality. Herself a wife and
mother, Leckey stresses that "God and grace are indeed present in all kinds
of families" and writes for single parents and intentional Christian communities as well as members of the more traditional nuclear family.   Sensitive, imaginative, helpful.

392. Dorn, Lois with Penni Eldredge-Martin. Peace in the family: a workbook
     of ideas and actions. New York: Pantheon, 1983. ix, 177p. illus.
     photogs. bibliog. notes. LC 83-42823. ISBN 0-394-71580-2. OCLC 9645603.
     pap. (also cloth).
This grew out of the Parent Support Project of the Nonviolence and Children
program, grounded in the peace commitment of the Religious Society of
Friends (Quakers) and initiated by the Friends' Philadelphia Yearly Meeting.
Its first chapters outline a foundational belief in affirmation and support
as key factors in personal growth and human relationships.   Thereafter
working principles and exercises are presented with the aim of helping
people evaluate their own attitudes and determine where they need more support so as to follow through on an affirmative parenting style.   Deals
with conflict resolution, journaling, and individual/family/classroom and
support group activities that stress negotiating limits, accepting feelings,
etc.   Large paper format with black and white photos, drawings.

393. McGinnis, James and Kathleen McGinnis. Parenting for peace and justice.
     Maryknoll, NY: Orbis, 1981. viii, 142p. notes. LC 81-3917. ISBN 0-
     88344-376-7. OCLC 7462153. pap.
The McGinnisses are directors of the Institute for Peace and Justice in
St. Louis. Believing that parenting can be one way to live out the Gospel's

call, they offer a personal account of how they have tried to integrate
social and family ministry in raising three adopted children through activities like multi-cultural training, dealing with sex-role stereotyping
and, of course, prayer. Suggestions are focused and specific; resource
items (like newsletters, manuals) are scattered throughout the text as
well as being brought together in a final appendix. Will please socially
conscious readers in public, church, seminary libraries.

394. Haessly, Jacqueline. Peacemaking: family activities for justice and
     peace. New York: Paulist,\ 1980. 86p. illus. photogs. bibliog. LC
     79-92008. ISBN 0-8091-2269-3. OCLC 7196773. pap. (o.p.).
A parent, author, and coordinator of the Milwaukee Peace Education Center
presents a variety of activities for a mix of age levels to promote cultural awareness, networking, and forms of service in the global community.
Thematic organization is around concepts of affirmation, respecting differences, cooperating, conflict-resolution, global interdependence, steward-
ship/service, and celebration. Includes family prayers, games, reflective
exercises, etc., enhanced by photos and drawings.

395. True, Michael. Homemade social justice: teaching peace and justice
     in the home. Chicago: Fides/Claretian, 1982. xiii, 160p. bibliog.
     LC 82-7291. ISBN 0-8190-0648-3. OCLC 8452143. pap.
A father of six (ages 15-22) with past experience as a draft counselor discusses ways of rearing children and adolescents so they will become sensi-
tized to issues of feminism, civil rights, and nuclear disarmament. True
advises substantial, open talk about one's own values and the reasons for
them and underlines the importance of using a light touch (e.g., celebrating victories rather than keeping things overly grim). Many references
to Catholicism, though Protestants could find this useful as well; includes family prayers for justice, but on the whole, a bit less specific
in terms of suggested activities than the McGinnis book, above.

396. Scheuring, Tom and Lyn Scheuring. God longs for family. Huntington,
     IN: Our Sunday Visitor, 1980. 149p. LC 79-92535. ISBN 0-87973-533-3.
     OCLC 6734444. pap.
The Scheurings' basic premise is that individual nuclear units cannot be
family in the full sense of the word until all the world is a family; God's
unconditional love pours out first into the person, then progressively into the marriage, the family, the community (church) and the whole world.
They reflect on this process together and in separate sequences, touching
also on healing prayer, spousal love, being a spiritual family for others,
involvement in the world's needs, etc. In so doing, they share personal
experiences they have had in various mission settings. Foreword by the
Scheurings' children.

K. FACING CRISIS

397. Stewart, Charles. When a caring family faces crises. St. Meinrad, IN:
     Abbey (When Books), 1980. 96p. illus. bibliog. LC 80-69089. ISBN
     0-87029-169-6. OCLC 7109856. pap.
Stressing Christ's spirit as the model and context, Stewart discusses the
components of real caring--strong love, nurturing, empathy, compassion,
setting limits--and ways of caring with family members at times of growth
and in times of crises like separation, divorce, accident, or death.

Crisis caring involves making contact, identifying the real problem, seeking outside help if necessary; with "growth" caring it is important to realize developing youth need space to learn to relate to God directly, not just via parental expectations.   A look, too, at the marriage relationship and the empty nest syndrome.

398. Welter, Paul. The family: stronger after crisis. Wheaton, IL: Tyndale, 1977. 251p. illus. notes. index. LC 81-86693. ISBN 0-8423-0861-X. OCLC 9625662. pap. (leader's guide available).
Based on the Bible, psychological insights, personal experience and experience with counselees, this treats common predicaments in family living. Chapters are arranged in triads: in each group, Welter examines (1) the predicament, (2) the situation as seen through the eyes of the one most closely involved, and (3) the reality as it appears through the eyes of family members offering help.   Deals with anxiety, hurt and anger, depression, and the struggle for independence.   The final part discusses working to understand each person's unique learning style and method of expression.   Clear and very substantive.

399. Oates, Wayne E. Your particular grief. Philadelphia: Westminster, 1981. 116p. LC 81-3328. ISBN 0-664-24376-2. OCLC 7459739. pap.
Oates is a prolific author in the area of pastoral counseling. This book, written in a warmly personal style, looks at five kinds of grief people may suffer in the wake of loss: anticipatory grief, sudden or traumatic grief, "no-end" grief, "near-miss" grief, and pathological grief requiring medical attention.   Devoting a separate chapter to each category, Oates describes representative situations to foster reader identification and offers helpful advice, some of which, incidentally (like dealing with a child's suicide) cannot be readily found elsewhere.   Recommended for public, church, seminary libraries.

400. Gilmore, G. Don. No matter how dark the valley: the power of faith in times of need. San Francisco: Harper, 1982. 141p. notes. index. LC 81-48208. ISBN 0-06-063121-X. OCLC 8280515. pap.
Gilmore shares his conviction that "the secret of overcoming a crisis is the direct result of personal companionship with our Lord." Chapters discuss the importance of living in faith; the soul as a "hidden higher self," how to become a "kingdom person" via "generation from above" and triumph over a divided mind; Jesus' "sharp-edged love" that is, besides being comforting, also "surgical, antiseptic, and purging"; and the power of hope and prayer.   Several cuts above the typical self-help guide, this is recommended for public and church libraries.

401. Skoglund, Elizabeth. Your troubled children. Elgin, IL: David C. Cook, 1974. 105p. LC 74-19440. ISBN 0-912692-50-2. OCLC 1323739. (o.p.).
Really a book on relationships, with a practical thrust, by a Christian counselor, this covers problem areas like sex, drugs, and school difficulties, as well as disturbances in family interaction and in one's faith relationship with God.   Skoglund favors reality therapy and places a strong emphasis on issues of self-esteem.   The best relationships, she suggests, are those that allow latitude for growth; sharing one's relationship with Christ is healthy, but it should never be forced (never, for instance, force a child to pray aloud).   She advocates a "reality spirituality," reflected in loving concern for others, and a self-esteem based on the reality of one's behavior, so that psychology and Christianity complement each other.

402. Dollar, Truman E. and Grace H. Ketterman. Teenage rebellion. Old
    Tappan, NJ: Revell, 1979. 206p. notes. LC 79-18957. ISBN 0-8007-
    1059-2. OCLC 5286253. (o.p.).
A conservative Baptist minister and child psychiatrist join forces to discuss the results of an attitudes/behavior questionnaire given to one hundred young people representing different geographical, religious and cultural backgrounds on the subject of rebellion. About two thirds of the
book discusses what to do with rebellious adolescents, integrating biblical guidelines and research, and stressing positive influences which can
prevent trouble at different developmental stages, as well as cures for
rebellion that has already fully emerged. Emphasis on the role of the
father, and on dynamics of guidance and reconciliation.

403. Benton, John. Do you know where your children are? Old Tappan, NJ:
    Revell, 1982. 158p. illus. LC 81-8633. ISBN 0-8007-1268-4. OCLC
    7555947. (1983 pap. ed. in BIP).
Drawing on his experiences with the Walter Hoving Home, a ministry to run-
away girls, Benton writes here for parents of potential--or actual--runa-
ways. He discusses danger signals of a potential runaway, what to do if
one's children leave, dealing with guilt and feelings of failure, processes
of reconciliation, and some practical concerns vis-a-vis religion (What
can prayer really accomplish? Should I make my children go to church?).
Includes some positive thoughts on enjoying one's children and keeping
them out of trouble.

404. Brogan, Frankie Fonde. The snare of the fowler. Lincoln, VA: Chosen-
    Zondervan, 1982. 198p. LC 82-17740. ISBN 0-310-60280-7. OCLC 8806228.
Here is a mother's deeply felt, beautifully told story of how she lost her
son Bob to the Children of God cult, was led as a consequence to venture
beyond her nominal Christianity into a genuine faith relationship with
God, and--after the prayerful involvement of many--eventually saw Bob return home. Striking for the way it combines a spiritual critique of both
cults and shallow church life with compassion and objectivity, this is
recommended for both public and church libraries.

405. Chambers, Mary Jane. Get me a tambourine! New York: Hawthorn, 1975.
    164p. LC 75-216. ISBN 0-8015-2948-4. OCLC 1901023. pap. (o.p.).
Sensitively and humorously written, this is a mother's story of her efforts
to understand her teenage son's need for and relationship with a congregation of "Jesus people" (or a "New Testament" church). Unlike the situation
with many contemporary cults, Craig's involvement with his church did not
mean that he must leave home or renounce his family; on the contrary, this
mother and son were very much mutually engaged over the years in struggling
to make the other understand his/her respective views, and the book includes commentary from Craig as well. Most interesting.

406. Greenfield, Guy. The wounded parent: coping with parental discourage-
    ment. Grand Rapids, MI: Baker Book House, 1982. 135p. bibliog. LC
    82-70463. ISBN 0-8010-3779-4. OCLC 8846340. pap.
Written by a Baptist professor of Christian ethics for parents whose children have rejected their faith, this explores early signs of rebellion,
typical responses when the rebellion becomes overt, and positive ways for
parents to deal with their feelings and attitudes. The emphasis is on
learning to transcend self-pity, guilt and fear by practicing listening,

understanding, and unselfish concern, and on learning how to build a better relationship with one's child in the future, regardless of what has happened in the past. An extremely compassionate, helpful book which, while intended for evangelicals, could also be useful to a wider Christian audience.

407. Lewis, Margie M. with Gregg Lewis. The hurting parent. Grand Rapids, MI: Zondervan, 1980. 143p. LC 80-10264. ISBN 0-310-41731-7. OCLC 5992471. pap.
Written for parents who are hurting because of spiritual estrangement from their children, this book by a mother and her son shares real-life stories of both heartbreak and reconciliation. The basic principles, emphasized again and again, are the importance of openness, acceptance, forgiveness, unconditional love, and hope; and, conversely, the dangers of shame, rejection, anger, guilt and despair. The Lewises look, also, at the impact of certain practical strategies and the importance of fellowship with other hurting parents. A most compassionate book.

408. White, John. Parents in pain: a book of comfort and counsel. Downers Grove, IL: InterVarsity, 1979. 244p. notes. LC 78-24760. ISBN 0-87784-582-4. OCLC 5555926. pap. (study guide available).
The main point in psychiatrist White's book is to speak helpfully to the feelings of parents whose children have, by rebellion or alienation, caused them deep pain; it is only incidentally, he stresses, about childrearing itself. In three main sections, he explores why childrearing has become so complicated today (proliferating specialties, etc.), the dynamics as a parent/child relationship seems to be disintegrating, and the parents' responsibility to cling to God's truth and the biblical principles of right and wrong, not to be seduced by a secular pragmatism. Theologically strict yet also compassionate, emphasizing that while parents can love and teach their children, they can never control their destinies.

409. Switzer, David and Shirley Switzer. Parents of the homosexual. Philadelphia: Westminster (Christian Care Books), 1980. 118p. bibliog. LC 80-13748. ISBN 0-664-24327-4. OCLC 6196608. pap.
Written by a minister and psychologist, this is for parents who have recently discovered, or who suspect, their child is a homosexual--and especially for those to whom Christianity has "some meaning." The Switzers discuss typical responses to the discovery, ways of clarifying what's actually going on, looking for someone with whom to discuss it, patterns of blame, guilt, recrimination etc., to try and avoid. They look, too, at current research findings re homosexuality and what they believe the Bible actually says. (Yes, it's a sin, but don't we all sin in some fashion? Besides, the Bible doesn't really address the issue of committed homosexual partnerships.) Closes with a look at what the young person needs from the parents.

410. Jones, Clinton R. Understanding gay relatives and friends. New York: Crossroad-Seabury, 1978. viii, 133p. bibliog. LC 77-28704. ISBN 0-8164-2179-X. OCLC 3609063. pap. (o.p.).
By a minister who has counseled numerous young people in the area of homosexuality, this offers advice and guidelines for relatives (parents, siblings, spouses, children, etc.) and closely involved non-relatives like clergymen or teachers. Each chapter opens with a representative letter from a gay individual to a person in one of the above categories, expressing feelings and needs (a gay son writing his mother; an angry girl writ-

ing her judgmental sister; a gay clergyman, writing for his counselor's
eyes only, confessing his yearning to share his condition with his parishioners). Following each letter Jones offers advice, definitely from the
liberal end of the spectrum.

411. O'Brien, Bev. Mom, I'm pregnant. Wheaton, IL: Tyndale, 1982. 127p.
     bibliog. LC 82-50437. ISBN 0-8423-4495-0. OCLC 9612915. pap.
Here is a mother's personal narrative of how she coped with her teenage
daughter's pregnancy: battling urges to interfere in decisions of whether
to marry and whether to keep or relinquish the baby, continually turning
to her faith for guidance and grounding. Mixed in with the story of this
particular case is some sound, compassionate discussion of the range of
alternatives which should be useful to others, regardless of which action
they finally choose. (O'Brien's daughter relinquished her daughter for
adoption.)

412. Linkletter, Art and George Gallup, Jr. My child on drugs?: youth and
     the drug culture. Cincinnati, OH: Standard, 1981. 128p. bibliog. LC
     81-50355. ISBN 0-87239-456-5. OCLC 7571712. pap.
Linkletter's daughter died before her twentieth birthday when she jumped
from a window during an LSD flashback. In the first part of this book he
sorts through his own feelings and questions in the wake of that tragedy,
with some special thoughts for Christians, stressing that they are not
exempt from repercussions of the drug culture. The discussion includes
factors involved in drug addiction, family contributors (competition, etc.)
the need to transcend guilt, faith in God as the best antidote to drug use,
and the virtues of clear parental authority. Part Two, "Statistics,"
draws on Gallup surveys to present data re drug use on campus, issues
surrounding marijuana, and the extent of alcohol abuse among youth.

413. Wilkerson, Don. Facts every parent should know about marijuana. Old
     Tappan, NJ: Power-Revell, 1983. 130p. LC 82-21627. ISBN 0-8007-
     5107-8. OCLC 9017524. pap.
Wilkerson discusses facts about the drug (its effects, widespread use,
social permissiveness regarding it, etc.), attitudes toward it, life-styles
the drug industry, medical arguments against it, the option of decrimi-
nalization (which he opposes), and ways parents can help exercise influence
against its use (listening, being a consistent role model, nurturing self-
esteem, and not demanding perfection). He stresses religious motivation
to stay away from drugs and offers some thoughts for young people themselves as well as for parents. Rev. ed. of Shocking new facts about marijuana, 1980.

414. Neff, Pauline. Tough love: how parents can deal with drug abuse. Nash-
     ville, TN: Abingdon, 1982. 160p. LC 81-17682. ISBN 0-687-42406-2.
     OCLC 7947914.
Primarily an introduction to the Palmer Drug Abuse Program (PDAP), a non-
sectarian fellowship for drug users aged 13-29, this draws on the experiences of seven families whose children conquered their habits with the
help of the techniques involved. The approach, modeled after AA, was
examined semi-critically on "Sixty Minutes" in the early 80's, after which
certain changes were introduced. A look, too, at hospitalization as an
alternative in some cases.

415. Vecchio, Holly Lee. Return from a far country. Philadelphia: West-
      minster, 1971. 155p. LC 71-136751. ISBN 0-664-24907-8. OCLC 125861.
      pap. (o.p.).
Told via excerpts from transcribed interviews and reflective/analytical
passages by the author, this is the true story (names changed) of a teenage girl who, after running away from home and getting heavily into drugs,
finally came back to her parents. Offered as a representative case history,
it explores the healing/reconciliation process rather than analyzing "causes" in any detailed way. Includes a look at helpful vs. unhelpful styles
of Christianity.

416. Mehl, Duane. You and the alcoholic in your home. Minneapolis, MN:
      Augsburg, 1979. 141p. LC 78-66947. ISBN 0-8066-1697-0. OCLC 4956603.
      pap.
Mehl himself is a recovered alcoholic, so this book of guidance for spou-
ses/family members has a particularly insightful and empathic viewpoint.
He discusses trouble signs, the process of deterioration and loss of control, confronting the alcoholic, and options for counseling or for Al-Anon
or Alateen. Considers, too, the alcoholic woman or teenager, other addic-
tive drugs, the process of surrender, and the need for specifically Christian treatment centers. Very direct (e.g., in its clear counsel re sex
and the alcoholic).

417. Klewin, Jean and Thomas Klewin. When the man you love is an alcoholic.
      St. Meinrad, IN: Abbey (When Books), 1979. 96p. photogs. notes. LC
      79-51276. ISBN 0-87029-149-1. OCLC 5530396. pap.
Al-Anon oriented, with frequent refrains of the "Let go and let God" slogan,
this emphasizes keeping one's own mental health intact while remaining in
a "reality-oriented" love relationship with an alcoholic. (It does not
offer counsel on helping a spouse to leave an alcoholic marriage.) Stresses the need to change oneself, rather than simply responding to the alcoholic's manipulative tactics; spiritual resources can give insight and
inner strength to cope with the problem, the Klewins suggest, but there is
no magical solution. Advice on assessing guilt/responsibility, learning
self-acceptance, and helping children to cope. A short list of resource
organizations is included.

418. Drews, Toby Rice. Getting them sober. Plainfield, NJ: Haven-Logos,
      1980. xvii, 204p. notes. LC 80-82751. ISBN 0-88270-460-5. OCLC
      7062911. pap. (available through Bridge).
This compassionate, pull-no-punches guide is written by a counselor and
free-lance writer specializing in issues of alcoholism. Philosophically
compatible with AA and Al-Anon, it will help readers see their situations
more clearly while "hanging in there" or, if necessary, leaving. The text
is crowded with helpful references to actual cases and runs the gamut in
topics covered, all the way from whether to hide car keys to how to respond
to incestuous behavior. Each chapter closes with a brief prayer. Highly
recommended for public and church libraries.

419. Marsh, Jack. You can help the alcoholic: a Christian plan for inter-
      vention. Notre Dame, IN: Ave Maria, 1983. 88p. LC 82-74499. ISBN 0-
      87793-270-0. OCLC 10100390. pap.
The author, a recovered alcoholic, is now alcoholism consultant for Seat-
tle's Archdiocese; the book is for family members, friends, or employers

of alcoholics. Marsh writes especially for "co-alcoholics," stressing the
desirability of professional counseling if at all possible, but encouraging
the concerned individual to take steps even if a counselor is not available. His guidance recommends sticking one's neck out, remembering "God
is on your side," prayer, Al-Anon, the resource of an "intervention group"
of concerned others, planned confrontation, and continued support.

420. Costales, Claire and Priscilla Barack. A secret hell: surviving life
     with an alcoholic. Ventura, CA: Regal, 1984. 138p. notes. LC 83-21275.
     ISBN 0-8307-0915-0. OCLC 10046037. pap.
The author is a recovered alcoholic, founder and President of the Alcoholic's Hope Foundation, and told her own story in Alcoholism: the way
back to reality (entry 084). This is for the co-alcoholic: simple,
practical, with discussion of the characteristics of a co-alcoholic personality, warning signs of developing alcoholism, a look at why co-alcoholics are attracted to alcoholics, manipulative strategies used, etc.
Stresses the need to recognize the problem and to take active responsibility in channeling anger constructively, as well as the importance of turning to God for help. Includes blank pages to fill in with sentence completion exercises on feelings, attitudes.

421. Mattison, Judith. I'm worried about your drinking. Minneapolis, MN:
     Augsburg, 1978. 104p. LC 77-84093. ISBN 0-8066-1620-2. OCLC 3914675.
     pap.
Mattison knows the problems of the alcohol-involved family through growing
up in a home where her father drank. These free verse reflections trace a
typical cycle of feelings that may emerge among family members as the
problems deepen: confusion, self-pity, anger, protection, fear, analysis,
despair, avoidance, and--at the end--a growing self-determination to make
decisions and take action. Concludes with a list of resource groups and
a "Basic facts about alcoholism" list.

422. Monfalcone, Wesley R. Coping with abuse in the family. Philadelphia:
     Westminster (Christian Care Books), 1980. 120p. bibliog. LC 80-15125.
     ISBN 0-664-24326-6. OCLC 6446450. pap.
This volume looks at subtle and overt abuse that occurs in families. We
all abuse others in some way, says Monfacone,--he presents a chart depicting a range of "abusive" behaviors along a continuum from "ignore/with-
drawal" to "homicide/suicide"--and there are even some forms of specifically "religious" abuse. Thus, the "severe abuse" (child abuse, spouse
abuse) is just an exaggeration of our destructive potential. Stresses
that redemption, for the Christian, does not eliminate sin, and that con-
fession/forgiveness are still necessary.

423. Olson, Esther Lee with Kenneth Petersen. No place to hide. Wheaton,
     IL: Tyndale, 1982. 144p. LC 82-80967. ISBN 0-8423-4721-6. OCLC
     8734845. pap.
Here is a disturbing, thought provoking book by an evangelical Christian
counselor in which she shares what happened as she sought to counsel a
battered woman who felt trapped in her marriage. Olson openly acknowledges
the dangers inherent in a legalistic emphasis on wifely submission and her
concern to walk the fine line between a biblical and an unbiblical approach
to self-love. She tells of bringing her client to the point where she
could leave the abusive marriage and openly express feelings of anger, only
to be reluctantly drawn back once more when her husband became a Christian.
Ends on a very ambiguous note; a book that leaves many questions unanswered

424. Edwards, Katherine. <u>A house divided</u>. Grand Rapids, MI: Zondervan, 1984.
     157p. bibliog. notes. LC 83-27329. ISBN 0-310-43501-3. OCLC 10301038.
     <u>pap</u>.
Probably the most useful book examined by the compiler on the subject of
incest, this first person narrative shares Edwards' experiences of sexual
abuse at the hands of her adoptive father and the later repercussions on
her life, as well as offering thoughtful and intelligent guidance to
others--both victims and concerned helpers. Edwards entered counseling at
the time she was preparing her manuscript, to help resolve unfinished business and to produce a more objective book. She has succeeded remarkably
well, and offers, as well as her own story, some rich reflections on the
power of the faith relationship with God to facilitate forgiveness, healing, and creative growth.

425. Ricks, Chip. <u>Carol's story</u>. Wheaton, IL: Tyndale, 1981. 202p. LC
     81-51321. ISBN 0-8423-0208-5. OCLC 7948800. <u>pap</u>.
Here is a first-person narrative, names changed, that tells the painful
story of an incest victim, raped as a girl by her father. Designed as an
aid for other victims and to help concerned individuals and society at
large understand, this is an honestly written account. Beyond the childhood experience, the narrative deals with Carol's subsequent growth: her
conversion to Christianity as a teenager; her difficulties in believing in
her own worth or in her new life in Christ, on a gut level, as a result of
the early trauma; her terror of sharing the truth with her fiance; ambivalence and anxiety at the prospect of being a mother herself; and eventual
psychological/spiritual victory.

426. Roberts, Deborah. <u>Raped</u>. Grand Rapids, MI: Zondervan, 1981. 159p.
     illus. LC 81-11408. ISBN 0-310-43680-X. OCLC 7653472.
At the age of 19, while working at an inner city church in Chicago, Deborah
Roberts was raped. In this honest, extremely well written book she tells
of the horror of that experience and of her subsequent struggles to work
through the problems it caused in her relationship with God and, after
marriage, in her sexual adjustment with her husband. Ultimately a tale
of triumph, this is remarkable for the tasteful, effective way it explores
topics often considered taboo in religious circles. Highly recommended
for public and church libraries.

427. Reid, Clyde H. <u>Help! I've been fired</u>. Philadelphia: Pilgrim, 1971.
     64p. illus. bibliog. notes. LC 76-170106. ISBN 0-8298-0224-X. OCLC
     213947. (o.p.).
A nice combination of the substantive/compassionate and the gently joking,
this has amusing line drawings interspersed with the text and is genuinely
empathic as it counsels leaning into the pain and growing through it. Reid
suggests a common pattern among those who have been fired is to fluctuate
between hopeful activity and immobilized depression, and he offers ideas
on resources (including prayer), concluding with a bilbiography. (The
latter is dated, but the text is very good.)

428. Schuller, Robert H. <u>Tough times never last, but tough people do</u>. Nash-
     ville, TN: Thomas Nelson, 1983. 237p. LC 83-4160. ISBN 0-8407-5287-3.
     OCLC 9393191.
Here is more "Hour of Power" preaching-cum-pep-talk, ostensibly for the
unemployed: catchy slogans ("play it down and pray it up"), the Ten
Commandments of Possibility Thinking, etc. But, actually,there is little

on unemployment here--just a pot-pourri of motivational exercises and anecdotes (mainly on how Schuller raised money for his Crystal Cathedral).

429. Larsen, John A. When a member of the family needs counseling. St. Mein
     rad, IN: Abbey (When Books), 1979. 95p. illus. LC 79-51274. ISBN
     0-87029-147-5. OCLC 5277494. pap.
In addition to guidance on seeking counseling, this offers reflections on
the experience of the individual as part of a family, family development,
signs of developing trouble, and skills to exercise before consulting a
professional (effective communication and listening, "I" statements, definition of the problem, etc.). Then Larsen, a pastoral counselor, looks
briefly at different schools of counseling and how to evaluate them.
(Note: there is very little explicit discussion of the Christian framework here.)

430. Andreasen, Nancy. Understanding mental illness: a layman's guide.
     Minneapolis, MN: Augsburg (Religion and Medicine Series), 1974. 110p.
     bibliog. LC 73-88610. ISBN 0-8066-1413-7. OCLC 867652. pap. (o.p.).
Basic information on specific types of mental illness: schizophrenia, af-
fective disorders, organic brain syndrome, neuroses, alcoholism/drug abuse,
and children's disorders. Andreasen is a physician who teaches psychiatry;
she examines causes (medical, psychodynamic and behavioral), types of treat
ment and facilities, how friends and relatives can help, and the relationship between religion and psychiatry: the problems of evil, moral responsibility and guilt (can one be too religious?), and faith as a resource.

431. Bennett, George. When the mental patient comes home. Philadelphia:
     Westminster (Christian Care Books), 1980. 118p. bibliog. LC 79-23809.
     ISBN 0-664-24295-2. OCLC 5675727. pap.
The Dean of Students at a Presbyterian seminary and Chaplain Supervisor at
a medical facility discusses practical and psychological/spiritual issues
surrounding the homecoming of hospitalized relatives. Examines, among othe
topics, guilt, tuning in on feelings, handling overactivity, coping with
past memories, acknowledging mistakes, facing fears of relapse, preventing
suicide or homicide, and coping with suicide or homicide if they actually
occur. Sensitive exploration of faith as a resource.

432. Blackburn, Bill. What you should know about suicide. Waco, TX: Word,
     1982. 154p. notes. LC 82-50517. ISBN 0-8499-0302-5. OCLC 9100046.
Written by a Baptist pastoral counselor for friends and family members of
potential suicides, this explains how to recognize signs and prevent the
catastrophe from occurring. Chapters cover the reasons people may be
tempted to suicide, warning signals, ways of intervening (including prayer
and sharing Jesus as a healing resource), and the feelings of the person
involved. Blackburn stresses that he is not writing for the potential
suicide himself or herself,--any such person coming on the book should
instead seek counseling--nor is he dealing with ethical fine points for
ambiguous situations such as terminal illness.

433. Coleman, William L. Understanding suicide. Elgin, IL: David C. Cook,
     1979. 172p. bibliog. LC 79-51742. ISBN 0-89191-186-3. OCLC 5614471.
     pap. (o.p.).
An excellent book aimed mainly at people who have known a suicide or potential suicide close to them. Looks first at the impact of the problem on
those involved--taboos surrounding it, the need to forgive, the need to

bring feelings out into the open as to causes, assessing blame, etc. Next come some objective facts: the extent of suicide among the young and the elderly, signs of potential suicides, and how to get help, refer, use resources. Guidance, too, on handling personal troubles in the wake of a suicide/suicide attempt, resolving feelings and seeking counseling if need be. Potentially very helpful for other family members involved.

434. Petersen, J. Allan. The myth of the greener grass. Wheaton, IL: Tyndale, 1983. 222p. notes. LC 82-50997. ISBN 0-8423-4656-2. OCLC 9176696.
Petersen's concern here is to offer hope to the Christian couple where there has been adultery, and to teach husbands and wives who have not yet gone through this trauma how they may spot danger signals and take steps to "affair proof" their marriages. The book explores the dynamics of temptation, stressing that it can be an opportunity for growth if resisted, how unmet needs for acceptance, etc., can make a partner vulnerable, and, if one spouse has succumbed, how to work through the devastation toward reconciliation and forgiveness.

435. Thomas, Joan. Tempted by love. Grand Rapids, MI: Eerdmans, 1976. 61p. LC 76-18898. ISBN 0-8028-1653-3. OCLC 2318170. (o.p.).
Here is a six-week program of lessons, exercises, reflections, and words of guidance (one page for each day of the week) aimed at helping men and women, married or single, pull away from adulterous relationships. Thomas begins with some practical suggestions (look after your spiritual health, stay away from romantic novels, do not communicate with "X" in any way at all), then continues with thoughts on Bible reading, immersion in work/ family, and general meditative exercises plus Scripture passages.

436. Vigeveno, H. S. I'm in love with a married man. Philadelphia: A. J. Holman, 1976. 132p. LC 76-22495. ISBN 0-87981-067-X. OCLC 2331515. (o.p.).
Vigeveno shares the stories of four of his female Christian counselees, who discuss their love affairs with married men and how they broke free, finding new strength in Christ. Thereafter he explores some issues the narrative raises: the problem of needs and desires, the process of pulling free (as reflected in correspondence from another client), and finding resolution in God.

437. Kilgore, James E. Try marriage before divorce. Waco, TX: Word, 1978. 158p. notes. LC 78-57551. ISBN 0-8499-0056-5. OCLC 4492478.
Mainly for couples whose marriages are on the rocks, but also for those who just want to improve their partnerships, here is advice from a professional counselor on making relationships work. Controlling and competitive unions spell disaster, says Kilgore; complementarity and honest effort is the key to success. Standard common-sense advice on communication, balance, sex, etc., with the special feature of a 30-day marriage improvement guide (special self-disclosure/sharing exercises to do together). Includes some brief reflections on the importance of a relationship with God in growing toward a better relationship with one another.

438. Hudson, R. Lofton. Is this divorce really necessary? Nashville, TN: Broadman, 1983. 173p. notes. LC 81-86665. ISBN 0-8054-5649-X. OCLC 9450879. pap.
Hudson, a marriage and family counselor, thinks that sometimes a marriage may seem dead, but hidden potential may still exist for bringing it back

to life. He looks at elements of a good marriage and factors for success, the value of child-like qualities (vs. destructive childishness), how to deal with anger without causing alienation (including biblical guidance on anger), the inevitability of ambivalence within love, nipping an affair in the bud, and ways grace can heal once legalism has been trancended. Includes a look at various Christian views toward divorce.

439. Chapman, Gary D. Hope for the separated. Chicago: Moody, 1982. 119p. bibliog. LC 81-18667. ISBN 0-8024-3616-1. OCLC 7945943. pap.
A pastor offers practical, biblical advice for dealing with the separation period--a topic very inadequately covered in most books. Believing that separation need not necessarily lead to divorce but may actually pave the way for a restored, healthier marriage, Chapman stresses that the key question to ask is not "Do you want to work on your marriage?" but "Will you work on your marriage?" Reconciliation requires mutual repentance (marital failure always involves both parties) and attention to three main areas: self-development, developing a relationship with God, and developing a relationship with one's mate. "Growth assignments" (exercises, questions are appended to each chapter; concludes with a discussion of divorce in case reconciliation fails.

440. Arnold, William and others. Divorce: prevention or survival. Philadelphia: Westminster, 1977. 128p. LC 77-22066. ISBN 0-664-24142-5. OCLC 3168499. pap.
This is intended both for those definitely getting a divorce and for those who might be able to gain insights to continue successfully with their marriages. The first section, "Before divorce," looks at early and advanced warning signals, issues concerning sex and money, and the church's attitude The second section, "After divorce," deals with emotional and practical problems faced by the newly single person. The co-authors are three divorced individuals who were participants in a divorce group led by Arnold.

L. DIVORCE, SINGLE PARENTING, AND REMARRIAGE

441. Smoke, Jim. Growing through divorce. Irvine, CA: Harvest House, 1976. 168p. bibliog. LC 76-21980. ISBN 0-89081-081-8. OCLC 2805912. pap.
Practical advice on letting go, seeing the ex-spouse more clearly, assuming responsibilities for self, children and the future, finding and granting forgiveness, dating, remarriage, the role of the church as extended family, and learning to help others. Chapters include questions for reflection and testimonies from individuals Smoke has counseled in his former job as Minister to Single Adults at Robert Schuller's Garden Grove Community Church in California.

442. Peppler, Alice Stolper. Divorced and Christian. St. Louis, MO: Concordia, 1974. 93p. LC 74-4505. ISBN 0-570-03189-3. OCLC 897870. pap.
A deeply empathic, poetic book whose brief chapters deal with shock, despair, seeking help, telling the family, coping with the ex-spouse, money matters, times of feeling abandoned by God, dating and sexual struggles, and eventual recovery and readiness for new life and love. Stressing feelings over practical detail, this emphasizes the renewal of faith.

443. Correu, Larry M. Beyond the broken marriage. Philadelphia: Westmins-
     ter, 1982. 126p. bibliog. LC 82-13661. ISBN 0-664-24446-7. OCLC
     8666984. pap.
Addressed to "abandoned" rather than "abandoning" parties, this book by a
minister/editor whose wife chose divorce shares discreetly from personal
experience but focuses on guiding others. Correu's suggestions are consistently "scriptural" (he stresses forgiveness, fair legal arrangements,
a conservative stance on post-marital affairs); still, direct Bible quoting
is kept to a minimum. An alternative to "secular" divorce writers like
Mel Krantzler or Morton Hunt.

444. Bustanoby, Andre. But I didn't want a divorce: putting your life back
     together. Grand Rapids, MI: Zondervan, 1978. 174p. notes. index. LC
     78-15531. ISBN 0-310-22171-4. OCLC 4056533. pap. (also cloth).
Advice from a Christian counselor that combines contemporary psychological
insights with a scriptural approach, including a brief theological look at
biblical passages on divorce and remarriage. Most of the book offers emo-
tional/practical advice re separation dynamics, loneliness, dangers of
falling prey to sexual vulnerabilities, coping with children, etc. Emphasis on learning to develop a healthy self-love so as to bring one's own
sense of value (and values) into life and new relationships.

445. Rambo, Lewis R. The divorcing Christian. Nashville, TN: Abingdon,
     1983. 95p. notes. LC 83-6361. ISBN 0-687-10994-9. OCLC 9412883. pap.
Written by a divorced pastoral psychology professor and Church of Christ
minister, this is, first of all, confessional, as Rambo shares intimately
from his own experience with divorce and, secondly, a counseling effort
aimed at helping others. His denomination (Church of Christ) tends to be,
he tells us, narrowly and sometimes legalistically biblical. It is surprising, then, that he comes across so liberal: assuming most Christians
will go through a series of post-divorce affairs, sharing openly his own
ambivalence about recommitment, etc. Something of a curiosity; and it
certainly offers a different view.

446. Greteman, Jim. Coping with divorce: from grief to healing. Notre Dame,
     IN: Ave Maria, 1981. 80p. illus. bibliog. LC 81-65334. ISBN 0-87793-
     226-3. OCLC 7785698. pap.
A spiralbound book of resources by a counselor for Catholic Charities, this
is a unique volume designed to "appeal to the child in you." Highly imaginative graphics deal with feelings, needs, stages in the process of grieving. Explores three phases of divorce--the death of the relationship,
mourning, and healing--and how the pain involved evokes childhood trauma,
good/bad, either/or perceptions, etc. Emphasizes the importance of coming
to like oneself and of forgiving the ex-spouse.

447. Becker, Russell J. When marriage ends. Philadelphia: Fortress (Pocket
     Counsel Books), 1971. 56p. notes. LC 74-152366. ISBN 0-8006-1102-0.
     OCLC 151661. pap. (o.p.).
The author, a Jungian therapist, writes from the premise that all divorced
individuals can profit from counseling regardless of whether or not they
consider themselves the "injured party." His aim is to introduce the
reader to some concepts and themes that will be useful background for a
subsequent counseling experience. Chapters deal with the nature of grief
work, the damage to pride, the "inner child-self," the influence of animus/

anima archetypes in relationships involving real-life partners, the "dark side" or shadow archetype and ways it may be destructively projected onto others, the needs of children, and finding a counselor.

448. Crook, Roger H. An open book to the Christian divorcée. Nashville, TN: Broadman, 1974. 159p. notes. LC 73-87064. ISBN 0-8054-5217-6. OCLC 1046740. pap.
The guiding theme is that Christians are divorcing, but they differ from others as they struggle to relate their actions to God's will. The Bible is seen as a resource, but, Crook believes, some contemporary circumstances were unforeseen in biblical times, so Scripture is not quoted as the one solution to every problem. Discusses how to decide whether divorce is the best alternative, accepting responsibility for one's role in the failed marriage, ambivalence toward possible reconciliation, Jesus' redemptive attitude toward sinners, identity as a single, sex, children, remarriage, and the effects of women's lib in making women potentially stronger independent agents and better able to withstand the destruction of divorce. A bit more permissive toward post-marital sex than most others, though Crook does affirm celibacy as an admittedly difficult ideal.

449. Laz, Medard. Helps for the separated and divorced: learning to trust again. Liguori, MO: Liguori, 1981. 64p. ISBN 0-89243-147-4. OCLC 9428066. pap.
The theoretical basis for Fr. Laz's advice is drawn from Sr. Josephine Stewart's "Beginning Experience" workshops which help people work through grief and guilt, learn to trust again, discover a deeper relationship with God, and experience closure on the marriage. Brief, simple, and with a mix of spiritual/practical guidance (on listing gains and losses, say, or seeking an annulment), this makes a good resource for separated or divorced Catholics.

450. Zwack, Joseph P. Annulment: your chance to remarry within the Catholic Church. New York: Harper, 1983. xiii, 129p. bibliog. notes. LC 83-47739. ISBN 0-06-250990-X. OCLC 10450255. pap.
By a Roman Catholic and practicing civil attorney, this presents updated information on the Revised Code of Canon Laws in language accessible to the lay reader. Zwack discusses answers to the questions he receives most often on annulment, covering the procedure itself, step by step, the selection of grounds and rise of psychological cases, and Internal Forum operations. Practical guidance rather than moral or theological evaluation; includes sample forms.

451. Ripple, Paula. The pain and the possibility: divorce and separation among Catholics. Notre Dame, IN: Ave Maria, 1978. 143p. LC 78-67745. ISBN 0-87793-162-3. OCLC 4468584. pap.
First this is concerned with the spiritual dynamics of healing in the wake of divorce: the need for forgiveness and a new beginning; a look at Elisabeth Kubler-Ross' stages of response to imminent death and their application to the divorce situation. Secondly, it deals with the actual and poten tial relationship between divorced individuals and the Catholic church, emphasizing what such people can bring to the Church (a deeper understanding of suffering, compassion for others in need, etc.) as well as what they need to receive.

452. Johnson, Margaret. <u>Divorce is a family affair</u>. Grand Rapids, MI: Zondervan, 1983. 127p. notes. LC 83-1109. ISBN 0-310-45831-5. OCLC
9196465. <u>pap</u>.
A mother shares her reactions when she learned of the impending break-up
of her daughter's marriage: denial, dread of divorce, theological struggles
over the situation, and then, as events unfolded, taking her daughter back
into her home temporarily, and moving from a strictly parental role to that
of friend. Johnson looks closely at some of her own failings--a refusal to
recognize early warning signals and to deal with her own hostility--and at
how the divorce affected her and her circle of friends. Closes with a
prayer God will use the experience for everyone's growth.

453. Coleman, William L. <u>What children need to know when parents get di-
vorced</u>. Minneapolis, MN: Bethany House, 1983. 91p. illus. LC 83-6006.
ISBN 0-87123-612-5. OCLC 9392995. <u>pap</u>.
Here is an excellent book for children (ages six to eleven) which parents
can read and discuss with them as an aid to helping them work through feelings vis-a-vis divorce. Brief reflections touch on all phases of feelings
and concerns (fear, anger, bewilderment about the future and about possibilities of marriage in general, worries over whether parents still love them
and whether they are somehow at blame). Coleman is clear in his reassurance
but does not gloss over the sad realities, and he encourages readers to pray
honestly, sharing their real feelings with God. A good catalyst for genuine sharing.

454. Swihart, Judson J. and Steven L. Brigham. <u>Helping children of divorce</u>.
Downers Grove, IL: InterVarsity, 1982. 125p. bibliog. LC 82-8945.
ISBN 0-87784-373-2. OCLC 8720541. <u>pap</u>.
A counselor specializing in family/child development issues offers practical
suggestions for parents, teachers and relatives on helping children deal
with the divorce crisis. Topics examined include surviving divorce, telling
the children, seeing it through their eyes, common reactions (loners, bul-
lies, clinging vines, etc.), adolescent reactions, and the use of prayer.
Brief, simple, practical.

455. Vigeveno, H. S. and Anne Claire. <u>Divorce and the children</u>. Glendale,
CA: Regal, 1979. 127p. bibliog. LC 78-67855. ISBN 0-8307-0645-3.
OCLC 5103118. <u>pap</u>.
Offering biblical, practical advice for adults concerning children's needs,
this is written from the children's point of view (explaining the effects
of divorce via sample questions and answers with children of all ages) and
from the parents' (detailed interviews with both a man and a woman having
custody). Second marriages and step-parenting also are discussed. The
authors interviewed over 100 children and young people ages six to twenty
in preparation for this book.

456. Arnold, William V. <u>When your parents divorce</u>. Philadelphia: Westminster
(Christian Care Books), 1980. 118p. bibliog. LC 79-20055. ISBN 0-664-
24294-4. OCLC 5333531. <u>pap</u>.
One of the "Christian Care Books" offering guidance for life crises, this
explores for the teenage and young adult reader his/her feelings, thoughts
and actions in response to parental divorce. Both practical and spiritual
issues are discussed.

457. Smoke, Jim. Suddenly single. Old Tappan, NJ: Revell, 1982. 192p. bib-
     liog. LC 82-629. ISBN 0-8007-1312-5. OCLC 8219027. pap.
This is for people to use after the crisis of death or divorce; it is not
on dealing with those crises themselves. Smoke, a minister to singles,
discusses the importance of living in the present, identity problems, loneliness, forming friendships and dating, fears, new career beginnings, possibilities of remarriage, etc. A very fine combination of practical wisdom and spiritual guidance; God-centered without being theologically heavy-
handed.

458. Hensley, J. Clark. Coping with being single again. Nashville, TN:
     Broadman, 1978. 136p. bibliog. LC 78-52623. ISBN 0-8054-5420-9. OCLC
     4228540.
A book by "at least a semi-professional counselor," with chapters on coping
with grief, loneliness, boredom, stigmatization, health and money matters,
sexual needs, the demands of single parenthood, remarriage, and considera-
tion of whether one should counsel others. An especially gentle book--"God
forgets--God forgives--God loves--so forgive yourself"--which suggests for-
mulating ethics (including sexual ethics) according to the Golden Rule.
Suggested resources for coping include your knowledge of yourself, your experience with God, your practice of prayer, and the church family.

459. Smith, Harold Ivan. A part of me is missing: how to cope with life
     after divorce. Irvine, CA: Harvest House, 1979. 144p. bibliog. notes.
     LC 79-65543. ISBN 0-89081-209-8. pap. (different title in BIP).
Most unusual among popular Christian divorce books, this is devoted to the
subject of post-marital sexual behavior. Working with responses to questionnaires he administered at church seminars with the divorced, Smith
reports and comments on people's actions, responses, and attitudes. Himself
divorced and the author of several other inspirational/self help books, he
seems to hold the underlying premise that, biblically speaking, post-marital
activity is wrong, and emotionally it is often destructive, but it nonetheless exists and therefore deserves exploration. No easy answers are offered, and one senses that Smith has not fully resolved his own feelings
and attitudes in this area.

460. Peppler, Alice Stolper. Single again--this time with children: a
     Christian guide for the single parent. Minneapolis, MN: Augsburg, 1982.
     136p. LC 81-52278. ISBN 0-8066-1910-4. OCLC 8532362. pap.
Here is a practical, compassionate book of guidance on single parenting.
Peppler examines children's and parents' needs, various developmental
stages and their implications for childrearing practices, ways to discipline
and draw children into family activities, etc. Emphasizes the importance
of spiritual and psychological dynamics, including the importance of forgiving the ex-spouse no matter what has happened.

461. Reed, Bobbie. "I didn't plan to be a single parent!" St. Louis, MO:
     Concordia, 1981. 158p. bibliog. LC 81-1305. ISBN 0-570-03837-5. OCLC
     7283769. pap.
Counsel for the Christian single parent (either widowed or divorced, with
or without custody) based on interviews with a variety of parents, children, pastors, counselors, and attorneys. Practical advice covers new
roles, expectations, developing a support network, dating, legal issues,
letting offspring go emotionally. (The author's husband asked for a divorce when her sons were four and six, and she shares from her own experience along with interview material drawn from others.) See also Reed's
Christian family activities for one-parent families (Standard, 1982).

462. Richards, Larry. Remarriage: a healing gift from God. Waco, TX: Word, 1981. 144p. LC 80-54548. ISBN 0-8499-0265-7. OCLC 7812272.
Richards suggests that evangelicals often "legalize grace" by transforming Jesus' guiding principles into rigid rules and then taking it upon themselves to judge others whose spiritual circumstances don't allow them to meet these strict expectations. Actually, he argues, there is always a tension between the ideal to which we are called and the sinful circumstances in which we are still partially involved. Approaching divorce and remarriage in this perspective, he concludes that remarriage after divorce is a legitimate option for those who feel led to it.

463. Brown, Bob W. Getting married again: a Christian guide for successful remarriage. Waco, TX: Word, 1979. 138p. LC 78-59433. ISBN 0-8499-0105-7. OCLC 5051484.
While the Bible upholds the sanctity of permanent marriage, Brown argues, it also upholds the possibility of redemption, of beginning anew. Moreover, those who take an excessively legalistic position on divorce should, to be consistent, also take an absolute stand against all war (for example), which they clearly do not do. Besides theological justification for remarriage, this includes guidance on making marriage work, addressing such topics as coping with guilt, handling children, life-style changes, etc.

464. McRoberts, Darlene. Second marriage: the promise and the challenge. Minneapolis, MN: Augsburg, 1978. 157p. bibliog. LC 77-84087. ISBN 0-8066-1612-1. OCLC 4203664. pap.
A personal narrative-cum-guide, this brings compassion and a sense of humor to bear on the fears, problems, challenges and rewards of remarriage. Looks honestly at the doubts and considers practical issues involved in dating, the wedding, post-marital adjustment, "instant parenthood," the value of counseling, etc.

465. Twomey, Gerald S. When Catholics marry again. Minneapolis, MN: Winston, 1982. xiv, 187p. bibliog. LC 82-70487. ISBN 0-86683-633-0. OCLC 8995822. pap.
A thorough book covering a wide variety of topics, this looks first at the psychodynamics of becoming single again, then at religious issues in terms of biblical passages, Catholic theology (the ideal vs. the real), and current Catholic practices (annulments and "internal forum" or behind-the-scenes solutions). Twomey considers, too, questions of excommunication and access to the Eucharist, stressing again the ways the church seeks to accommodate to real-life situations without denying the ideal. Closes with a discussion on preparing fully for remarriage and adjusting to the marriage itself with new extended families. A mix of ecclesiastical practice, biblical/Catholic theology, and psychology. (Note: Catholics planning remarriage may also want to look at A redeeming state: manual and handbook for couples planning remarriage in the Church, by Judith Tate O'Brien and Gene O'Brien, Paulist, 1984.)

466. Bustanoby, Andre. The readymade family: how to be a stepparent and survive. Grand Rapids, MI: Zondervan, 1982. 144p. notes. index. LC 82-16099. ISBN 0-310-45361-5. OCLC 8763484. pap.
Most books on this subject, says counselor Bustanoby, seem to stress the differences between stepfamilies and biological ones, but he believes that the same basic principles of family living are actually applicable to both cases. Opening with an attitudes survey to reveal differences in spouses' views and catalyze discussion, this goes on to examine theological vs. psy-

chological guilt, the needs/wants/roles of stepmothers and stepfathers, what to expect of stepchildren, and how to work with one's own family system. Emphasis on the importance of keeping the marriage relationship primary and on respecting the husband's authority in the total constellation, even if he is not the natural father.

467. Juroe, David J. and Bonnie B. Juroe. Successful stepparenting. Old
     Tappan, NJ: Revell, 1983. 191p. bibliog. index. LC 82-20449. ISBN
     0-8007-1339-7. OCLC 8907456.
The authors, counselors with children from previous marriages, are now remarried to each other; in their book they draw on their own experiences as well as experiences of their counselees. Chapters examine various problems and patterns of response, ways children try to cope with restructured families, suggestions on what parents can do, and discussion questions for reflection. A practical approach, with biblical guidance, in a low-key style.

468. Reed, Bobbie. Stepfamilies: living in Christian harmony. St. Louis,
     MO: Concordia, 1980. 143p. bibliog. LC 79-20168. ISBN 0-570-03798-0.
     OCLC 5336865. pap.
An extremely useful book on stepparenting, chock full of down-to-earth advice, exercises, worksheets, real-life examples, and scriptural helps/verses offered in a comfortable sort of way. Focuses on understanding step relationships (the importance of recognizing sources of stress and breaking out of cycles of failure), demystifying roles (a look at stepfathers, stepchildren, stepmothers and the parents without custody), and various challenges (communicating, confronting, forgiving, finding equal time, etc.). Based on interviews with stepfamilies, counselors, pastors, lawyers, and on personal experience.

M. HEALTH AND ILLNESS

469. Ellingson, David R. and Darcy D. Jensen. My body, my life. Minneapo-
     lis, MN: Augsburg, 1981. 126p. bibliog. index. LC 79-54122. ISBN
     0-8066-1761-6. OCLC 7732623. pap.
A guide to "body spirituality" in which prayer and physical fitness are viewed as complementary paths to personal wholeness. Ellingson first offers an "experience guide"--a personal inventory assessing general data on oneself and one's spirituality in terms of habits, exercise, eating, and activities--plus nutritional charts, self-directed exercise programs, and instructions on charting activity/progress. Successive chapters then explore the body and spirituality, the body and prayer, the body and food, the body and movement, and the body and play.

470. Heller, Alfred L. Your body His temple. Nashville, TN: Thomas Nelson,
     1981. 194p. illus. bibliog. LC 81-1897. ISBN 0-8407-5769-7. OCLC
     7275290. pap.
Aiming at a balanced view of body/mind/soul/feeling integration, this covers a variety of general issues re health, nutrition, exercise, etc. Heller discusses the ten "big killers" and how to take preventive action, caring for the heart, dangers of obesity, a step-by-step program for weight control, outdoor activity, the twenty-five most often asked questions about exercise, the dangers of fad diets, how to use behavioral modification

constructively, making a "contract" with God, etc. Emphasizes the framework of a relationship with Christ and includes a biblical survey on eating/
exercise. By a physician.

471. Meiburg, Albert L. Sound body/sound mind. Philadelphia: Westminster
     (Potentials: Guides for Productive Living), 1984. 120p. bibliog. LC
     84-10356. ISBN 0-664-24532-3. OCLC 10779478. pap.
A hospital chaplain explores the mind-body relationship, offering guidance
on taking a personal health inventory, interpreting signals our bodies send
us, understanding the influence of emotions on physical health (just as
negative feelings are destructive, so positive ones can be healing), responding to external "stressors" in internally beneficial ways, taking charge
of general well-being, and hooking up with personal support systems. Theologically low-key.

472. Skoglund, Elizabeth R. The whole Christian. New York: Harper, 1976.
     xii, 113p. notes. LC 75-12288. ISBN 0-06-067391-5. OCLC 1863336. (o.p.).
Stressing that the balanced Christian life must include attention to physical and psychological health as well as spiritual issues, Skoglund looks
at the body's effect on the mind, particularly medical problems like hypo-
glycemia, the question of self-esteem, when and how to seek professional
help. Rather than an in-depth examination of the above topics, this is
more a statement of encouragement (Christ is a wonderful resource, but counseling can also be a God-given tool) and a low-key pep-talk to pay attention to one's whole range of needs.

473. Blitchington, W. Peter. The energy and vitality book. Wheaton, IL:
     Tyndale, 1981. 143p. notes. LC 80-52559. ISBN 0-8423-0687-0. OCLC
     7344726. pap.
Assistant Director of Behavioral Sciences at the Florida Hospital in Orlan-
do, Blitchington begins with the premise that while we may not be able to
change the basic energy levels that are "given" with our personalities, we
can become "effectively energetic" by learning to use energy resources wisely over the years, avoiding burn-out. Discusses basic principles--some
neurophysiology, influence of personality styles and emotion/stress/depres-
sion on energy output, how energy is generated and maintained--plus specific techniques for working effectively and conquering procrastination. Occasional low-key references to Christian faith and principles with closing
thoughts on the energizing power of love.

474. Collins, Gary R. Spotlight on stress. Santa Ana, CA: Vision House,
     1982. 217p. notes. index. LC 82-50239. ISBN 0-88449-087-4. OCLC
     9081324. pap.
An evangelical psychologist discusses stress in all its dimensions--its nature, physical/psychological/spiritual effects, and emotional/social/spi-
ritual causes--with a focus on the different areas in which it appears:
in response to everyday occurrences, family life, sexuality, developmental
stages, special crises (like divorce or unemployment), religious issues,
and the job world. This is a very practical commentary, interspersed with
specifically evangelical discussion (e.g., the chapter on "crisis stress"
includes reflections on the stress to be experienced during God's final
judgment). Closes with a look at false escapes and effective coping me-
chanisms. Published in 1977 as You can profit from stress.

475. Osgood, Don. Pressure points: the Christian's response to stress.
Chappaqua, NY: Christian Herald, 1978. 219p. illus. bibliog. LC
78-56975. ISBN 0-915684-40-3. OCLC 4193244. (also pap.).
The basic thesis of this book is that stress is caused by external "pressure points," but since the stress itself is experienced internally, our
response is the key to stress management, and a relationship with Christ is
the best context for a healthy response; we are not to avoid stressful situations, but rather to let Christ within us create the response. Osgood
looks at sources of stress (including personality types), specific pressure
points we confront (parenting, over-controlling people, financial troubles,
poor health, etc.) and the process of transcendence.

476. Sehnert, Keith W. Stress/unstress. Minneapolis, MN: Augsburg, 1981.
222p. illus. bibliog. LC 81-65647. ISBN 0-8066-1883-3. OCLC 7544270.
pap.
A Christian physician committed to a holistic philosophy discusses the nature of stress, its bodily signs, and how to manage it. His five management
modes involve different dimensions of living: changing the workplace and
general environment (exercise more control, renew relationships); understanding emotions; practicing remedies like massage; caring for the body
(nutrition, exercise); and spirituality/prayer. Draws from other work in
the field, e.g., Seyle's writing, Type A personality research, stress tests,
etc. Many exercises and practical helps.

477. Keller, W. Phillip. Taming tension. Grand Rapids, MI: Baker Book House,
1979. 224p. LC 77-94259. ISBN 0-8010-5407-9. OCLC 5690674. pap.
Acutely anxious as a child and seriously ill as a young man, the author--
now healthy and active in lay ministry, wildlife/conservation activities,
and spiritual writing--shares the holistic approach to living that helped
him master his own tensions. Discusses the physical life, the mental/emo-
tional life and the spiritual life, with a stress (in Part I) on outdoor
living, and (in Parts II and III) on learning to discipline thought processes, cultivate sound attitudes, and grow in faith, in the context of a full
knowledge of God's character. Very simply and effectively presented.

478. Hansel, Tim. When I relax I feel guilty. Elgin, IL: David C. Cook,
1979. 150p. illus. notes. LC 78-73460. ISBN 0-89191-137-5. OCLC
5102963. pap.
The author, a former Young Life staffer and subsequent director of a moun-
taineering wilderness survival school for spiritual seekers, discusses the
hows and whys of a relaxed and joyous (but still Godly) lifestyle. Spiritual strength, Hansel stresses, lies in quiet confidence, not in frantic
efforts; work and leisure should both be understood on a deeper level than
they usually are, and then integrated in our lives. When we understand
Christ's message and personal life-style more fully, we will truly be able
to live in the present, taking life one day at a time.

479. Oates, Wayne E. Your right to rest. Philadelphia: Westminster (Potentials: Guides for Productive Living), 1984. 103p. bibliog. LC
83-26045. ISBN 0-664-24517-X. OCLC 10277396. pap.
Westminster's new series presents advice to help readers deal with challenges in a way that will nurture others as well as themselves. Psychologist Oates, the series' general editor, here offers a look at the importance of rest as a spiritual resource: how to balance work and recreation, understand life's rhythms and the need for proper breathing and

sleep, transcend greed, and find true rest through prayer and Jesus' presence. Theologically low-key with references to secular as well as Christian writers, this should appeal to a wide audience.

480. Perry, Charles E. Why Christians burn out. Nashville, TN: Thomas Nelson, 1982. 167p. notes. LC 82-2098. ISBN 0-8407-5800-6. OCLC 8170309. pap.
A pastor who himself experienced and recovered from burn-out discusses its causes, symptoms and effects in a book aimed mainly at professionals in people-helping careers, but potentially useful to others as well. In exploring preventive and healing decision making, Perry stresses that he offers not a formula but a guide, for obeying God's will involves sensitivity to one's interests and inclinations, rather than relying on simplistic blueprints.

481. Chapian, Marie. Free to be thin. Minneapolis, MN: Bethany House, 1979. 179p. illus. bibliog. LC 79-15656. ISBN 0-87123-560-9. OCLC 5101485. pap. (study guide by Neva Coyle).
The author, a therapist who worked with Neva Coyle, founder of Overeaters Victorious, stresses that her book is not really about fasting or dieting but rather about learning to eat. Lots of upbeat biblically based pep-talk on, for instance, learning to "shop in the Spirit" rather than "in the flesh." Chapters cover making the initial commitment, motives, goals, obedience, rebellion, why we are attracted to the wrong foods, self-control, goal maintenance, nutrition, exercise, etc. Success stories from Over-eaters Victorious, Bible verses, check lists, motivational prayers. See also Neva Coyle's Free to be thin cookbook (Bethany House, 1982).

482. McMillen, S. I. None of these diseases. Revised, updated and expanded ed. by David E. Stern. Old Tappan, NJ: Revell, 1984. 224p. illus. notes. LC 84-6807. ISBN 0-8007-1207-2. OCLC 10711790.
Originally written two decades ago by a medical missionary/Bible scholar, and now revised by his grandson, a medical student, this has been a popular volume and is included as representative of a conservative biblical approach to health issues. The thesis is that one area in which the Bible's infallibility is reflected is in the area of advice on health matters. In terms of the Old Testament Law, for instance, McMillen claims that circumcision (in spite of modern medical trends against it) actually correlates with an absence of penile cancer, and that biblical instructions for treating lepers reflect effective preventive medicine for contagious disease. Includes thoughts on smoking, homosexuality, psycho-somatic ailments, and such topical issues as AIDS and herpes.

483. Bittner, Vernon J. Make your illness count. Minneapolis, MN: Augsburg, 1976. 126p. LC 76-3862. ISBN 0-8066-1532-X. OCLC 2507290. pap.
The central message of this strong, empathic book by a hospital chaplain is that, paradoxically, we must sometimes become sick before we can become better, and therefore what matters is how we choose to respond when illness strikes. Bittner goes step by step through the predictable stages a patient may experience (doubt, denial, fear, anger at God, etc.), exploring how we can find God's love even in helplessness and can reach the point of discarding old resentments and learning to forgive in the midst of the crisis. There are numerous case illustrations here, and Bittner shares some of the struggles with illness and despair he himself has weathered.

484. ten Boom, Corrie. He cares, He comforts. Old Tappan, NJ: Revell, 1977.
     95p. LC 77-8260. ISBN 0-8007-0891-1. OCLC 2966455.
Elsewhere Corrie ten Boom has written of her concentration camp experiences
as a consequence of her family's resistance activities during World War II
(see The hiding place, Revell, 1974). The reflections here are intended
for those who are seriously ill and frightened, as ten Boom draws on past
experience with sick friends--a terminally ill girl in a children's hospital, people she knew in the concentration camp, etc.--and offers comforting thoughts on Jesus as resource, the importance of forgiveness, and
more. Devotional in style, but set apart from typical examples of the
genre by virtue of the author's unquestionable spiritual authority. One
of a trilogy, the "Jesus is Victor" series.

485. Coleman, William L. My hospital book. Minneapolis, MN: Bethany House,
     1981. 83p. illus. LC 81-10094. ISBN 0-87123-354-1. OCLC 7578071. pap.
For children in grades 2-7, billed as "interesting activities and information for your hospital stay," this is comfortably reassuring as it explains
how hospitals work, what happens when you have an operation, etc., and suggests an assortment of entertaining activities to turn the potentially
scary experience at least partially into one of adventure and fun. The
opening chapter stresses that God will be there throughout the hospital
stay, and Bible quotes appear at the end of each section. Also, numerous
cartoons, illustrations, fill-ins, and check-lists (which of the above does
your hospital room have?).

486. Belgum, David. When it's your turn to decide. Minneapolis, MN: Augs-
     burg, 1978. 124p. bibliog. LC 77-84091. ISBN 0-8066-1616-4. OCLC
     3997971. (o.p.).
A pastoral counselor and hospital chaplain explores various problematic
questions that arise for patients in hospital/treatment contexts to help
them work their way through to personal decisions. Discussing the shifting
policies in medical decision-making, how to talk with professionals, and
specific steps in working through issues, Belgum focuses on the areas of
prolonging life, organ transplants, human experimentation, having children,
and abortion. Very clear and helpful with a religious approach that emphasizes a Gospel-based nurture rather than legalistic guidelines.

487. Belgum, David. What can I do about the part of me I don't like? Min-
     neapolis, MN: Augsburg (Religion and Medicine), 1974. 102p. illus.
     bibliog. LC 73-88609. ISBN 0-8066-1412-9. OCLC 867651. (o.p.).
Sharing the fact that he stuttered as a child, Belgum writes here for anyone who is self-conscious over some hidden or overt disfiguration: whether
of their physical body (birthmarks, club foot), of their senses (such as
blindness or deafness), as a result of surgery (colostomy), or in regard to
capacity or physiology (cerebral palsy, high blood pressure, mental retardation). He discusses feeling dynamics and responses, encouraging readers
to see any potential humor the situation may hold. Translating Jesus'
teaching into practical guidelines, he advocates patience while waiting for
others' damaging attitudes to change. Includes list of specialized and
self-help groups.

488. Cassie, Dhyan. So who's perfect! Scottdale, PA: Herald, 1984. LC 84-
     12948. ISBN 0-8361-3372-2. OCLC 10949881. pap.
Fulfilling a ten-year dream, a teacher of the deaf and pastor's wife sought
out handicapped or physically "different" people (men and women with MS,

spina bifida, or birthmarks; amputees; an Albino; tall, short, overweight
individuals, etc.) and interviewed them as to experiences in childhood,
school, social/work life, religious faith, and what they would like to
share with society at large. Their responses, presented Studs Terkel style,
cover a wide range indeed; in terms of faith, for instance, some demonstrate deep belief in God's sovereignty over their handicaps, while others
opt for an "accidental" cosmology. Well done.

489. Cox-Gedmark, Jan. Coping with physical disability. Philadelphia:
     Westminster (Christian Care Books), 1980. 119p. bibliog. LC 79-28275.
     ISBN 0-664-24297-9. OCLC 5831544. pap.
Cox-Gedmark deals mainly with the process of accepting the realities of
disability and working through denial and "why me?" dynamics in this very
useful book. She briefly explores answers others have found to suffering
(e.g., in the Book of Job) but stresses that the important thing is to live
with one's questions, since by experiencing suffering one comes to know
God better. With the turning point of acceptance comes the need to discover possibilities, unfreeze feelings, discover a deeper understanding
of one's sexuality, and get back into the stream of living.

490. Eareckson, Joni with Joe Musser. Joni. Grand Rapids, MI: Zondervan,
     1980. 256p. illus. photogs. LC 76-10450. ISBN 0-310-23982-6. OCLC
     2151056. pap. (available in multiple editions by various publishers).
Joni Eareckson, who became a quadriplegic as a result of a diving accident
during a happy, athletic adolescence, has become a rallying center in the
evangelical community with her truly inspiring attitude and her beautiful
artwork, rendered with a pencil clamped in her mouth. This is her personal
story: of the accident, and of her long, tortuous road through suicidal
depression and into a deep, revitalizing faith in God's sovereignty.

491. Rushing, Phillip. Empty sleeves. Grand Rapids, MI: Zondervan, 1984.
     156p. LC 84-2289. ISBN 0-310-28820-7. OCLC 10375823.
Born on Senator Eastland's Mississippi plantation, "Bud Doggy" Rushing was
an ordinary black teenager when one day he innocently touched a live uti-
lity wire and found himself, overnight, without arms. Despair followed;
at last he decided to end it all. The vision he experienced that day as
he tried to jump from a bridge but felt himself mysteriously restrained,
and the words he heard spoken, as from God, are set forth here with the
quiet simplicity of absolute authority. Indeed, the whole book, which goes
on to detail his subsequent growth and how the "hands" of others helped him
(he eventually attained a full ministry as social worker/public servant)
has the same authentic ring. A fine book.

492. Armstrong, April Oursler. Cry Babel: the nightmare of aphasia and a
     courageous woman's struggle to rebuild her life. Garden City, NY:
     Doubleday, 1979. ix, 252p. illus. LC 77-26511. ISBN 0-385-13529-7.
     OCLC 4593634. (o.p.).
In the biblical story of the Tower of Babel, proud men with a common language are changed by the Lord so they can no longer communicate. April
Armstrong, mother of seven, author and professor of theology, became a
victim of aphasia at the age of 45 and found herself suddenly trapped in
a private Babel of her own. This book--rich with courage, terror, pain,
laughter, and joy--is the record of her comeback, learning to "translate
Babel" (and, in moments of deepest anguish, being compelled to "cry Babel")
to those on the other side. It is most essentially a witness of faith,

naked faith from the guts, no prettied-up greeting card variety. For those
tough enough and caring enough to stand it, this book will speak eloquently,
complementing rather than duplicating other "aphasia narratives" now available. Highly recommended.

493. Reuss, Edith A. A glimpse of the sunshine. Wheaton, IL: Tyndale, 1979.
      87p. LC 78-57961. ISBN 0-8423-1036-3. OCLC 5526360. pap. (o.p.).
A pastor's wife with a severe form of lupus tells her personal story: of
the diagnosis/discovery, seeming improvements only to be followed by set-
backs, struggling with fear and growing in faith. Dreams were dashed (the
Reusses had hoped to adopt a child but decided not to at one point in the
revised prognosis), but there is ecstasy here too, as in the author's reaction to her success as a writer. On the whole, a real tale of victory.

494. McConkey, Clarence. When cancer comes. Philadelphia: Westminster,
      1974. 140p. bibliog. notes. LC 74-1330. ISBN 0-664-24987-6. OCLC
      811061. pap. (o.p.).
A pastor who has battled cancer himself and lost his wife to it discusses
characteristics of the disease, who gets it (including its geographical in-
cidence), how it begins and spreads, methods of prevention and treatment,
and--at length--how people respond to it: states of shock, fear, and hope,
and ways faith can serve as resource. Closes with a look at issues of
living and dying.

495. Dawson, John. The cancer patient. Minneapolis, MN: Augsburg (Religion
      and Medicine), 1978. 128p. notes. LC 78-52192. ISBN 0-8066-1662-8.
      OCLC 4493299. pap.
"Live! Don't just survive" is the message of this book by a pastoral counselor who has worked with cancer patients and their families over many
years; here he explores cancer's range of meanings--some facts about different kinds of the disease, the body/mind interaction--as well as the
phenomenon of faith healing (he encourages being grounded in reality and
balancing emotional desires with hard facts, though he does emphasize the
importance of a positive attitude). Examines, too, coping with cancer,
adjusting to circumstances, cancer and children, and finding spiritual
meaning in suffering.

496. Moster, Mary Beth. Living with cancer. Chicago: Moody, 1979. 179p.
      notes. LC 78-23665. ISBN 0-8024-4947-6. OCLC 4493584. pap. (o.p.).
Moster has worked extensively with Nell Collins, a nurse and cancer patient
who, as a result of her own experience, has developed a widespread counseling ministry to cancer patients (see The valley is bright by Nell Collins,
Thomas Nelson, 1983). This book discusses various forms of cancer, courses
the illness can take, common treatments, family dynamics and spiritual
needs, self-image problems, and the whole difficult area of the patient's
fear, distrust in God, etc. Designed to reassure patients and their families, this should be a valuable resource.

497. Pendleton, Edith. Too old to cry, too young to die: 35 teenagers talk
      about cancer. Nashville, TN: Thomas Nelson, 1980. 174p. bibliog. LC
      80-18463. ISBN 0-8407-4086-7. OCLC 6487268. (o.p.).
Here is information on various types of cancer and case history accounts
by actual teenage patients who share their experiences and responses. Includes comments on faith dynamics in the midst of suffering, plus discussion of treatments, tests and side effects, life inside a hospital, meet-

ing the outside world as a cancer patient (dating, family relations, reactions of friends, going bald, keeping a positive attitude), and facing the possibility of death. Glossary, resource list, and suggestions for further reading.

498. Paterson, George W. The cardiac patient. Minneapolis, MN: Augsburg
     (Religion and Medicine), 1978. 125p. illus. bibliog. LC 78-52187.
     ISBN 0-8066-1661-X. OCLC 4432581. pap.
Heart disease is presented here as a spiritual crisis, not just a health problem. Paterson, a hospital chaplain, discusses biological factors in heart damage, preventing its development, recovering from an attack, surgery, children as patients, and living with heart disease, with a stress on the holistic dimension and on spiritual problems/opportunities involved. Some interesting discussion of neurotic vs. healthy uses of religion in responding to the disease, and a look at how to let God effect change within us so as to prevent trouble developing.

499. Schemmer, Kenneth E. Between faith and tears. Nashville, TN: Thomas
     Nelson, 1981. 131p. notes. LC 81-1467. ISBN 0-8407-5770-0. OCLC
     7271961. pap.
A Christian physician explores the relationship between faith and healing. Part I presents six personal histories illustrating a range of encounters with severe illness, including the seemingly miraculous healing of the author's infant daughter. Part II is devoted to Schemmer's reflections on the nature of "miracle," the relationship between natural and supernatural, the dangers of magical thinking and of confusing faith with superstition. At the core of the book is an emphasis on spiritual wholeness as the most essential factor. Discussion questions conclude each chapter.

500. Althouse, Lawrence W. Rediscovering the gift of healing. Nashville,
     TN: Abingdon, 1977. 144p. bibliog. notes. LC 77-9290. ISBN 0-687-
     35860-4. OCLC 3017018. pap. (2nd ed., Weiser, in BIP).
Althouse is a Methodist minister (former national president of the Spiritual Frontiers Fellowship) with a "soft sell and low-key" healing ministry. Believing that God's will for us is wholeness, but that illness is one of the consequences of free will, fear, and resistance, he discusses healing as part of the natural order (never magic), and encourages readers to develop healing attitudes: to seek the meaning of their diseases, make indicated changes in life-style, build spiritual support, and use meditation as an aid.

501. MacNutt, Francis. The prayer that heals: praying for healing in the
     family. Notre Dame, IN: Ave Maria, 1981. 116p. notes. LC 80-69770.
     ISBN 0-87793-219-0. OCLC 7461728. pap.
In very simple, brief words this affirms a belief that Jesus still heals today and wants Christians to pray for one another's healing. Then MacNutt describes the various elements of such prayer—praying aloud together, in your own words, touching the sick person, allowing time, stressing the importance of forgiveness and genuine faith—with a look, at the end, at psychological inner healing. A very childlike book in its simplicity as it urges the reader to expect healing (though not immediately) as a matter of course. Charismatic or Pentecostal readers will feel most at home here. (A lengthier, more substantive work is MacNutt's Healing, Ave Maria, 1974, which has been described as the first comprehensive Catholic book on healing; the present title, however, is more of a "self-help" work.)

502. Stanger, Frank Bateman. God's healing community. Nashville, TN: Abing-
     don, 1978. 143p. bibliog. LC 78-8017. ISBN 0-687-15332-8. OCLC
     3869720. pap.
Stanger believes all Christians are called to be ministers of healing and
that healing itself is a holistic process of mind/body/spirit, whose op-
timal context is a right relationship with Christ. He looks here at biblical references to healing, its relationship to Christian faith, steps on
the way (relaxation, purging, clarification etc.), how to be healed and to
pray for healing, stories of people who have been healed, hindrances, and
how to become a minister of healing for others.

503. Drahos, Mary. To touch the hem of His garment: a true story of healing.
     New York: Paulist, 1983. vii, 215p. bibliog. index. LC 83-60371.
     ISBN 0-8091-2548-X. OCLC 1048970. pap.
The author, a wife and mother, has suffered for some twenty-five years from
multiple sclerosis, experiencing both periods of remission and recurrent
deterioration. Drawing from personal experience and extensive study, she
reflects on ways that different approaches to healing--medical, holistic,
charismatic--interact, stressing that in an ultimate sense, all healing
comes from God. Though not a "how to" book in the strict sense of the
word, the thoughtful insights and real life examples shared here should be
very helpful to others.

504. Parker, Larry. We let our son die: a parent's search for truth. Irvine,
     CA: Harvest House, 1980. 204p. LC 80-80457. ISBN 0-89081-219-5. OCLC
     7176235. pap. (o.p.).
Here is an anguished and very disturbing story of how the Parkers, devout
fundamentalists, inadvertently let their diabetic son die by withdrawing
insulin treatments while waiting for a healing by faith alone. The distortions to which they fell prey are evident in anecdotes like the one in which
they interpreted test results of a continued need for insulin as Satanic
lies. In retrospect, Parker sees all this as presumption, not faith, and
tries to help readers distinguish between the two.

N. WHEN A LOVED ONE DIES

505. Davidson, Glen W. Living with dying. Minneapolis, MN: Augsburg (Reli-
     gion and Medicine), 1975. 111p. bibliog. notes. LC 74-14186. ISBN
     0-8066-1468-4. OCLC 1323697. pap. (study guide also).
For relatives and friends of seriously ill people, this draws on interviews
with over 600 patients and their families, offering thoughts on the various
"meanings" of dying (it means loss, change, conflict, suffering, and--in a
faith context--triumph). Suggestions, as well, for handling one's own feelings and being creatively present for the individual facing death. By a
psychiatrist specializing in thanatology.

506. Burnham, Betsy. When your friend is dying. Lincoln, VA: Chosen-Zonder-
     van, 1983. 96p. LC 82-17725. ISBN 0-310-60341-2. OCLC 8785246. pap.
Written during the final year of the author's own battle with cancer (she
died in January, 1983), this offers practical, sensitive guidance on kinds
of behavior that help and hurt terminal patients. Burnham's advice and illustrative examples will be very useful, but what is most remarkable is her
tone: simple and dignified in the face of death, embodying a quiet courage

that is bound to reassure anxious readers and thereby help them make use of her suggestions. Highly recommended for all popular collections.

507. Sherrill, John L. Mother's song. Lincoln, VA: Chosen-Zondervan, 1982.
      134p. LC 82-9527. ISBN 0-310-60190-8. OCLC 8493481.
Simultaneously intimate and broadly relevant, this is Sherrill's story of how he and his family decided to abide by his mother's Living Will and to disconnect the I.V. tubes that were preserving her life in her bout with pneumonia at 82. Freed from the hated tubes, incapable of speech, his mother was able to devote all her remaining energies to completing the spiritual and psychological closure of her life, as Sherrill movingly relates. This deals honestly with the family's self-doubt, but concludes on a note of conviction that God's will was, indeed, served.

508. Nouwen, Henri J. M. A letter of consolation. San Francisco: Harper,
      1982. 96p. LC 81-48212. ISBN 0-06-066327-8. OCLC 8221426.
Six months after his mother's death in 1978, Nouwen composed this long letter to his father; he publishes it now in the hope it will help other bereaved individuals. Written during Holy Week, 1979, it reflects on the mysterious interrelationship between life and death; on how his mother's death, even as it caused deep grief, freed Nouwen's father to discover qualities in himself that were previously submerged; on our need to "befriend" our own death; on our utter dependence on God. Deeply personal yet of universal significance, this is highly recommended.

509. Landorf, Joyce. Mourning song. Old Tappan, NJ: Revell, 1974. 184p.
      LC 74-9938. ISBN 0-8007-0680-3. OCLC 922863.
This is a very personal book on the process of living through a loved one's terminal illness and death. Having already lost her young son and grandfather, Landorf shares the experience of her mother's illness with cancer and, eventually, her death. Denial, anger, a desperate need for honesty in facing the reality and confronting a range of feelings lie at the core of the story; included are reflections on the grieving process as a healing, restorative experience and on prayer as a resource.

510. Bishop, Joseph P. The eye of the storm. Minneapolis, MN: Bethany House,
      1983. 126p. LC 76-20567. ISBN 0-87123-263-4. OCLC 2318341. pap.(Chosen
      Books ed., 1976, examined).
"The way out of heartbreak, as out of every storm of human existence, is always and only the way through the center." That is the core message of this deeply honest book in which the pastor/counselor/author shares two losses--the death of his teenage son in an auto accident (briefly described), and the gradual death of his wife to cancer (detailed at length). Interspersed with Bishop's reflections on ways he and his family fought the urge to deny and struggled through to confrontation, there is clear, gentle guidance for others. Very stark and honest, full of spiritual and psychological complexity but presented with remarkable simplicity.

511. Price, Eugenia. Getting through the night. New York: Dial-Doubleday,
      1982. 84p. LC 81-17390. ISBN 0-385-27658-3. OCLC 7947477.
The metaphors of night and morning, darkness and light, weave their way through this gentle yet firmly positive guide for coping with loss. Nominally addressed to all suffering loss (the divorced as well as the widowed), this is actually most appropriate for the bereaved since Price's message of comfort is centered in the promise of ongoing life in Christ after

death. Expecting rebellion, she nonetheless gently insists that morning
<u>will</u> come and urges her readers to cling to that conscious hope amid their
pain.

512. Miller, Jolanda. <u>You can become whole again: a guide to healing for</u>
     <u>the Christian in grief</u>. Atlanta, GA: John Knox, 1981. 99p. illus.
     LC 80-84652. ISBN 0-8042-1156-6. OCLC 7774521. <u>pap</u>.
Miller's advice on coping with bereavement comes, as she says in her preface, from both the heart and the head: in 1971 she was left a widow with
two small children when a boating accident took her husband's life, and
since then she has learned from experience what it means to grieve constructively. What she has written, though, is a straight guidebook rather
than a "how-it-was-with-me" account. The chapters are brief and follow a
consistent pattern: a few paragraphs of practical psychological/spiritual
advice; relevant scriptural passages; a summing-up prayer.

513. Brown, Velma Darbo. <u>After weeping, a song</u>. Nashville, TN: Broadman,
     1980. 164p. bibliog. notes. LC 79-53321. ISBN 0-8054-5425-X. OCLC
     6157380.
Intended as a kind of "road map" for someone embarking on the "pilgrimage"
of grief, this shares the experiences of two people--the author's late husband, who lost his first wife to a serious illness, and the author herself--
as they encountered the experience of bereavement. Believing that grief
has two purposes--to mark the passing of the loved one and to bring the
griever through turbulence into new life--Brown first explores the stages
of grief work, then shares the personal stories.

514. Nye, Miriam Baker. <u>But I never thought he'd die: practical help for</u>
     <u>widows</u>. Philadelphia: Westminster, 1978. 150p. notes. LC 78-9644.
     ISBN 0-664-24208-1. OCLC 3912753. <u>pap</u>.
Drawing on her own experience and that of others, Nye discusses the dynamics of bereavement and how to cope with practical problems arising in its
wake re money, decision-making, socializing, changing residence, etc. This
is well written, with some interesting thoughts on the potential spiritual
growth which can come as one works through grief after loss, how to grow
from immature to mature prayer habits, and the widow's relationship to the
church.

515. Fabisch, Judith. <u>A widow's guide to living alone</u>. Grand Rapids, MI:
     Zondervan, 1978. 122p. LC 78-6724. ISBN 0-310-43481-5. OCLC 10212288.
     <u>pap</u>. (1983 ed. in <u>BIP</u>).
Fabisch, widowed at 35, shares lessons from her own and others' experiences.
Emphasizing the need to focus on God through the transition if one is to
avoid self-pity, she discusses practical questions surrounding funeral arrangements, insurance, financial readjustments, plus emotional issues like
how to handle memories fruitfully and find a new sense of purpose. Some
thoughts, too--very traditional--on coping with sexual desire and reinforcing a sense of feminine identity in the midst of celibate living. Concludes with a look at options for remarriage. Formerly titled <u>Not ready to</u>
<u>walk alone</u>.

516. Vogel, Linda Jane. <u>Helping a child understand death</u>. Philadelphia:
     Fortress, 1975. x, 86p. bibliog. notes. LC 74-26325. ISBN 0-8006-
     1203-5. OCLC 1323801. <u>pap</u>.
A wife, mother, and teacher of Christian education tells of her own first
encounter with death's full reality (when her father fell ill with brain

cancer) and, stressing that one cannot share children's feelings about death
without facing one's own, offers many helpful guidelines. Includes suggestions on working through the mix of feelings to find acceptance, on listening to what children are really asking at different developmental levels,
on pitfalls to avoid (e.g., destructive euphemisms), on the death of pets,
and on sharing religious faith.

517. Klopfenstein, Janette. Tell me about death, Mommy. Scottdale, PA: He-
     rald, 1977. 110p. LC 77-76989. ISBN 0-8361-1821-9. OCLC 3223304. pap.
A young widow with two children offers guidance on discussing death with
youngsters and shares from her own experience. She looks at the need behind
the questions (what it feels like to be orphaned), ways of putting such concepts as immortality into simple and accessible language, plus harder concepts she would not try to explain at times of bereavement--e.g., God's will.
Extremely sensitive and thoughtful, with the compassionate stamp of one who
has been there.

518. Biebel, David B. Jonathan: you left too soon. Nashville, TN: Thomas
     Nelson, 1982. 192p. notes. LC 80-28276. ISBN 0-8407-5809-X. OCLC
     7206328. pap.
In this moving and potentially very useful book the pastor of an Evangelical Free Church shares the grief and turmoil he experienced in the wake of
his three-year-old son's death: his initial encounter with the boy's mysterious illness; his obsessive guilt and anger after the death itself; and,
finally, the gradual restoration of his faith. The narrative is striking
above all for its honesty, reflecting Biebel's conviction that seemingly
unorthodox feelings should be accepted and allowed to run their course--
even (or especially!) for pastors. Poems, letters, and journal fragments
add considerably.

519. Derksen, Sandy with Connie Nash. The other side of sorrow. Minneapolis,
     MN: Augsburg, 1982. 124p. LC 81-52281. ISBN 0-8066-1913-9. OCLC
     8532364. pap.
Derksen's daughter, injured in an accident at a neighbor's pool, never re-
gained consciousness; after an anguished period during which she was cared
for first in a nursing home and later with the family, she eventually died.
This account, written five years after the death, is an effort to sift
through feelings of anger and guilt and find some sort of healing. Primarily a straight narrative, this will be useful to others in providing them
another's experience with which to empathize; actual guidance, though, is
kept to a minimum.

520. Hewett, John H. After suicide. Philadelphia: Westminster (Christian
     Care Books), 1980. 119p. bibliog. LC 79-24373. ISBN 0-664-24296-0.
     OCLC 5706924. pap.
One of the "Christian Care Books," this is addressed specifically to sur-
vivors in the wake of a loved one's suicide. Hewett examines statistics,
explanations and myths regarding suicide, what to expect in coping with
acute grief, dynamics among surviving family members, and the possible need
for counseling. A look, too, at the religious dimension and how the Judeo-
Christian tradition has regarded suicide; Hewett urges believers to reject
the idea that God "took" the suicide as part of some "plan" and stresses
instead God's role in sharing the pain in the wake of tragedy. The bibliography at the end suggests titles for additional study, focusing on the different issues in the narrative, chapter by chapter, and including some titles specifically written for children in suicide's aftermath.

O. MID-LIFE, AGING, AND FACING DEATH

521. White, Jerry and Mary White. The Christian in mid-life. Colorado
     Springs, CO: NavPress, 1980. 287p. illus. notes. LC 80-83388. ISBN
     0-89109-448-2. OCLC 8033298. pap.
By a regional director of the Navigators and his wife, this is intended to
identify typical mid-life problems and offer biblical guidelines for solving
them. Believing that all problems have a spiritual base but are reflected
in concrete, practical ways, the Whites discuss the special situations of
women and men, and then, in successive chapters, examine success and
failure (God's view vs. that of the world), depression, marriage and children, singleness, roots, ruts and recreation, mid-life ministry, and new
vistas. With a stress on dangers and opportunities, this is explicitly
biblical as it deals with a wide range of situations.

522. Olson, Richard P. Mid-life: a time to discover, a time to decide.
     Valley Forge, PA: Judson, 1980. 160p. illus. notes. LC 80-10709. ISBN
     0-8170-0859-4. OCLC 6016372. pap.
A look at the various dimensions of the mid-life crisis by a Baptist minister who, while generally biblical in orientation, is not explicitly evangelical. Olson explores what mid-life is all about (including personal
statements by a man and a woman), health management, the process of reas-
sessing, questions of marriage/singleness/remarriage, relationships between
the generations, new inner and outer opportunities for growth, and theological issues re pilgrimage, rebirth, and grace.

523. Conway, Jim. Men in mid-life crisis. Elgin, IL: David C. Cook, 1978.
     316p. notes. LC 78-67098. ISBN 0-89191-145-6. OCLC 4627884. pap.
A professor of practical theology active in conference/writing ministries
who went through his own acute mid-life depression (and shares it here)
discusses the nature of the crisis, "inside" pressures the man experiences,
dead-end roads that may tempt him (early retirement, affairs), stages of
adult development, the wife's crisis, ways of working on the related marital
problems, jobs, parenting, and sources of help. Psychological, scriptural,
and experiential insights.

524. Conway, Jim and Sally Conway. Women in mid-life crisis. Wheaton, IL:
     Tyndale, 1983. 394p. bibliog. LC 83-50127. ISBN 0-8423-8382-4. OCLC
     1006 1867.
The Conways have both written previously on mid-life issues (Jim Conway's
Men in mid-life crisis, above, and Sally Conway's You and your husband's
mid-life crisis, David C. Cook, 1980). This present book, jointly authored,
is a very substantive look at the social/psychological causes and dynamics
of women in crisis, exploring how roles can entrap and stultify, pressures
from outside (cultural, marital, parenting demands, aging, etc.), the dynamics of depression, low self-esteem and escapist fantasies, and positive
guidance for growth and change. In spite of its clear Christian orientation, this ranges far beyond strictly biblical topics and attitudes to deal
with controversial topics like affairs and to cite clearly "secular" authors.

525. Brewi, Janice and Anne Brennan. Mid-life: psychological and spiritual
perspectives. New York: Crossroad, 1982. x, 146p. bibliog. LC 81-
19512. ISBN 0-8245-0417-8. OCLC 8032060.
Brewi and Brennan are active leaders of mid-life workshops. Their main emphasis here is on Jung's notion of the two halves of life (childhood/youth
vs. mid-life/old age), with the first involving external conformity and ego-
building skills and the second calling for adaptation to the inner world
and a realization of the Self. The narrative is poetic/reflective (with
a fair amount of repetition), and the authors equate the mid-life realign-
ment they advocate with Jesus' call to a second birth. Recommended for
spirituality collections.

526. O'Collins, Gerald. Second journey: spiritual awareness and the mid-
life crisis. New York: Paulist, 1978. v, 86p. notes. LC 77-99303.
ISBN 0-8091-2209-X. OCLC 4186195. pap.
If the first "journey" is from childhood to adulthood, and the third is
that of approaching death, the second or mid-life "journey" arises when
identity props of early adulthood fail, and one experiences disorientation
and the need to redefine meaning. O'Collins gives some examples of particular people's crises, instigated by failure, war, or sickness, and he
explores general patterns of responses and ways of coping, either by moving
into new covenant relationships or by reaffirming the old. The final chapter explores special needs of men and women religious.

527. Johnson, Barbara Mary. Saying yes to change: how Christian women at
life's turning points can discover unexpected growth and joy. Minneapolis, MN: Augsburg, 1981. 128p. illus. LC 81-65649. ISBN 0-8066-
1885-X. OCLC 8302919. pap.
Johnson interviewed approximately one hundred women from meetings, classes,
church, chance encounters, etc., as background for preparing this book.
The book itself is organized thematically around three kinds of transi-
tions--developmental ones, unexpected ones, and "subtle" ones--and draws
extensively from the experiences and words of the women interviewed as they
share responses to situations like going back to work, facing illness,
spiritual struggle, etc. There is a wide range here, from the woman who
found herself suddenly speaking in tongues after engaging in a "screaming"
prayer to the woman who finally mustered her courage to leave her abusive
husband. No one theological perspective emphasized; rather, God is seen as
resource in a variety of contexts.

528. Lester, Andrew D. and Judith L. Lester. Understanding aging parents.
Philadelphia: Westminster (Christian Care Books), 1980. 120p. bibliog.
LC 80-17832. ISBN 0-664-24329-0. OCLC 6423083. pap.
By a husband and wife team of pastoral counselors, this gives practical advice plus real-life illustrative examples on a variety of topics: relating
to one's aging parents, physical changes they will experience, loss and
grief in later years, the crisis when one parent dies, living arrangements,
community resources, etc. Though the faith/spirituality dimension is mentioned occasionally, this tends in general to be more of a look at concrete
situations and ordinary human feelings than at specifically Christian concerns.

529. Gillies, John. A guide to caring for and coping with aging parents. Nashville, TN: Thomas Nelson, 1981. 208p. LC 81-1138. ISBN 0-8407-5772-7. OCLC 7283201. pap.
"This book is a record of learned experiences," Gillies writes. Specifically, it is a highly practical guide to resources for meeting the needs of elderly parents, integrated and personalized by Gillies' own story of how he and his wife have been caring for his mother and her father: at home when possible, and in nursing homes when necessary. Each chapter discusses a different area of need or type of service: medical personnel, transportation, the role of the church, etc.; most conclude with a resource list. While much of the book concerns practicalities, there is some attention paid to emotional issues too, and a Christian awareness and concern permeate the narrative. Highly recommended.

530. Anderson, Margaret J. Your aging parents: when and how to help. St. Louis, MO: Concordia, 1979. 126p. bibliog. notes. LC 78-31502. ISBN 0-570-03789-1. OCLC 4550083. pap.
By the wife of a retired pastor, this touches on a variety of issues that may arise for offspring of aging parents: roles and responsibilities, emotional, financial and health issues, dealing with behavioral change, home vs. institutional care, the question of respect, and preparing to say good-bye. Explores supportive vs. care-taking roles, ways the church may help, how to nurture the individual's active involvement in his/her own aging, and a variety of specific physical syndromes that may appear from chronic brain disease, at one end of the spectrum, to mere forgetfulness, at the other. Touches on death periodically (avoiding explicit biblical agendas), gently underlining the importance of last opportunities for reconciliation and, sometimes, faith.

531. Nouwen, Henri and Walter J. Gaffney. Aging: the fulfillment of life. Garden City, NY: Image-Doubleday, 1974. 152p. photogs. notes. LC 74-1773. ISBN 0-385-00918-6. OCLC 867917. pap.
Here is a reflective, contemplative book on aging as "a way to light," looking towards death as eventual "unmooring" and also on caring as a way to understand oneself and others more deeply. Written for younger adults as well as for the elderly, the thrust is toward integrating the aging process into the total context of a life fully lived, so that when death comes we can "be what we have given." Expressive photos accompany the text.

532. Bianchi, Eugene C. Aging as a spiritual journey. New York: Crossroad, 1982. 285p. notes. index. LC 82-17103. ISBN 0-8245-0486-0. OCLC 8729597.
Reflections by a professor of religion intended to provide a context for a spirituality of aging: primarily Christian, broadly interpreted, with occasional references to Judaism and Eastern religions, heavily influenced by Jungian theory with a stress on the inner dialogue between the conscious ego and the deep, unconscious archetypes. There is concern, too, with the realm of social responsibility in that Bianchi suggests that the "inward conversions" of mid-life and old age have a key bearing on issues of peace, justice, ecology. The thesis is that mid-life and "elderhood" both offer challenges for spiritual deepening and active re-commitment in the world. Scholarly in approach but accessible to the serious reader.

533. Smith, Tilman. In favor of growing older. Scottdale, PA: Herald, 1981.
     200p. LC 81-6996. ISBN 0-8361-1978-9. OCLC 7737884. pap.
Here are guidelines and practical suggestions for planning one's retirement
years, with a stress on the need to think about these matters early and to
develop resources. Smith discusses mental activity as compensation for physical slow-down, the natural aging process, the value of exercise and humor,
middle age, a theology of sexuality, and more concrete retirement issues,
like housing options, rip-offs to avoid, etc. Imaginative and well done.

534. Reynolds, Lillian Richter. No retirement: devotions on Christian dis-
     cipleship for older persons. Philadelphia: Fortress, 1984. 96p.
     LC 83-48916. ISBN 0-8006-1779-7. OCLC 10072414. pap.
In five sections--on enjoying pleasures, seizing opportunities, coping with
difficulties, surviving tragedies, and living one's faith--Reynolds presents
brief reflections, about 300 words each, that blend spiritual uplift
with practical advice. The guidance in some cases is more concrete than
in others--e.g., the new trend of elders sharing apartments is mentioned
in a piece on living arrangements, but in the one on reading, large print
books are not. By and large, though, a very useful contribution that
stresses on-going involvement nurtured by faith, personal reflection,
prayer.

535. Hale, Charlotte. The super years. Old Tappan, NJ: Revell, 1984. 155p.
     LC 83-19224. ISBN 0-8007-1349-4. OCLC 9971525.
Almost fervently exuberant, this is a pep talk on the possibilities for
joyful living in the later years (over 50), emphasizing on-going activity
and involvement with virtually no mention of serious problems or obstacles
that might stand in the way. Hale, a free-lance writer, starts with pre-
liminaries (attitude is where it all begins), then covers jobs, physical
health and beauty, money, cures for loneliness, the importance of envision-
ing and going after desires, giving oneself away, etc. Lots of inspiring
examples (Gloria Vanderbilt, George Burns, Ben Franklin), "things to do,"
and occasional biblical challenges (the Lord will give you the "desires of
your heart").

536. Boyle, Sarah-Patton. The desert blooms: a personal adventure in grow-
     ing old creatively. Nashville, TN: Abingdon, 1983. 207p. LC 83-8800.
     ISBN 0-687-10484-X. OCLC 9557947. pap.
Widowed in her late 50's, the author moved from a small town to Arlington,
Virginia, planning to start an exciting new life. Instead she realized
that, in the eyes of most people she met, she was old. The encounters with
ageism (at church as well) coincided with exposure to a kind of "God-is-
dead" Christianity that stripped her of moorings till she hit bottom. Only
then did she begin to discover the strength that comes from accepting what
you cannot change, changing what you can, and living in the present. An
honest, strong, creative narrative (she started jogging at 72) about revitalizing faith and personal living.

537. Madden, Myron C. and Mary Ben Madden. For grandparents: wonders and
     worries. Philadelphia: Westminster (Christian Care Books), 1980. 118p.
     bibliog. LC 80-12778. ISBN 0-664-24325-8. OCLC 6200101. pap.
One of the "Christian Care Books," this is written by a husband and wife
who are themselves grandparents and are also active as pastoral counselors/
workshop leaders. Part One looks at the assets and opportunities of grand-
parenting, while Part Two explores some of the cares and concerns, espe-

cially regarding how to relate to children at various developmental periods, with some attention to special situations like living in the same house, or foster-grandparenting. Much personal sharing with occasional references to the Bible in a comfortable, low-key sort of way.

538. Rogers, Dale Evans with Carole C. Carlson. Grandparents can. Old Tap-
     pan, NJ: Revell, 1983. 128p. LC 82-18622. ISBN 0-8007-1343-5. OCLC
     8866337.
Very warm, and full of personal sharing to illustrate the low-key advice, this reflects on various functions grandparents can play: listening fully to children, creating fun times, building memories, comforting effectively, making connections past the generation gap, etc. Includes thoughts on grandparents' possible influence in leading children to Jesus and teaching them to pray. Some words, too, on the Foster Grandparent program.

539. Maves, Paul B. A place to live in your later years. Minneapolis, MN:
     Augsburg (Religion and Medicine Series), 1983. illus. bibliog. LC
     82-72650. ISBN 0-8066-1957-0. OCLC 9651553. pap.
This is intended to assist those who soon expect to retire, or already have retired, in planning for residential needs. Maves seeks to bring the Chris-tian perspective to bear on this question in concrete ways as he considers confronting and coping with change, ordering priorities, and transcending anxiety. A look, too, at specific housing options that may be available, including regrouping, sharing, and hospice facilities for the terminally ill.

540. Burger, Sarah Greene and Martha D'Erasmo. Living in a nursing home:
     a guide for residents, their families, and friends. New York: Con-
     tinuum, 1976. 178p. LC 76-17890. ISBN 0-8264-0126-0. OCLC 2238333.
By two registered nurses, this covers the whole range of issues and choices raised in evaluating/entering a nursing home and actually living there: feelings of guilt and loss, legal matters, relations between family and staff, bodily changes of the elderly, the aging process, death and bereave-ment, etc. The Christian perspective is not explicitly stated to any ex-tent in the narrative, though it is mentioned in the introduction. In terms of topics that are covered, this is very fine. For both residents and their families; includes glossary and appendixes detailing information on agencies, Ombudsman programs, licensure, private organizations, etc.

541. Sollenberger, Opal Hutchins. I chose to live in a nursing home. Elgin,
     IL: David C. Cook, 1980. 194p. bibliog. LC 79-57521. ISBN 0-89191-
     242-8. OCLC 6642891. pap.
A first-person account that shares the author's own experience in an up-beat style and tone, with implications for others in a similar situation. Sollenberger relates how and why she chose this option and covers details of daily life in her new home: religious activities/worship, the impor-tance of TV preachers to residents, ways faith has helped her. Appendixes on finding the right home, the proper questions to ask (very full and specific), sample application forms and letters, etc.

542. DuFresne, Florine. Home care: an alternative to the nursing home.
     Elgin, IL: Brethren Pr., 1983. 127p. illus. LC 82-24339. ISBN 0-
     87178-030-5. OCLC 9111906. pap.
The author cared for her elderly husband for three years prior to his death, and for his mother as well. This offers practical instruction in all phases of home care, presented in outline form. Included are detailed health assessment procedures, instructions in setting up equipment (complete

with an illustration showing how a hospital bed works), advice on getting
help and understanding the roles of nurse and doctor, plus guidance on
patient care and hygiene, body mechanics for exercise, nutrition, keeping
records, medication, safety procedures, etc. Appendixes list resources.
An extremely detailed, practical book with a concluding personal testimony
on the value of love and Christian faith.

543. Hamilton, Michael P. and Helen F. Reid, eds. A hospice handbook: a
     new way to care for the dying. Grand Rapids, MI: Eerdmans, 1980. xii,
     196p. illus. bibliog. filmography. notes. LC 79-19518. ISBN 0-8028-
     1802-1. pap.
Canon Hamilton is affiliated with the Washington Episcopal Cathedral and
Reid is a poet/editor; together they have compiled various essays that
deal with the needs of the dying, the hospice movement in England, and
styles of hospice organization/service, including reflections by a chaplain
on the spiritual dimensions of terminal illness. While lay readers seem
a secondary audience here, they might nonetheless find the material useful.
See also Robert W. Buckingham's Complete hospice guide (Harper, 1983) for
a useful, though not specifically Christian, treatment of related issues.

544. Herhold, Robert M. Learning to die, learning to live. Philadelphia:
     Fortress, 1976. 96p. photogs. notes. LC 76-7861. ISBN 0-8006-1232-9.
     OCLC 2654985. pap. (o.p.).
A book of spiritual/psychological reflections by a Lutheran pastor that
deals with the reality of death in the context of biblical insights and
the raw human struggle. Herhold expresses very movingly the tension between our vision of Jesus' perfect love/courage and our own limitations:
anger, fear, the need to cling to life and human bonds, etc. Occasional
pages are devoted simply to a free verse prayer/reflection set against an
evocative photograph. A very well written, honest expression of the emotions involved in facing our own, and our loved ones', mortality.

545. Gerber, Samuel. Learning to die. Scottdale, PA: Herald, 1984. 103p.
     bibliog. tr. by Peter J. Dyck. LC 84-10809. ISBN 0-8361-3369-2. OCLC
     10799172. pap.
A European Mennonite minister discusses preparation for death from a conservative evangelical perspective. He writes not just for those actually
facing terminal illness or old age (though they are clearly included) but
also for others; his emphasis is on the importance of facing one's own
mortality, taking the salvation issue seriously, making a conscious decision for Christ, and working with the accumulated guilts and negative
feelings of one's life thus far so as to be ready to let go of life in
peace. Reflections, too, on practical matters (tying up business activities, bequeathing possessions) and on the psychological/spiritual experience of death itself.

546. Kopp, Ruth Lewshenia with Stephen Sorenson. Encounter with terminal
     illness. Grand Rapids, MI: Zondervan, 1980. 238p. LC 80-10982. ISBN
     0-310-41600-0. OCLC 6042929.
The author is a specialist in Clinical Oncology; she writes a very supportive book for those facing death through terminal illness. Deals with
denial (in both patients and loved ones), the relationship between patient
and doctor (how to select a doctor and build good rapport), terminal illness and the family (including illness in a child), responses to the diagnosis, and how to prepare for and face death as a Christian. Very good in

balancing the human vulnerability shared by all, regardless of religious
affiliation, with the special resources that can come through Christian
faith.

547. Rawlings, Maurice S. Before death comes. Nashville, TN: Thomas Nelson,
     1980. 180p. notes. LC 80-13250. ISBN 0-8407-5191-5. OCLC 6195129.
     (o.p.).
By a doctor who became interested in life after death and religious faith
when a patient screamed that he was in hell during a "clinical death" experience, this suggests that some such experiences can be horrifying, and
presents a very conservative evangelical approach. In addition to stressing the need to accept Christ, Rawlings discusses the process of dying
itself: how it feels to die, institutional options to caring for the
dying, issues of euthanasia and suicide (God should remain in charge), and
stages of coming to terms with death, including planning for the funeral.
A few words should probably be said about the context in which this book
seems to have been written. Dr. Raymond A. Moody, Jr.'s Life after life
(Bantam, 1976), which discusses "near death" experiences as ineffably joyous, and the pioneering work of Dr. Elisabeth Kübler-Ross in preparing
terminally ill people and their loved ones for the process of dying (On
death and dying, Macmillan, 1969; Living with death and dying, Macmillan,
1981; Working it through, Macmillan, 1982) have been very influential in
recent years. Kübler-Ross's work, in particular, has radiated a deep,
empathic acceptance of the cycle of living and dying and a remarkable capacity to become involved with individuals facing the "transition," but because the thrust of her work seems to contradict orthodox Christianity,
some evangelicals have been disturbed. Such an attitude seems to underlie
certain evangelical books, such as this present title by Rawlings.

548. Linn, Mary Jane, Dennis Linn, and Matthew Linn. Healing the dying:
     releasing people to die. New York: Paulist, 1979. xiii, 109p. illus.
     notes. LC 79-53111. ISBN 0-8091-2212-X. OCLC 5678213. pap.
Written by a registered nurse and Catholic sister, together with two Jesuit
priests, this approaches inner healing of the dying through Jesus' last
words and acts, as models and embodiments of the processes the authors believe are required for spiritual readiness for death. Each chapter explores
the implications of one of the final sayings; prayers and reflection questions are included. Appendixes consist of liturgical sequences, hymns, a
sample uniform donor card, and additional commentary in the form of notes.

549. Peachey, Mark. Facing terminal illness. Scottdale, PA: Herald, 1981.
     72p. illus. LC 80-84364. ISBN 0-8361-1948-7. OCLC 7402723. pap.
Peachey, a Mennonite pastor and mission executive, learned in September,
1977, that he was suffering from cancer of the bone marrow. Between then
and his death in February 1979 he composed these notes and in the process
transcended pain, fear, and doubt by his faith in God and his commitment
to the perspective of common human experience. The book is very brief--it
can be easily read in one sitting--but it should stimulate much thoughtful
reflection. A good choice for paperback collections in public and church
libraries.

550. Conley, Herbert N. Living and dying gracefully: reflections on death
     as an opening to a richer life. New York: Paulist, 1979. x, 70p. LC
     79-65569. ISBN 0-8091-0298-6. OCLC 5614721. pap. (o.p.).
A rich blend of personal reflections and guidance for the reader who fears
his/her own death, this is a remarkably moving book by a Catholic priest,

written during his own encounter with terminal cancer. Fr. Conley takes
on all the inevitable struggles--"But I feel so alone"--and works them
through to show why the fears are actually false; he explores beneficial
by-products of terminal illness, e.g. that we learn instantly how to receive from God and others as our defenses melt away; he talks about the
importance of ordering priorities, doing what really matters. Closing with
a Christian perspective on death as a great adventure in God, he confesses
he doesn't know what's there but he does know Who is. A beautiful and
courageous book.

3.
IN THE WIDER
COMMUNITY

A. SPIRITUALITY FOR SERVICE

551. Foster, Richard J. Celebration of discipline: the path to spiritual growth. San Francisco: Harper, 1978. x, 179p. notes. index. LC 77-20444. ISBN 0-06-062831-6. OCLC 3870394. (study guide available).
Here is an exceptionally fine study of the value of the classic spiritual disciplines, both inward and outward, as a way of discovering the true life of the kingdom and attaining liberation from "good things" of the world. Foster, a Quaker, discusses the inward disciplines of meditation, prayer, fasting, and study, and the ways in which energies they generate then become expressed in such outward disciplines as simplicity, solitude, submission and service. Ultimately, the goal is corporate discipline manifested in confession, worship, guidance, and celebration.

552. Keating, John. Strength under control: meekness and zeal in the Christian life. Ann Arbor, MI: Servant (Living as a Christian), 1981. 129p. notes. ISBN 0-89283-104-9. OCLC 8642447. pap.
Another in Servant's biblically based, psychologically helpful series, this argues that meekness and zeal are intimately related as key components of Christian servanthood. Keating distinguishes true meekness (characterized by courtesy, forebearance, respect, and teachable obedience) from that mild timidity the word often suggests and defines zeal as "determined, aggressive dedication" rather than unpredictable emotional enthusiasm. Then he contrasts the life of servanthood with the "gospel of selfism" pervading today's society. This is clear, readable, intelligent, and practical.

553. Berry, Jo. The Priscilla principle: making your life a ministry. Grand Rapids, MI: Zondervan, 1984. 178p. bibliog. LC 84-2188. ISBN 0-310-42631-6. OCLC 10323767. pap.
Noting people's unfortunate tendency to label according to stereotypical assumptions, conservative evangelical author Berry suggests that we often do this same thing with the concept of "ministry." Rightly understood, "ministry" far transcends those church-oriented activities to which the word is often applied; for a Christian, one's whole life should be a ministry, expressed via roles, neighborhood/work activities, personal relationships, etc. Growing out of reflections nurtured by a year's retreat

from "business as usual" to re-evaluate her faith relationship, this book
explores personal qualities demonstrated by the biblical Priscilla and
underlying principles crucial to a life of full service.

554. Hinson, E. Glenn. A serious call to a contemplative life-style. Phila-
     delphia: Westminster, 1974. 125p. bibliog. notes. LC 74-9658. ISBN
     0-664-24992-2. OCLC 915898. pap.
A Baptist professor of church history, Hinson here addresses the problem of
secularization and loss of transcendence in the "space age." We must learn
to see God in what is happening today, he believes, and can do so by cultivating contemplative prayer in the midst of daily life, so as to adopt a
centered style of greater simplicity. Includes a look at "Aids to meaningful devotion" including AV's, journaling, devotional reading, fellowship, etc. A list of "Selected devotional reading" is included.

555. Green, Thomas H. Darkness in the marketplace: the Christian at prayer
     in the world. Notre Dame, IN: Ave Maria, 1981. 128p. notes. LC 81-67559.
     ISBN 0-87793-230-1. OCLC 7818494. pap.
Intended as a sequel to Opening to God (Ave Maria, 1977) and When the well
runs dry (Ave Maria, 1979), this presupposes the vision of prayer outlined
in these earlier books. The thrust here is to relate prayer dynamics to
one's experience with the "marketplace," or world, which sometimes appears
attractive, sometimes undesirable, reflecting the inherent tension between
contemplation and action, prayer and service. Green explores how inner
dryness and outer reality are integrally related, and how life in the world
plays a crucial part in inner growth: "darkness" at times envelops apos-
tolic activity, just as "dryness" comes at certain stages of the prayer
journey. By a Jesuit spiritual director.

556. Doherty, Catherine de Hueck. Poustinia: Christian spirituality of the
     East for western man. Notre Dame, IN: Ave Maria, 1975. 216p. LC 74-
     19961. ISBN 0-87793-083-X. OCLC 1229502. pap.
Doherty founded Friendship House in the Toronto slums and in Harlem and
Madonna House in Ontario. Born into a wealthy Russian family but now vol-
untarily poor in response to the Gospel's call, she writes here on the
"silence of God" to which she felt called as a pilgrim. The "poustinia"
she describes is a spiritual place of quiet solitude for restorative prayer,
an essential resource for those called to witness in the "marketplace" of
the world. Doherty's language is direct and down-to-earth, sometimes even
witty, as she describes this Russian concept for western novices. In subsequent books (Sobornost, Ave Maria, 1977; Molchanie, Crossroad, 1982;
Urodivoi, Crossroad, 1983) she moves deeper in sharing her faith vision,
becoming progressively more intense.

557. Carretto, Carlo. The desert in the city. New York: Crossroad, 1982.
     106p. LC 81-70877. ISBN 0-8245-0423-2. OCLC 8467156. pap. (also
     Collins ed.).
In Letters from the desert (Jove, 1976) Carretto, one of the Little Brothers
of Jesus, wrote of the time he spent in the Sahara and his spiritual quest
in its absolute silence. The present title, inspired by the voiced needs
of those he met on a trip to Hong Kong, aims in the format of a week's retreat (seven meditations/guided reflections for the seven days of the week)
to help readers discover God wherever they are, in the midst of their particular crowded lives: to discover the spiritual "desert" of silence and
prayer (as in Doherty's Poustinia, above) so as to view all of their circumstances as a single whole, a context for creative love.

558. Coburn, John B. A life to live, a way to pray. New York: Seabury, 1973
     x, 143p. notes. LC 72-96340. ISBN 0-8164-2079-3. OCLC 658184. pap.
A guidebook on prayer which also explains the dynamics of the prayer relationship in clear, simple terms, this starts with the assumption that
prayer and social responsibility belong together, the journey inward always involving a complementary journey outward. The essays are directed
at Christians, but Coburn sees Christ as praying for all who pray. The
first section deals with daily living as prayer's starting point; the second considers certain issues in the context of the Lord's prayer (love,
justice, sexuality, death, discipleship, etc.); the third meditates on
Christ. Emphasizes the importance of feelings, and that we meet Christ in
a dynamic two-way process leading to transformation when prayer rises from
the depths of who we really are.

559. Crosby, Michael H. Thy will be done: praying the Our Father as sub-
     versive activity. Maryknoll, NY: Orbis, 1977. viii, 254p. notes.
     indexes. LC 77-5118. ISBN 0-88344-496-8. OCLC 2873557. (also pap.).
To pray the Lord's Prayer authentically, Crosby argues, is to be drawn into serious questions about one's own life vis-a-vis the social and economic injustices in the world. Exploring what it would mean for people to
pray seriously that God's will be done, he examines the various phases of
the prayer in an in-depth analysis, and their implications as guidelines
for being in participative community, transcending mere ritual for immersion in reality, seeking truth, justice, and peace, and understanding the
Cross as a sign of conflict among worldly kingdoms. (See also The Lord's
Prayer: the prayer of integral liberation, by liberation theologian and
Franciscan priest Leonardo Boff, Orbis, 1983.)

560. Juel, Donald H. Living a biblical faith. Philadelphia: Westminster,
     1982. 117p. notes. LC 82-8652. ISBN 0-664-24429-7. OCLC 8476146. pap.
Working with Ephesians, Juel interprets key passages that relate to Christian ways of living in community, in the broader world, in work situations,
in family life, and vis-a-vis the state. His concern is to identify guidelines for a "biblical faith" while recognizing the Bible as a storehouse
of pluralistic meanings rather than a manual setting forth one rigidly defined way. Thus, the book provides a context for honest searching and personal application.

561. Skinner, Tom. If Christ is the answer, what are the questions? Grand
     Rapids, MI: Zondervan, 1974. 219p. LC 73-22696. OCLC 1176976. (o.p.).
Skinner is a well known black evangelist. Here, in question and answer
format, are his thoughts on some theological issues and on such practical
topics as the role of young people in society, the nature of social responsibility, the church as new community, and relations between black and
white Christians. Skinner takes a classical evangelical position with a
stress on involvement; his premise is that it does little good to keep re-
peating "Jesus saves" without entering into caring relationships and addressing issues of social concern.

562. Soelle, Dorothee. Beyond mere obedience. New York: Pilgrim, 1982.
     xxii, 73p. notes. LC 81-15431. ISBN 0-8298-0488-9. OCLC 7814149. pap.
German theologian Soelle states in her foreword that this is an attempt to
work through oppressive aspects of the tradition of obedience she inheri-
ted as a Christian woman in Germany. She advocates learning from Christ,
worshipping a God of justice rather than mere power, and moving from obe-

dience as submission to a person (the authoritarian model) into "objectivity" and a "liberated spontaneity" in proclaiming Jesus. Well translated
by Lawrence W. Denef, this makes more accessible reading for a general
audience than some of Soelle's books. Intended, in part, as a response
to what she sees as the authoritarianism of the Moral Majority.

563. Doherty, Catherine de Hueck. The Gospel without compromise. Notre
     Dame, IN: Ave Maria, 1976. 150p. LC 75-28619. ISBN 0-87793-104-6.
     OCLC 2072410. pap.
Drawn from various works by the author over a period of years, the reflections here are united by a single theme: the commandment to love
others, living out the Gospel "without compromise" in the world at large.
Rather than specifically analyzing social problems that pervade our culture, Doherty stresses constant prayer for an ever-deepening faith so as
to empty one's consciousness of self and facilitate radical sharing. Discussions of community, gifts, prayer, poverty of the heart, and related
topics, by a woman who has truly "sold all" and now lives in voluntary
poverty as she serves through the lay Catholic ministries she has founded.

564. Carmody, John. Holistic spirituality. New York: Paulist, 1983. 145p.
     bibliog. notes. LC 83-62468. ISBN 0-8091-2564-1. OCLC 10672584. pap.
Within a liberal theological context emphasizing love as the central uni-
fier, Carmody outlines and explores the possibility of a Christian spirituality that emphasizes connections between all interests. Discusses how
spirituality can infuse activities in the realms of ecology, economics,
politics, grass-roots community development, exercise, sexuality, education, and meditation. Reflective and verging on the scholarly, but with
guidelines for living included.

565. Palmer, Parker J. The promise of paradox: a celebration of contradic-
     tions in the Christian life. Notre Dame, IN: Ave Maria, 1980. 125p.
     notes. LC 80-68134. ISBN 0-87793-210-7. OCLC 6912176. pap.
In an intelligent and discerning book, Palmer suggests that there are bound
to be contradictions in the Christian life and that rather than hiding from
them by oversimplifying issues, we should accept a creative tension as the
framework for growth and celebrate the possibilities of experiential paradox. Faithful living involves presenting ourselves to God where and as we
are without straining to "get it all together" first, and true Christian
community emerges as private problems are translated into corporate issues
and as people move dynamically from resistance to acceptance, affirmation,
and liberation while encountering the mystery of the Cross.

566. Tubesing, Donald A. and Nancy Loving Tubesing. The caring question:
     you first or me first? choosing a healthy balance. Minneapolis, MN:
     Augsburg, 1983. 220p. illus. LC 83-70501. ISBN 0-8066-2007-2. OCLC
     9869086. pap.
Opening with some thoughts on the need for a good "self-care/other-care"
balance in living, and for yardsticks with which to measure "health-
fulness," this proceeds to discuss "reaching in" (physical, mental, relational, spiritual and holistic self-care) and "reaching out" (to family,
as a single, to a spouse, to one's neighbors, and to the wider world).
Very concrete and down-to-earth, with reflective exercises, "thought
provokers," guidelines for "internal dialogs," etc. An attempt to operationalize the "love your neighbor as yourself" principle.

567. Collins, Gary R. Joy of caring. Waco, TX: Word, 1980. 198p. notes.
     index. LC 80-52130. ISBN 0-8499-2928-8. OCLC 7068548. pap.
Psychologist Collins discusses basic principles of caring (who, where, why
and how), essential priorities (caring about ourselves, others, our families, our community, our leaders, and doubters), and the practice (sharing,
being open to feelings, maintaining self-control, practicing forgiveness,
etc.). Aims at being practical and specific, a real "how to" sort of
book, by helping readers learn to care and to accept caring from others
as well. Includes a look at covenant groups.

568. Colson, Charles. Loving God. Grand Rapids, MI: Zondervan, 1983. 255p.
     notes. LC 83-14769. ISBN 0-310-47030-7. OCLC 9826730.
In his third book, Colson goes beyond the autobiographical style of Born
again (Revell, 1977) and Life sentence (Revell, 1981) to explore, with illustrations from the Bible, church history, and his own experience, what
it means truly to love God and to live out that love concretely in the
world. Stressing obedience, getting grounded in the Bible, personal repentance, and individual/corporate holiness, he issues a real challenge
that unites faith in biblical infallibility with a response to life from
the perspective of the broken and oppressed.

569. McNeill, Donald P. and others. Compassion: a reflection on the Chris-
     tian life. New York: Image-Doubleday, 1983. xii, 142p. illus. LC 83-
     45045. ISBN 0-385-18957-5. OCLC 7305940. pap.
These reflections on compassion originated in a series of discussion/
prayer meetings McNeill, Douglas A. Morrison, and Henri Nouwen shared some
years ago. Organized around the themes of God's compassion as revealed in
Christ, compassionate living among Jesus' early followers, and the disciplines of prayer and action, the essays acknowledge that radical compassion runs counter to human nature in its "downward pull" toward identification with suffering. It is only when service is inspired by desire for
God as well as for social change that true compassion is possible. The
drawings are by Joel Filartiga, a Paraguayan doctor/artist whose son was
tortured to death by the police. Highly recommended.

570. McNamara, James. The power of compassion. New York: Paulist, 1983.
     82p. bibliog. LC 83-62463. ISBN 0-8091-2567-6. pap.
Unlike Donald P. McNeill's Compassion, which explored the subject in a
radical, even disturbing way, this takes a more intellectually distanced
look, stressing insights of contemporary psychology. Drawing heavily from
Rollo May, McNamara argues that powerlessness and pseudo-innocence are
enemies of compassion, blinding us to our own evil and leaving us vulnerable to outside manipulation. Best taken as a place to start rather than
a fully developed exploration of the Gospel's radical thrust.

571. Bruland, Esther Byle and Stephen Charles Mott. A passion for Jesus:
     a passion for justice. Valley Forge, PA: Judson, 1983. 159p. notes.
     LC 83-4379. ISBN 0-8170-0994-9. OCLC 9393824. pap.
Here is a workbook to help lay people encounter a theology of Christian
social responsibility and to equip them to become personally active.
Early chapters deal with God's grace, love, and justice; subsequent ones
suggest different ways of acting out concern through politics, citizens'
groups, noncooperation, etc.; the final one examines problems and conflicts
that may occur, and offers guidance. Each chapter has a narrative section
and "Engage" exercises and reflections.

572. Betz, Sr. Margaret. Faith and justice: living as Christians on a small planet. Winona, MN: St. Mary's Pr., 1980. 176p. photogs. index. LC 80-50259. ISBN 0-88489-114-3. OCLC 6366684. pap.
A consciousness-raising pot-pourri of images, photos, data, and open-ended narratives encouraging imaginative empathy ("You be the white parent"), together with profiles of change-agents (a missionary sister; Pete Seeger; Dorothy Day). Chapters deal with perspectives and habits of perception, beginning with one's unique talents and values, decision-making re work or lifestyle, cultural conflicts, population/pollution crises, hunger, and sources of energy. Review questions encourage the reader on his/her journey.

573. Wallis, Jim. The call to conversion: recovering the Gospel for these times. New York: Harper, 1983. xviii, 190p. bibliog. index. LC 80-8901. ISBN 0-686-92025-2. OCLC 7553793. pap.
Wallis is founder/leader of the Sojourners in Washington, D.C., a community of socially and politically active Christians who live and work in the inner city and publish Sojourners magazine. The purpose of the present book is to explore in historically specific terms what true conversion might mean in America today: the birth of a public rather than a merely private consciousness, a biblically consistent stand against the cultural status quo, and a commitment to fight injustice and the threat of nuclear war. Wallis is extremely dedicated and intelligent, but his book would have been strengthened by more concrete examples of Sojourners' struggles.

574. Watson, David. Called and committed: world-changing discipleship. Wheaton, IL: Harold Shaw, 1982. xii, 226p. bibliog. LC 82-824. ISBN 0-87788-101-4. OCLC 8195526. pap. (also cloth). (British ed. published as Discipleship).
Christ's plan for the world is one of radical discipleship, Watson stresses; having our personal needs met in Jesus is only the first half of the story. With this assumption he presents a systematic look at various dimensions of the full call: into God's family with its priorities for an alternative style of community; into a real capacity and resolve to bear with one another; into the effort to make new disciples, to live in the spirit, to pray, to study the Bible, to live simply, and to pay the necessary cost. Appendixes reprint the Lausanne Covenant on Simple Lifestyle plus basic and follow-up discipleship courses.

575. Fenhagen, James C. More than wanderers: spiritual disciplines for Christian ministry. New York: Seabury, 1978. xiii, 105p. notes. LC 77-17974. ISBN 0-8164-0386-4. OCLC 3447302.
Written by an Episcopal priest for all within the Christian tradition (but open as well to interested others), this is a guide for establishing an inner discipline as a resource for living "in the way"--to link meditation and ministry. An outgrowth of the theme in Fenhagen's Mutual ministry (Seabury, 1977) that people must be enabled to become "journeyers" rather than "wanderers," this discusses a theology of the Christian journey (struggle with oneself, encounter with the Lord, and the role of community), aspects/dimensions of ministry (including covenant prayer), growing beyond "ought" and into "thirst," hearing the "still small voice," using a journal as discipline, spiritual companionship, and the role of the local church. Heavily influenced by Henri Nouwen and Elizabeth O'Connor.

576. Manning, Brennan. The gentle revolutionaries: breaking through to
Christian maturity. Denville, NJ: Dimension Books, 1976. 140p. ISBN 0-
87193-012-9. OCLC 4951758. pap.
Exploring three centers of consciousness which Christ rejected (security,
sensation and power) and four which he affirmed (consciousness of the
Father, the disciples, the reign of God, and the world's cosmic oneness),
this encourages the reader to embark on a journey to higher Christian
consciousness by letting go of undesirable attitudes/orientations and nurturing Christlike ones. While recognizing natural routes (via psychology,
etc.), this affirms Christ crucified and the power of Pentecost as the
essential resource in transformation. Includes a look at techniques of
growth, e.g., consciousness-focusing to enable the "schizoid Christian"
to move toward integrity.

577. Driver, John. Community and commitment. Scottdale, PA: Herald, 1976.
92p. LC 76-41463. ISBN 0-8361-1802-2. OCLC 3001282. pap.
A Mennonite theologian active in missions work explores the meaning of
Christian "renewal" grounded in return to Jesus Christ as normative reference point, enabling people to leap over later cultural/ecclesiastical
distortions and take his actual Person as standard. Coming out strongly
against an evangelism that polarizes the spiritual and social dimensions,
he discusses the church as a community of radical sharing ("koinonia") in
which discipline is always in the service of reconciliation/forgiveness,
gifts are exercised for the whole body, all social/cultural barriers are
eliminated in the spirit of peace, and the Great Commission is understood
as a mandate for making whole disciples, not merely preaching salvation.

578. Camara, Dom Helder. Hoping against all hope. Maryknoll, NY: Orbis,
1984. 96p. LC 83-19348. ISBN 0-88344-192-6. OCLC 9968904. pap.
The widely loved Brazilian Archbishop who combines deep spirituality with
commitment to the oppressed has once again written a truly remarkable book,
ably translated by Matthew J. O'Connell. In parables, poetry, and brief
reflective essays, Camara ranges over a variety of topics, evoking the
special innocence of children, the arresting wisdom of the mad ("God's
Simpleton"), and unexpected breakthroughs into hope in the face of suffering, persecution, and obsession with "national security." Brief and
eloquent, this embodies the heart of the Gospel.

579. Stott, John R. W. Christian counter-culture. Downers Grove, IL: Inter-
Varsity (The Bible Speaks Today), 1978. 222p. notes. LC 77-27687.
ISBN 0-87784-660-X. OCLC 3943796. pap.
One of "The Bible Speaks Today Series" (Old and New Testament expositions
relating Scripture to contemporary life), this work by a leader in evangelical Christianity (Rector Emeritus of All Souls Church in London) is a
detailed examination of the Sermon on the Mount, as Christ's description
of the alternate cultural lifestyle to which disciples are called. Discusses mandated attitudes toward values, money, ambition, lifestyle and
personal relationships as contrasted to those of the "secular" world.

580. Merton, Thomas. A Thomas Merton reader. Rev. ed. by Thomas P. McDon-
nell. Garden City, NY: Image-Doubleday, 1974. 516p. LC 74-29. ISBN
0-385-03292-7. OCLC 897842. pap.
Admittedly, this substantive compilation of Merton's writings--reflecting
his many faceted gifts as contemplative and poet and his varied thoughts
on subjects ranging from spirituality to peacemaking--can in no way be

called a "self-help" book. Yet it seemed essential to include at least
something by Merton, so influential has he been in nurturing a new consciousness among those seeking to integrate contemplation and active service. Here, then, is a rich sampling from his many works over the years.

B.   THE WORLD OF WORK

581. Dayton, Edward R. and Ted W. Engstrom. Strategy for living: how to
     make the best use of your time and abilities. Glendale, CA: Regal,
     1976. 191p. illus. bibliog. LC 76-3935. ISBN 0-8307-0424-8. OCLC
     3634504. pap. (also cloth).
Life is a process, the authors explain, so the best strategy for living
is dynamic and circular: identifying goals and priorities, planning how
to enact them, living out the plan, and then returning to the goals and
priorities stage once again. The book's chapters are designed around the
components of this circular process and touch on aspects of living like
family commitments, time with God, one's job, etc. There are some biblical
quotations and some discussion of the spiritual dimension, but this is
less heavily scriptural than some such titles.

582. Zehring, John William. Preparing for work: get ready now for life
     after school. Wheaton, IL: Victor, 1981. 159p. illus. LC 79-92001.
     ISBN 0-88207-582-9. OCLC 7811558. pap.
An excellent book by Earlham College's career planning director that con-
cisely combines practical techniques/resources, psychological exercises/
guidelines, and a clear Christian approach to vocational issues (e.g.,
applying stewardship concepts to the decision-making process). Zehring
assumes that the reader is a Christian, believes in prayer, and wants to
act with the Holy Spirit's guidance, and this viewpoint is smoothly integrated into his very practical, useful discussion of common myths, church
vs. "secular" jobs, getting experience, analyzing attitudes, making contacts, finding summer jobs, writing letters/resumes, and being interviewed.

583. Clark, Martin E. Choosing your career: the Christian's decision manual.
     Phillipsburg, NJ: Presbyterian and Reformed, 1981. ix, 106p. bibliog.
     ISBN 0-87552-205-X. OCLC 7818549. pap. (also Baker Book House ed.).
This is, Clark tells us, intended for Christians who want to make career
decisions responsibly; he takes great pains to stress that it is, indeed,
biblical to use counseling tools as vehicles for setting goals, as if he
feels readers may regard such activities with suspicion, and he spends
considerable time discussing the theology of work, God's sovereignty,
spiritual gifts vis-a-vis career, etc. After this justification for the
rational decision-making process, there is actually comparatively little
space devoted to counseling techniques per se. There are some inventories
for self-evaluation, but on the whole this might better serve to get the
reluctant individual to a career counselor than as a "do-it-yourself"
substitute. Primarily for the younger reader.

584. Mattson, Ralph and Arthur Miller. The truth about you: discovering
     what you should be doing with your life. Old Tappan, NJ: Revell,
     1977. 153p. LC 77-24446. ISBN 0-8007-0887-3. OCLC 3167223. (o.p.).
The authors argue on the basis of extensive interviewing (in over 3,000
cases, they claim, they haven't found an exception) that each person shows

a pattern of voluntary behavior throughout the life cycle, and that by
analyzing this pattern (in terms of such categories as organize/operate,
serve/help, shape/influence, etc.) it is possible to identify a person's
unique motivational thrust or design which, when channeled into an appropriate vocation, results in successful and fulfilling work experience.
Much of the book presents exercises and techniques for identifying and
analyzing one's own pattern; there is also some discussion of the principles involved, including theological assumptions about God as Prime
Designer. (Readers may also wish to examine Mattson's and Miller's second book, Finding a job you can love, Thomas Nelson, 1982. This goes
more fully into theological questions raised but imperfectly resolved
in the first, but spends less time on techniques to identify the motivational pattern.)

585. Gentz, William. Career opportunities in religion: a guide for lay
     Christians. New York: Hawthorn, 1979. ix, 252p. bibliog. indexes.
     LC 79-84206. ISBN 0-8015-3200-0. OCLC 5969667. pap.
A sort of Occupational outlook handbook for careers in religion, this describes an assortment of job possibilities with a look at responsibilities,
preparation/training, and prospects. Covers careers in the local church,
in church-wide institutions and offices, in interdenominational and interfaith councils and agencies, and in non-church-related organizations, plus
international career opportunities and part-time, seasonal, volunteer and
independent careers. Appendixes list useful majors, centers, and resources.

586. Fisher, Doug, ed. Why we serve: personal stories of Catholic lay
     ministers. New York: Paulist, 1984. 144p. ISBN 0-8091-2640-0. pap.
Vatican II's statement on lay ministry and the reality of dwindling orders
forms the context for this cross-section of vivid personal statements from
non-ordained men and women, married and single, who are all engaged full
time, as their sole means of support, in some active ministry: Christian
education, peace activity, foreign missions, communal living, even a clown
ministry. Recurring themes are the challenge/necessity of a simple lifestyle and--very interesting--a trend away from more conventional, struc-
tured work into free-lance, individually evolving efforts.

587. Schumacher, E. F. and Peter N. Gillingham. Good work. New York: Harper,
     1980. xi, 223p. illus. index. LC 76-5528. ISBN 0-06-090561-1. OCLC
     6259093. pap.
Schumacher's widely read Small is beautiful (Harper, 1976) argued for a
human-scale technology from a Buddhist point of view. The present book,
published after his death, is much more explicitly Christian, drawn mainly
from lectures given in the U.S. during the 1970's and earlier essays. In
it he suggests some implications of the Gospels for an industrial society:
that life (including work) should be a training ground toward "the kingdom
of heaven" rather than pursuit of more comfort, and that today's techno-
logical culture nurtures avarice, in opposition to Jesus' teachings.

588. Beckmann, David M. and Elizabeth Anne Donnelly. The overseas list:
     opportunities for living and working in developing countries. Min-
     neapolis, MN: Augsburg, 1979. 192p. notes. indexes. LC 79-50095.
     ISBN 0-8066-1719-5. OCLC 5802446. pap.
A handbook for people interested in obtaining jobs in Third World countries,
primarily with a service thrust and a commitment to help alleviate hunger
and malnutrition. Covers issues pertaining to "global living," some op-

portunities with church missions, private development agencies, international organizations, U.S. government jobs, business situations, study,
teaching, and journalism. Concludes with a look at living in the Third
World and a Christian rationale for such service. Indexes to occupations,
organizations and geographic locations. Royalties go to Bread for the
World Educational Fund.

589. Wilson, J. Christy, Jr. Today's tentmakers: self-support--an alter-
     native model for worldwide witness. Wheaton, IL: Tyndale, 1979. 160p.
     bibliog. LC 79-90737. ISBN 0-8423-7279-2. OCLC 5972804. pap.
The author, professor of Missions and Evangelism at Gordon Conwell, worked
as a teacher in Afghanistan some time ago as a "tentmaker"--i.e., one engaged in missionary activities while earning support through secular employment. Arguing that this sort of missions work on the part of lay
Christians best matches the biblical models and is the answer to burgeoning
expenses straining church budgets, Wilson discusses examples of "tent-
making," advantages and disadvantages, locating employment overseas, relationships with missions boards, preparation/orientation, resource groups,
etc.

590. Anderson, Margaret J. The Christian writer's handbook. New revised ed.
     San Francisco: Harper, 1983. 322p. bibliog. notes. index. LC 82-48917.
     ISBN 0-06-060195-7. OCLC 9194877. pap.
A complete guidebook for the aspiring Christian writer. Deals with "pre-
liminaries" (like commercial possibilities and developing discipline) and
offers advice on writing poetry and devotionals, articles of all kinds
(narrative, how-to, personality sketches, etc.), short stories, book
length fiction and non-fiction, drama, educational materials, and church
outreach tools. Concludes with some words on the business end of writing
and a motivational pep-talk.

591. Hybels, Bill. Christians in the marketplace. Wheaton, IL: Victor, 1982.
     144p. LC 82-50135. ISBN 0-88207-314-1. OCLC 8850039. pap.
The minister of a growing community church in Illinois offers advice on
how to glorify God in the context of one's work-life: not through evangelical gimmicks, but by effectiveness in our work, who we are, what we
say. Advice on handling anger (the mandate of living harmoniously is
stressed), loving confrontation, avoiding "workaholism," prioritizing
time, handling money responsibly (disciplined spending habits and tithing),
building self-confidence, avoiding temptation. Closes with a brief evangelical presentation of the Gospel.

592. Catherwood, Fred. On the job: the Christian nine to five. Grand Rapids,
     MI: Zondervan, 1983. 185p. notes. indexes. LC 82-23716. ISBN 0-310-
     37261-5. OCLC 9082396. pap.
Here is a challenge to apply one's faith to job activities, professional
ethics, views on income, wealth, etc. Topics discussed include involvement with labor unions, sales and advertising practices, creative vs.
destructive kinds of competition, and styles of being a manager or employee.
There is little about specific techniques here; it is, rather, a discussion
of Christian ethics in the context of various sets of circumstances. The
subject index, together with the index to scriptural passages, should make
this particularly useful as a resource for those wishing to do more exploration of the issues involved, and while the perspective is British, references to the American scene are provided. (Revised edition of The Christian
in industrial society.)

593. White, Jerry and Mary White. Your job: survival or satisfaction? Grand
     Rapids, MI: Zondervan, 1977. 191p. LC 76-45191. ISBN 0-310-34321-6.
     OCLC 2493621.
This is on blending one's Christian faith and one's job in the world; the
job, say the Whites, is our training ground, the context in which we must
apply our faith. They discuss, first, foundational principles (all related
to the above assumption), then move on to look at practical circumstances
in a variety of different settings: for the hourly employee, the salaried
employee, the homemaker, the working woman, the government employee, sales-
men, military people, the self-employed. In each case, they discuss ad-
vantages/disadvantages, spiritual dangers, and practical guidelines.

594. Eims, LeRoy. Be the leader you were meant to be: what the Bible says
     about leadership. Wheaton, IL: Victor, 1975. 132p. LC 75-5392. ISBN
     0-88207-723-6. OCLC 1637824. pap.
Written by the evangelism director of the Navigators, an international discipleship organization, this stresses the spiritual psychodynamics of effective leadership (being centered in one's own relationship with God,
having a servant's heart, etc.) before moving on to look at more strategic
processes like setting goals, increasing efficiency, etc. The spiritual
discussion includes a look at the psychology of famous biblical leaders,
and the book should be more useful for individuals working with Christian
groups than for leaders in other settings.

595. Alexander, John W. Managing our work. Second rev. ed. Downers Grove,
     IL: InterVarsity, 1975. 104p. bibliog. LC 75-320308. ISBN 0-87784-
     352-X. OCLC 1583215. pap.
The president of Inter-Varsity Christian Fellowship and an active member of
the American Management Association discusses the "management cycle" (plan-
ning--execution--review) as a process that can be useful in one's individual work (stewardship) and also as a leadership style. Grounded in the
assumption that all planning must begin with an awareness that God has
plans for us and that we must continually reaffirm our commitment to Him,
this attempts to relate the management process to biblical principles and
stresses the need for balancing family/work priorities against spiritual
ones.

596. Kraybill, Donald B. and Phyllis P. Good, eds. Perils of professionalism
     Scottdale, PA: Herald, 1982. 240p. bibliog. LC 82-3052. ISBN 0-8361-
     1997-5. OCLC 8345300. pap.
Various professionals from diverse fields share thoughts on the impact of
professionalism on persons, marriage, families, congregations, and pastors
themselves. Emphasis is on the dilemmas professionalism raises (disrupting
wholeness, causing distance from others, etc.); a look, too, at a theology
of professionalism and its impact on faith. Kraybill and Good devote
several chapters specifically to the Mennonite-Amish experience, but in
general this is broadly applicable and emphasizes concrete issues over
purely theoretical ones.

597. Kreider, Carl. The Christian entrepreneur. Scottdale, PA: Herald,
     1980. 222p. notes. indexes. LC 80-16836. ISBN 0-8361-1936-3. OCLC
     6421129. pap.
From his Mennonite perspective, an enconomics professor addresses ethical
problems faced by Christians in business and offers guidance for lay readers
who struggle with the dilemmas discussed. While strongly supporting in-

tentional communities as models of a new economic order, Kreider believes
that "economic nonconformity" can also be practiced by committed individuals
in the larger society, in ways he suggests here. His book covers biblical
teachings re the productive process, ethical problems of the business
person, personal decisions re. lifestyle and consumerism, and the use of
financial resources and individual gifts. Includes a look at alternative
forms of Christian business.

598. Van Vuuren, Nancy. Work and career. Philadelphia: Westminster (Choices:
      Guides for Today's Woman), 1983. 115p. LC 83-12338. ISBN 0-664-24539-0.
      OCLC 9683575. pap.
Not a straight career guide, this contribution to Westminster's new series
on women's issues seeks to make the readers aware of the wide range of
options open to them today but stresses, at the same time, that work should
be understood holistically: not just in terms of career, but more broadly,
as all that one does in integrating life's activities into a framework of
faith. Van Vuuren looks at expectations, challenges and problems in the
workplace, family relationships, the meaning of money, etc. Excellent in
terms of providing a philosophical framework within which to use more traditional career manuals.

599. Ward, Patricia and Martha Stout. Christian women at work. Grand Rapids,
      MI: Zondervan, 1981. 242p. notes. LC 81-13021. ISBN 0-310-43700-8.
      OCLC 7672650.
Based on interviews with 100 Christian women in various vocational and
personal situations (working class, professional, married, single, widowed,
and divorced), this explores issues like the meaning of vocation, creative
potential, and home/work conflicts; case histories complement the general
discussion. While respecting Christian doctrine, the authors deal realistically with changing roles and demands facing women today and appeal for
more supportive treatment from the church. Appendix includes resource
items on education, part-time work, apprenticeships, etc.

600. Oates, Wayne E. Confessions of a workaholic: the facts about work ad-
      diction. Nashville, TN: Abingdon, 1978. 112p. bibliog. LC 75-136606.
      ISBN 0-687-09393-7. OCLC 137090. pap.
Pastoral counselor Oates claims this is intended as "a serious jest" in his
Preface. The "workaholic" (he coined the term) is one who is addicted to
work as a compulsion, and this is the personal story of his own struggles
with the malady and how he learned to overcome it with the support of family. Discusses, too, social factors in America conducive to the syndrome,
situations of wives and children of the workaholic, the workaholic on the
job and vis-a-vis religious faith, the woman workaholic, and remaking one's
life. Grace, Oates suggests, is the ultimate antidote: freely given,
accomplishing what work (and one's own efforts) cannot do alone. (See also
the author's Workaholics, make laziness work for you, Doubleday, 1978.)

601. Diehl, William E. Thank God, it's Monday!. Philadelphia: Fortress
      (Laity Exchange Books), 1982. xi, 196p. LC 81-71390. ISBN 0-8006-
      1656-1. OCLC 8451699. pap.
Like most others in this series, this is a substantive, thoughtful look
at some issues confronting lay people who are seriously attempting to live
the Christian life. More an exploration of key problem areas than a "how
to" book, this examines the dilemma of feeling caught in the middle between worldly and spiritual demands, biblical implications for life in a

competitive society, questions posed by "principalities and powers" (re occupation, security, status, etc.) and thorny issues like how to balance national loyalties against the priorities of discipleship. Concludes with a look at the role of the church.

C. TOWARD A WIDER CALL

602. Zehring, John William. Making your life count: finding fulfillment beyond your job. Valley Forge, PA: Judson, 1980. 111p. notes. LC 79-25309. ISBN 0-8170-0869-1. OCLC 5798729. pap.
Zehring has found his own spiritual fulfillment in the area of avocation rather than simply career, and he urges readers to consider this approach to spiritual growth in a prayerful, Christ-centered context. With many exercises, fill-ins, and career-counseling techniques adapted to identify avocational interests, this makes a most useful book.

603. Elliott, Douglas A. Any Christian can: a personal guide to individual ministry. Waco, TX: Key Word-Word, 1981. 100p. LC 79-66522. ISBN 0-8499-4125-3. OCLC 6304013. pap.
Written to help the ordinary person minister to others in practical ways, this discusses helpful attitudes (putting the other first; the importance of flexible caring and patient waiting on the Spirit), embodied compassion, recognizing resources, removing such hindrances as destructive inhibitions, and establishing helpful relationships in everyday encounters. Elliott then looks at some specific modes of ministry such as listening, appreciation, encouragement, and keeping balance. Very clear and simple in its approach, with many concrete examples.

604. Schultejann, Marie. Ministry of service: a manual for social involvement. New York: Paulist, 1976. 113p. bibliog. LC 76-16901. ISBN 0-8091-1967-6. OCLC 2493235. pap. (o.p.).
Designed for concerned individuals as well as for social action groups and parish councils, this offers ideas for service projects, plans for organization, and extensive resource lists so that people can create new ministries. Discusses theology of service (learning to love as Christ loved us), building blocks (awareness, leadership, screening, etc.), constructing a support system, and ideas for specific programs: "friendly visitor" activities, "big-brother/big-sister" partnerships, "neighborhood book exchanges," tutorials, projects for the hungry, consumer education, and many more. Concrete and practical.

605. Keeler, Ronald F. To the work! what you can do after the sermon. Cincinnati, OH: Standard, 1976. 87p. LC 76-26296. ISBN 0-87239-135-3. OCLC 3186674. pap. (o.p.).
A host of brief, practical ideas for specific service ministries individual Christians can perform in their communities. Averaging a page or so in length, Keeler's suggestions include starting a Christian book club, paper route, or travel bureau, writing letters, taking a "favorite hymn poll," sharing modern parables, taking a "Bible hike," running a telephone or cassette ministry, and so on. While this does not address the dynamics of ministry with any depth, its suggestions might still be useful in facilitating brainstorming sessions among individuals wishing to become more active in some sort of service capacity.

606. Pennington, M. Basil. Called: new thinking on Christian vocation. New
     York: Seabury, 1983. xiii, 107p. LC 83-652. ISBN 0-8164-2472-1. OCLC
     9370820. pap.
Pennington's new book offers thoughts for lay readers and religious on
discerning one's call: to intimacy with God, in partnership with another
or in celibacy, and to specific "calls within [that] call," to service
in particular contexts. Christian vocation is for everyone, Pennington
stresses, and his descriptions of methods he uses to help people discern
their paths and his honest exploration of sensitive areas (e.g., can one
be "called" to a committed homosexual partnership?) make this a rich, re-
warding book.

607. Lange, Joseph and Anthony Cushing. Called to service. New York:
     Paulist (Living Christian Community Series), 1976. vi, 168p. LC 75-
     41813. ISBN 0-8091-1921-8. OCLC 2188552. pap.
Volume Four of the "Living Christian Community Series" which draws on experiences of the Children of Joy Community in Allentown, Pennsylvania, this
assumes as background spiritual issues discussed in the first three volumes:
entering into relationship with Jesus in the Spirit as described in
Friendship with Jesus, and processes of worship and personal liberation as
explored in Worshipping community and Freedom and healing (all published
by Paulist). Believing service gifts are but neutral tools and that love
is what really counts, the authors discuss issues of authority, states in
life (single, married, etc.), mission, and commitment, with a focus on
developing gifts to serve the community and to bring others to full spiritual maturity. Catholic spirituality grounded in communal living.

608. Wagner, C. Peter. Your spiritual gifts can help your church grow.
     Ventura, CA: Regal, 1979. 272p. notes. index. LC 78-53353. ISBN 0-
     8307-0644-5. OCLC 9277783. pap.
A specialist in church growth at Fuller Theological Seminary examines spiritual gifts in terms of how they can help individual Christians evangelize
and disciple more effectively. Touches on and defines twenty-seven gifts
in the course of the narrative, advocating a conscious effort to identify
one's own unique gifts so as to make the most of them. Wagner has an
eclectic Protestant background and sheds interesting light on attitudes
toward gifts in different denominations. Includes a list of "ten best
books" on the gifts in one of its chapters.

609. Hall, Robert Benjamin. Anyone can prophesy. New York: Seabury, 1977.
     v, 96p. LC 77-8267. ISBN 0-8164-2158-7. OCLC 2966448. pap.
Within an Episcopalian perspective, Hall's approach is to try and view
prophecy "from man's viewpoint"--how he (she) receives, verifies and passes
on God's inspiration--in the context of daily living. With stress on the
practical rather than the theoretical, Hall explores forms of prophecy,
specific tests we can apply (is the apparently prophetic message confirmed
by other people or events? does it fit the law of love?), and offers some
gentle words of warning about dangers of the occult. As the title indicates, the author believes that while not all Christians are full-fledged
"prophets," all can, on occasion, receive and transmit prophecy.

610. Kinghorn, Kenneth Cain. Gifts of the Spirit. Nashville, TN: Abingdon,
     1976. 126p. illus. index. LC 75-22268. ISBN 0-687-14695-X. OCLC
     1530816. pap.
A United Methodist minister and church history professor writes for the
general reader on the biblical basis for spiritual gifts, how the gifts

function, the various categories ("enabling" gifts, "serving" gifts, and
the gifts of tongues/interpretation) and the process of discovering one's
own gifts and using them in the church. Kinghorn takes a biblical approach
with a stress on the mandate for Christian unity: Christ should be the
only "foundational" focus (not tongues, for instance). A balanced approach
with attention to psychological/human factors as well as scriptural principles.

611. Flynn, Leslie B. Nineteen gifts of the Spirit. Wheaton, IL: Victor,
      1974. 204p. LC 73-91027. ISBN 0-88207-701-5. OCLC 897710. pap.
A Baptist minister discusses nineteen gifts,--including prophecy, teaching,
knowledge, wisdom, hospitality, discernment, miracles, healing, and tongues/
interpretation--organized by category as "speaking gifts," "serving gifts,"
and "signifying gifts." Flynn stresses that all believers receive one or
more at the time of regeneration for the purpose of building up the whole
Christian body; all are responsible for developing their unique gifts and
exercising obedience even in "ungifted" areas (e.g., all should witness
when possible even without the specific gift of evangelism). Tongues--
discussed last--are not seen as a special sign of baptism in the Spirit but
as one gift among many. Concludes with thoughts on discovering gifts and
putting them to work.

612. Yohn, Rick. Discover your spiritual gift and use it. Wheaton, IL:
      Tyndale, 1974. 154p. bibliog. LC 74-80798. ISBN 0-8423-0668-4. OCLC
      1054496. pap.
Spiritual gifts--special abilities God bestows so people can help accomplish His work--are explored in this book by a pastor in an Evangelical
Free Church. Chapters on the gifts of physical healing, leadership, faith,
apostle/prophecy, etc., occupy most of the book; scriptural principles,
common misconceptions, and practical/contemporary application are also
included. A brief final chapter discusses how to discover one's own gifts
through faith, prayer, awareness, responsibility, and common sense, and
shares thoughts on putting the gifts to use in the framework of the local
church.

613. O'Connor, Elizabeth. Eighth day of creation: gifts and creativity.
      Waco, TX: Word, 1971. 115p. bibliog. LC 70-175725. OCLC 226179. pap.
      (o.p.).
Similar in format to Our many selves and Search for silence (see annotations), with which it forms a trilogy, this focuses on the importance of
identifying one's special gifts and bringing them to fruition. The "exercises" offered consist of meditational readings from secular/scriptural
sources chosen to facilitate awareness of talents, followed by instructions
on imagining particular works which might draw on gifts so identified.
O'Connor's introductory essay on creativity and resistances to its actua-
lization--nearly half of the book--is rich in discernment and implications.
Some may, in fact, find it even more valuable than the pot-pourri of
reflective readings she later offers.

D. EVANGELISM AND DISCIPLING

614. Kiemel, Ann. I'm out to change my world. Nashville, TN: Impact, 1975.
      119p. photogs. LC 74-81137. ISBN 0-914850-27-X. OCLC 1093844. pap.
In free-verse vignettes Kiemel describes representative chance encounters
she has had and ways she has nurtured friendships with people in her neighborhood to use everyday situations to share her relationship with Christ.
While occasionally verging on the sentimental, the interactions are often
quite powerful, and one senses that substantive change may really have
occurred. Evangelism-in-action, described (and practiced) with a youthful
spontaneity and lack of inhibition.

615. Posterski, Don. Why am I afraid to tell you I'm a Christian?: witnes-
      sing Jesus' way. Downers Grove, IL: InterVarsity, 1983. 114p. LC 83-
      12958. ISBN 0-87784-847-5. OCLC 9830626. pap.
Written by Ontario's director for Inter-Varsity Christian Fellowship of
Canada, this presents an approach to evangelism focusing on Jesus' own style
of communication. It emphasizes listening, discerning another's essential beliefs, communicating in a personal fashion, and thinking about the
process rather than just the doctrine. Talks about psycho-spiritual preparation for such evangelism, how to activate the mind of Christ, strategic
ways of communicating the Gospel, living like Jesus, and connecting with
one's culture in loving involvement. Brief, clear, and practical. Appendixes include a Bible study on the theme of reconciliation and techniques
for addressing both believers and nonbelievers.

616. Neville, Joyce. How to share your faith without being offensive. New
      York: Crossroad-Seabury, 1979. vi, 152p. notes. LC 78-25885. ISBN
      0-8164-2228-1. OCLC 4492904. pap.
There is a double focus here in this excellent and very clear book: first,
on witnessing (telling, doing, being) in a variety of one-to-one situations,
and second, on using Christian small groups as contexts for sharing, nurturing relationships, prayer and praise. The author has been active as a
teacher of lay witnessing and a developer of small groups in the Episcopal
church, and her style will make this accessible to readers who might be put
off by some of the more conservative evangelical titles.

617. Deville, Jard. The psychology of witnessing. Waco, TX: Word, 1980.
      126p. illus. LC 80-51447. ISBN 0-8499-2922-9. OCLC 7007561. pap.
      (o.p.).
By a psychotherapist and psychology professor, this draws on the psychodynamics of communication and decision-making as it discusses ways to share
one's faith. Examines issues of personal responsibility and maturity, interpersonal motivation and relationships, understanding resistance, listening with the heart, presenting the Gospel choice, maintaining interpersonal
trust, and asking for a decision. Very clear, with chapter summaries and
reflective questions.

618. Brestin, Dee. Finders keepers: introducing your friends to Christ and
      helping them grow. Wheaton, IL: Shaw, 1983. 179p. illus. notes. LC
      83-8522. ISBN 0-87788-265-7. OCLC 9557791.
This guide to personal and small-group evangelism views such activitiy as
a natural outgrowth of genuine friendships with non-Christians. "Finding"
refers to the importance of finding time for others, caring to develop

empathic friendships, and being ready to share Christ with non-believers
if they wish, to start small Bible study groups, etc. "Keeping" denotes
teaching new believers the principles of Christian obedience, or the process of "disciple-making." There are numerous anecdotes and real life
examples, making this more lively than evangelism guides that stay on the
level of general principles alone. "Try this" suggestions conclude each
chapter.

619. McPhee, Arthur G. Friendship evangelism: the caring way to share your
     faith. Grand Rapids, MI: Zondervan, 1978. 139p. bibliog. LC 78-17344.
     ISBN 0-310-37311-5. OCLC 3966270. pap.
Citing the dangers of a "care-less" evangelism (minimizing repentance, offering "cheap grace," etc.) McPhee describes a mode of evangelism that grows
out of genuine friendship and involvement. Words and actions must coin-
cide, he says (it is what you are that really communicates a message), and
one must earn the right to be heard by first being a caring person. Includes lessons in conversation and in ways of avoiding off-putting "religious" language, establishing relationships, and following through.

620. Petersen, Jim. Evangelism as a lifestyle: reaching into your world
     with the Gospel. Colorado Springs, CO: NavPress, 1980. 144p. bibliogs.
     LC 80-83874. ISBN 0-89109-475-X. OCLC 8174759. pap.
In addition to "proclamation" evangelism, says Petersen, there is a need
for "affirmation" evangelism, which involves visibly living out the Gospel
message once it has been initially verbalized. Here he concentrates on
this second mode of witnessing through one's lifestyle, looking at the
importance of congruence, the ways mutual fear can inhibit honesty, the
dynamics of adaptation and conversion, and modeling the Kingdom through
styles of corporate living. Petersen, a Latin America Navigators Division-
al Director, has been extensively involved in cross-cultural ministry.

621. Aldrich, Joseph C. Life-style evangelism: crossing traditional boun-
     daries to reach the unbelieving world. Portland, OR: Multnomah (Cri-
     tical Concern Books), 1981. 246p. indexes. LC 80-27615. ISBN 0-930014-
     46-4. OCLC 7168164.
Aldrich's central premise is that the process of living integrally in one's
faith creates a distinctive lifestyle which is in itself a most effective
witness: embodied love rather than mere words. Believers who keep Christ
at the center as their model, who refrain from judging others, and who recognize they are bound to meet people who believe and act differently, will
be able to practice a true neighborly love and establish genuine relationships with non-Christians rather than regarding encounters with non-believers
as forays into a kind of enemy territory. Though primarily intended for
pastors, this could also be very helpful to lay-people.

622. Pippert, Rebecca Manley. Out of the saltshaker and into the world:
     evangelism as a way of life. Downers Grove, IL: InterVarsity, 1979.
     188p. notes. LC 79-1995. ISBN 0-87784-735-5. OCLC 5450034. pap.
By an evangelism consultant for Inter-Varsity Christian Fellowship, this
focuses on Jesus as model, contrasting His way with that of the pharisees.
The thrust is to help Christians get past a fear of offending, and to develop a style that, indeed, will not offend. Discusses practicing Christ's
presence by seeing others in a loving and accepting fashion, developing an
easy conversational style to nurture dialogue, sharing reasons for one's
faith in an effective manner, etc. Appendix One outlines steps to God;
Appendix Two presents books for evangelism.

623. Galilea, Segundo. The Beatitudes: to evangelize as Jesus did. Maryknoll, NY: Orbis, 1984. iii, 108p. LC 83-19342. ISBN 0-88344-344-9.
OCLC 9946001. pap.
Here is an integration of liberation theology and evangelical faith by a
Chilean priest, author of Following Jesus (Orbis, 1981). The Beatitudes,
Galilea argues, demonstrate Christ's priorities in evangelization and
should be guidelines for our own: Luke's version identifies preferential
targets (the poor), while Matthew's sets forth attitudes of spiritual
poverty needed on the faith journey. With discussion also on prayer,
contemplation/vision, mercy, and criteria for a personal lifestyle of
evangelical poverty, this is provocative and rich.

624. Spande, Norma. Your guide to successful home Bible studies. Nashville,
TN: Thomas Nelson, 1979. 143p. LC 78-21036. ISBN 0-8407-5683-6. OCLC
4495132. pap. (o.p.).
In a comfortable, homey tone freelance writer Spande shares her own story
of how participating in a Bible study changed her life, then discusses a
range of practical questions re setting up and conducting such a group:
getting members, choosing materials, being a leader, making arrangements
for children, etc. This is definitely housewife-oriented, but there is
a chapter on groups for men in which a man shares his own point of view.
Very concrete and down-to-earth.

625. Ghezzi, Bert and John Blattner, eds. Prayer group workshop. Ann Arbor,
MI: Servant, 1979. 138p. LC 79-115574. ISBN 0-89283-066-2. OCLC
5446002. pap. (o.p.).
Originally published in New Covenant magazine, the 25 short articles here
explore diverse practical aspects of conducting prayer meetings: giving
effective sharing, identifying leadership, testing prophecy, forming music
groups, organizing book ministries, and much more. The authors are experienced prayer group leaders, primarily in the Catholic charismatic renewal. This is an excellent aid for those involved in prayer groups and
would be ideal for church collections.

626. Rinker, Rosalind. Teaching conversational prayer: a handbook for
groups. Waco, TX: Word, 1970. 140p. bibliog. indexes. LC 70-91946.
OCLC 62051. (o.p.).
"Conversational prayer," about which Rinker has written earlier (see, for
instance, her Prayer: conversing with God, Zondervan, 1959), involves spon-
taneous vocal prayer led by the Spirit in a group setting. The present
book is to encourage Christians to pass this method along to others. Besides teaching aids, it discusses how to discover and believe in God's
love and to communicate its reality. Defines and explains conversational
prayer, tells how to teach the basic steps, and offers guidelines for
groups. For additional titles by Rinker on conversational prayer, see
BIP.

E. DYNAMICS OF FELLOWSHIP

627. Couchman, Bob and Win Couchman. Small groups: timber to build up God's house. Wheaton, IL: Harold Shaw, 1982. 96p. LC 82-798. ISBN 0-87788-097-2. OCLC 8195450. pap.
This is an encouragement/guidance manual for people wishing to start small "growth" or "cell" or "koinonia" groups as an adjunct to (not instead of) the local church. The Couchmans discuss reasons for forming such groups, what goes on, how to decide on leadership, modes of worship, prayer, and inductive Bible study, possible service patterns for small groups, etc. They regard groups like these as a place for learning and growing through doing rather than just listening, and their study questions at the end of each chapter should facilitate discussion.

628. Trudinger, Ron. Cells for life: home groups--God's strategy for church growth. Plainfield, NJ: Logos, 1979. xi, 123p. LC 79-91748. ISBN 0-88270-416-8. OCLC 7218915. pap. (o.p.).
Here is a brief look at the role and nature of home "koinonia" groups and their sharing/discipling function. Chapters cover modes of nurture, warning/correction, provision, leadership, training, etc., with the integrating metaphor of a biological organism made up of numerous interdependent cells woven throughout the discussion. Includes practical advice re activities, member participation, pitfalls, ways of starting; Trudinger draws often on his own experience in such groups, which is very useful. Appendix lists scriptural references.

629. Evans, Louis H., Jr. Covenant to care. Wheaton, IL: Victor, 1982. 120p. LC 81-86104. ISBN 0-88207-355-9. OCLC 8815255. pap. (rev. ed. of Creative love, 1977).
Evans begins by sharing how difficult it once was for him to open himself to others, and how the turning point came when he could finally join a covenant group: a fellowship of committed Christians promising to be present for one another with affirmation, availability, prayer, openness, honesty, sensitivity, confidentiality, and accountability. Besides describing how such groups work and exploring in separate chapters each of the characteristics listed above, Evans makes some practical suggestions about working with covenant groups and examines the biblical basis.

630. Wagemaker, Herbert, Jr. A special kind of belonging: the Christian community. Waco, TX: Word, 1978. 126p. bibliog. LC 77-92473. ISBN 0-8499-0072-7. OCLC 4499300. pap.
Episcopalian psychiatrist Wagemaker has been involved in Christian community (mainly in the context of small sharing groups) for a number of years. Here he shares his experiences and reflections: on how such fellowship can facilitate self-discovery, wholeness, healing and liberation; on the demands it makes on participants; on various dimensions of community (community of love, service, evangelism); and on how to start such a fellowship. Distinguished by Wagemaker's clinical sensitivity to the psychodynamics involved as he discusses what he considers to be the necessary resources for community relationships--openness, trust, involvement, acceptance--and offers helpful guidelines to readers as yet unfamiliar with the experience and its rewards.

631. Henry, Mark and Mary Frances Henry. A patchwork family. Nashville,
     TN: Broadman, 1978. 160p. illus. notes. LC 77-82403. ISBN 0-8054-
     4486-8. OCLC 3837586. (o.p.).
Here are ideas, methods, and "a touch of theory" from a couple who have
been actively involved in creating intergenerational small groups: fellowship groups including children and adults of all ages. Experience in such
a fellowship, say the authors, can help families learn to communicate
better, and they examine the group process, Jesus as the key to abundant
relationships, behaviors to expect from people at different age levels,
leadership styles, plus general principles of Christian covenant groups.
Includes lists of written resource materials and contact people.

632. Allen, Donald. Barefoot in the church. Richmond, VA: John Knox, 1972.
     188p. notes. indexes. LC 72-1759. ISBN 0-8042-1540-5. OCLC 314226.
     (o.p.).
Based on experiences of and in his own house church (part of a cluster of
such groups in Virginia), Allen describes and explores strengths, weaknesses, and future potential of the house church movement (close groupings
of people grounded in mutual identity and mission, often affiliated with
established churches). Organized by the themes of becoming, discovering,
belonging, grounding, reaching, strengthening, celebrating, establishing,
and projecting, this offers transcripts of members' discussions, examples
from other house churches past and present, a look at linkages with the
human potential movement, and general guidelines. Subject index and index
of Christian communities.

633. Bubna, Donald L. with Sarah M. Ricketts. Building people through a
     caring, sharing fellowship. Wheaton, IL: Tyndale, 1978. 153p. LC 78-
     55984. ISBN 0-8423-0185-2. OCLC 4295473. pap. (also leader's guide).
Not a straight "how-to," this is rather a collection of stories and anecdotes in which Pastor Bubna shares interactions he has facilitated or wit-
nessed between parishioners and attenders which reflect honesty, acceptance, shared empathy, etc. Emphasis on people's needs to be accepted as
they are and to experience "koinonia" fellowship, and on the desirability
of witnessing while still allowing space for authenticity and openness
on the part of the other.

634. Getz, Gene A. Building up one another. Wheaton, IL: Victor, 1976.
     120p. LC 76-19918. ISBN 0-88207-744-9. OCLC 3186907. pap.
The theme here is that ordinary church members can help and strengthen each
other by practicing proper biblical behavior in their fellowship: being
members of one another; honoring, greeting, serving, accepting, and admon-
ishing each other; being of one mind and bearing one another's burdens.
The book is full of biblical references together with examples of how this
has worked at the Fellowship Bible Church where Getz is pastor.

635. Stedman, Ray C. Body life. Rev. ed. Glendale, CA: Regal, 1979. 182p.
     illus. LC 74-181764. ISBN 0-8307-0732-8. OCLC 3665778. pap.
First published in 1972, this is now revised to report on newer develop-
ments in the author's Peninsula Bible Church in Palo Alto, which he describes to illustrate some basic principles. One audience here is definitely pastors as Stedman discusses how and why PBC took its current shape
(not hierarchical; the pastor is not the "final authority"; great emphasis
on lay ministry outside the church walls; sharing services stressing im-

mediate, concrete response to one another's needs, etc.). Yet in his discussion of the importance of individual Christians discovering and exercising their own gifts for the building-up of the whole body, this is very
well suited to lay readers also, and directly addresses them in a clear,
immediate style. Based on Ephesians, with an extended metaphor of the
human body (skeleton, nervous system, circulatory system, etc.) used to
illuminate the role of different gifts. Emphasizes the process of maturing
in faith/service.

636. O'Connor, Elizabeth. The new community. New York: Harper, 1976. 121p.
    photogs. notes. LC 76-9964. ISBN 0-06-066337-5. OCLC 2542234. pap.
O'Connor has written previously of the founding and early growth of Washington, D.C.'s Church of the Saviour, and of that fellowship's understanding
of spirituality and mission (Call to commitment, Harper, 1963, and Journey
inward, journey outward, Harper, 1968). Here, in large format paperback
with many photos, she updates the story, writing about emerging new struc-
tures/missions that inner city crises have called forth, and how individuals involved have had to struggle against inner resistance and to work
through a process of creative tension. As always, O'Connor is discerning
and sensitive in sharing the psychodynamics involved in breaking through
to new modes of creative concern.

637. O'Connor, Elizabeth. Letters to scattered pilgrims. San Francisco:
    Harper, 1979. xvi, 147p. notes. LC 78-3361. ISBN 0-06-066333-2. OCLC
    5103410. (also pap.). (1982 ed. in BIP).
O'Connor's letters–really essays—were originally written to challenge and
encourage members of six new faith communities that branched off from the
inter-denominational Church of the Saviour in Washington, D.C., but familiarity with these groups and their missions is not necessary in order to
enjoy the poetic, thoughtful intelligence that penetrates these essays on
such matters as money, group living, journal writing, and identifying one's
vocational call. O'Connor's central concern is to integrate the historical,
intellectual, and emotional dimensions of Christian faith and life. A
fine addition to most religious collections.

F.   COUNSELING ONE ANOTHER

638. Bryant, Marcus D. The art of Christian caring. St. Louis, MO: Bethany
    Pr., 1979. 125p. illus. notes. LC 78-20791. ISBN 0-8272-0015-3. OCLC
    4515034.
Written for the lay reader unfamiliar with counseling techniques and vocabulary, this offers insights on helping skills in clear, everyday language.
The early chapters discuss the caring relationship in general, and how to
express such caring through listening, responding, etc. Then Bryant turns
to specific target groups for ministry, such as nursing home residents,
the retarded, prisoners, and mental patients, examining guidelines and
background information. The final chapter discusses how to gather one's
own resources for the helping process through worship, meditation, and
spirituality, stressing as a general guideline that Christian caring is sus-
tained by God's love and by our personal responses to that love as we experience it in our own lives. Underscoring the importance of commitment and
self-discipline in relations with others, this is a good introductory guide
that should be helpful to general readers.

639. Collins, Gary. How to be a people helper. Santa Ana, CA: Vision House,
     1976. 189p. notes. index. LC 76-15112. ISBN 0-88449-055-6. OCLC
     2597556. pap.
Collins, a pastoral counselor with a special interest in carving out a
Christian psychology (see annotation for The rebuilding of psychology)
takes as his point of departure the notion that counseling among laypeople
should be a basic part of a church's outreach. He stresses the need to
base all counseling on the Bible as God's Word, opening with a discussion
of the Great Commission and discipleship as the context/aim for "theocentric" outreach counseling. Thereafter he discusses principles of helping,
the importance of the helper's character, and various specific settings/
circumstances; friend-to-friend counseling, helping in a crisis and over
the phone, suicide referrals, preventive counseling, the Christian body
as a helping community, and helping oneself.

640. Drakeford, John W. The awesome power of the listening heart. Grand
     Rapids, MI: Zondervan, 1982. 178p. LC 82-17518. ISBN 0-310-70261-5.
     OCLC 8806050. pap.
Drakeford uses the term "listening heart" to signify that love is expressed
in focused attention, and in this book he seeks to help people acquire
skills needed to be present in this fashion for others. Chapters deal with
levels of listening, third-ear and body-listening, the use of listening in
leadership positions and marriage relationships, and advice on mastering
the arts involved. Drakeford's Christian perspective is reflected in occasional biblical references recalling something Jesus said or did rather
than in specifically evangelical discussion.

641. Hughes, Selwyn. Helping people through their problems. Minneapolis,
     MN: Bethany House, 1982. 192p. illus. index. LC 81-70198. ISBN 0-
     87123-201-4. OCLC 9499771. pap.
An introductory guide for those wishing to improve their effectiveness as
"people helpers" in everyday situations with their friends, this starts
with a look at physical/psychological/spiritual factors in human problems
and then examines basic skills (listening, accepting, evaluating levels
of need, etc.). Hughes devotes some space to Ellis' RET (rational-emotive
therapy) techniques as potentially useful tools and stresses memorizing
various scriptural passages to have at one's disposal. Includes an exploration of working with one's own personality and faith relationship, plus
common errors to avoid.

642. Miller, Paul M. Peer counseling in the church. Scottdale, PA: Herald,
     1978. 166p. bibliog. LC 78-9299. ISBN 0-8361-1854-5. OCLC 3913206. pap.
Here is a simple, clearly written book (no technical jargon) designed to
help ordinary Christians do peer counseling with one another. Miller
assumes many caring relationships are already underway, and he discusses
attitudes and skills that will be needed on the part of peer counselors,
ways to initiate the process, and specific ways of approaching issues in
vocational, premarital, and marital counseling contexts. There is some
exploration of the ideal Christian approach: e.g., shun inspirational
pep-talks, don't play God, do sit humbly before the unfolding mystery.

643. Worthington, Everett L. When someone asks for help: a practical
     guide for counseling. Downers Grove, IL: InterVarsity, 1982. 239p.
     illus. notes. LC 82-81. ISBN 0-87784-375-9. OCLC 8494404. pap.
An introductory guide for friend-to-friend counseling, this first sets
forth a framework for "Christian helping" and discusses how problems

develop, utilizing a five-stage model. Next it discusses various helping
skills that are needed at each stage, together with examples. Worthington
draws on the Bible, but he goes beyond it too, supplementing it with psychological insights he believes to be spiritually consistent with Scripture, albeit not explicitly stated.

644. Smith, Harold Ivan. Tear-catchers: developing the gift of compassion.
     Nashville, TN: Abingdon, 1984. 160p. ISBN 0-687-41184-X. pap.
Scheduled for publication in October, 1984, this was not actually examined
but is included because of the author's popularity in some evangelical
circles. Smith (who also has written as Jason Towner, e.g. in Jason loves
Jane, but they got a divorce, Impact, 1978) has recently been working in
a ministry to hurting individuals, and here, according to pre-publication
notices, he shares thoughts on the importance of tears as an expression of
grief and offers advice on how to be a compassionate presence for others
in need.

645. Adams, Jay E. Ready to restore: the layman's guide to Christian coun-
     seling. Grand Rapids, MI: Baker Book House, 1981. ix, 111p. notes.
     ISBN 0-8010-0171-4. OCLC 7642185. pap. (also Presbyterian and Reformed
     ed.).
An extremely conservative biblical counselor states the premise that "all
Christians must counsel" and offers "simple," non-technical guidance toward
this end in the form of biblical principles he deems relevant to the counseling situation. Considering goals and attitudes (the ultimate goal here,
as elsewhere, being to glorify God), Adams stresses meekness in a counselor,
total dependence on the Bible rather than on "worldly" wisdom, and the
impossibility of successfully counseling nonbelievers (who may only be
"precounseled," or evangelized). Adams is an influential author at the
extremely conservative end of the spectrum.

646. Grantham, Rudolph E. Lay shepherding: a guide for visiting the sick,
     the aged, the troubled, and the bereaved. Valley Forge, PA: Judson,
     1980. 112p. bibliog. LC 79-22678. ISBN 0-8170-0863-2. OCLC 5493211.
     pap.
Beginning with a look at authority issues and the context for lay ministry,
Grantham explores ways the biblical, humanistic and broadly spiritual perspectives relate to each other and looks at specific ministries lay people
can engage in: crisis intervention, bereavement counseling, hospital/
nursing home visiting, etc. Considers, too, the dynamics of healing, how·
to be an effective listener and to pray with the sick and personal lay
evangelism of beneficial and destructive kinds. Appendix includes discussion questions and additional study resources.

647. Keys, Joel T. Our older friends: a guide for visitors. Philadelphia:
     Fortress, 1983. 64p. bibliog. LC 83-8865. ISBN 0-8006-1724-X. OCLC
     9441264. pap.
A very brief but very useful guide for laypeople planning to spend time
with elderly individuals--as friends, family members, or volunteers. Keys
discusses various qualities of a good visitor, the importance of realistic
expectations, how different environments (nursing homes, private residences)
can impinge on the situation, physical/emotional/spiritual traits of elders,
and techniques for good conversation. The simple style makes this ideal for
the apprehensive novice, but the bibliography is sufficiently detailed that
readers wishing guidance in more specialized terms can also use it to locate
additional resources.

648. Hart, Thomas. The art of Christian listening. New York: Paulist, 1981.
128p. bibliogs. LC 80-82810. ISBN 0-8091-2345-2. OCLC 7526987. pap.
Recognizing a wide variety of helping relationships in the church today,
Hart discusses how laypeople as well as religious professionals can offer
effective spiritual direction. Some of the issues considered include
roles of helper and helpee, the difference between spiritual and secular
counseling, the place of prayer, the process of Christian growth. Hart
is sympathetic to process theology and stresses facilitating responsible
autonomy, helping people search for potential "purpose" rather than a pre-
designed "plan."

649. Dyckman, Katherine Marie and L. Patrick Carroll. Inviting the mystic,
supporting the prophet: an introduction to spiritual direction. New
York: Paulist, 1981. 112p. bibliog. notes. LC 81-80053. ISBN 0-8091-
2378-9. OCLC 8167030. pap.
To encourage lay people as well as Catholic sisters and priests to become
spiritual directors, this explores ways of building on natural gifts and
becoming an emphatic, helpful listener. In a poetic, discerning style,
the authors (a Catholic sister and a Jesuit priest) focus on "faithing,"
contemporary spirituality, the nature of spiritual direction, presuppositions about directors, problems and presuppositions in the area of prayer,
praying through the "desert" experience, prayerful decision-making, and
"mystics and prophets" in contemporary living. Emphasizes the importance
of a Christian faith that follows Jesus in doing rather than merely believing.

650. Bennett, Rita. How to pray for inner healing for yourself and others.
Old Tappan, NJ: Power-Revell, 1983. 126p. bibliog. LC 83-10981. ISBN
0-8007-5126-4. OCLC 9647152. pap.
Expanding on her book Emotionally free (see annotation), Bennett discusses
how to prepare and organize a lay ministry of prayer counseling ("soul
healing"). She begins by reviewing the nature of soul-healing prayer,
then looks at qualities needed in a soul-healing prayer-counselor and
techniques involved (reliving the scene with Jesus, followed by creative
prayer). Next comes working with a prayer partner and specific stages
in the process, reflections on the use of imagination, and particular
prayer helps for nineteen individual circumstances (dyslexia, depression,
alcoholism, divorce, failed suicide, rape or incest, abortion bereavement,
homosexual experience, etc.). Closes with additional thoughts on the
prayer process and on starting a ministry. Appendixes on praying for receiving Jesus as Savior, renouncing involvement in the occult, and a list
of churches with this type of ministry.

G.   TOWARD A SIMPLE LIFESTYLE

651. Crean, David, and Eric and Helen Ebbeson, eds. Living simply: an
examination of Christian lifestyles. New York: Seabury, 1981. x, 102p.
notes. LC 81-5834. ISBN 0-8164-2340-7. OCLC 7574299. pap.
Intended for use in adult discussion groups, this aims to help people increase their awareness of the importance of simpler lifestyles. There are
four thematic sections--on humanity as community, individuals in community,
transformation in community, and the world as community--in which various
individuals from different denominational backgrounds share reflections/
experiences. More of a motivational tool than a practical listing of
"how to" steps.

652. Finnerty, Adam Daniel. No more plastic Jesus: global justice and
     Christian lifestyle. Maryknoll, NY: Orbis, 1977. xiv, 223p. bibliog.
     LC 76-13174. ISBN 0-88344-341-4. OCLC 2597528. pap.
The first part of Finnerty's book analyzes the current global situation--
world-wide poverty, an unjust class system, tragic waste, etc.--as one of
impending disaster; thereafter he discusses the simple living movement,
embodied in the Shakertown Pledge, a "religiously grounded Simple Living
commitment" he actively advocates; finally he looks at the role of the
church, calling it to abandon its own wealth and embrace a Christian poverty. The appendix discusses the Shakertown Pledge more fully. See also
the author's book World citizen: action for global justice (written as Adam
Daniel Corson-Finnerty, Orbis, 1982), in which he analyzes socio-economic
crises of the "post-colonial world" more fully and discusses, in the final
chapter, specific movements/groups with which the reader might wish to
affiliate for involvement in issues of peace/disarmament, the environment,
economics, social justice, human rights, etc. Finnerty is affiliated with
the International Division of the American Friends' Service Committee.

653. Sider, Ronald J., ed. Lifestyle in the eighties: an evangelical com-
     mitment to simple lifestyle. Philadelphia: Westminster (Contemporary
     Issues in Social Ethics Series), 1982. 256p. LC 82-7067. ISBN 0-664-
     24437-8. OCLC 8430508. pap.
One of a new series, this reviews various evangelical statements on social
responsibility: The Chicago Declaration of Evangelical Social Concern,
the Lausanne Covenant, and the Evangelical Commitment to Simple Lifestyle,
which the present book discusses. The Commitment grew out of a 1980 International Consultation on Simple Lifestyle, held in England and attended by
evangelical leaders from 27 countries; here Sider reprints the Commitment,
together with background papers on biblical/theological issues, personal
testimonies and related Bible studies.

654. Sider, Ronald J., ed. Living more simply: biblical principles and
     practical models. Downers Grove, IL: InterVarsity, 1980. 206p. notes.
     LC 79-3634. ISBN 0-87784-808-4. OCLC 6329272. pap.
These papers were originally delivered at the U.S. Consultation on Simple
Lifestyle in 1979. The first chapters look briefly at Old and New Testament principles applicable as guidelines for living in America today; in
subsequent chapters (the true core of the book) individuals share personal
stories of how and why they have been shedding such "false securities" as
tenured jobs and expensive houses in their own lives. Will appeal to
counter-culture Christians.

655. Gish, Arthur G. Beyond the rat race. Rev. ed. Scottdale, PA: Herald,
     1973. 208p. bibliog. LC 73-9336. ISBN 0-8361-1985-1. OCLC 802817. pap.
This is a sort of consciousness-raising tool to help people think through
the issues involved in choosing to move toward a simple lifestyle. Topics
covered--the nature of the simple life, what's really wrong with being rich,
etc.--both explain the virtues of simplicity, as Gish sees it, and answer
specific objections that might be raised from the other side. Some specific suggestions as well as a discussion of general principles involved; includes a chapter on "Jesus our President and our Chairman," explaining the
biblical basis for adopting a simpler lifestyle. Church of the Brethren
perspective.

656. Foster, Richard J. Freedom of simplicity. San Francisco: Harper, 1981.
     vii, 200p. notes. index. LC 80-8351. ISBN 0-06-062832-4. OCLC 7196933.
For Foster, a Quaker, Christian simplicity is paradoxically highly complex;
it involves maintaining a creative balance between such seeming opposites
as grace and discipline, inner and outer reality, the goodness and the
limitation of material things. In this very thoughtful book he first looks
at scriptural guidelines in the Old and New Testaments and at some monastic
and traditional disciplines, then moves to a more personal discussion of
ways people can shift to simpler living. Foster's stress is on a sensitivity to individual differences and on avoiding any hints of a new legalism. Highly recommended for public, church, seminary libraries. (A
sequel to Celebration of discipline; see annotation.)

657. Longacre, Doris Janzen and others. Living more with less. Scottdale,
     PA: Herald, 1980. 294p. photogs. notes. indexes. LC 80-15461. ISBN
     0-8361-1930-4. OCLC 6378842. pap. (study/action guide by Delores
     Friesen).
Longacre wrote the popular More-with-less cookbook (Herald, 1976); when she
died in 1979 she had not quite finished this pot-pourri of ideas on living
more simply drawn from the actual experiences of Mennonites around the
globe. As her husband's preface suggests, the fact that others had to help
complete the manuscript reflects the truth that simple living must always
be cooperative and is never "finished." No legalistic manual, this is a
sort of gigantic brainstorming session captured on paper with something
for everyone depending on where they find themselves. For church and
public libraries.

658. George, Denise. The Christian as a consumer. Philadelphia: Westminster
     (Potentials: Guides for Productive Living), 1984. 113p. bibliog.
     LC 83-26062. ISBN 0-664-24518-8. OCLC 10277408. pap.
Another entry in the new "Potentials" series offers an introductory look at
the virtues of simple living by a theologically trained author, wife, and
mother. Beginning with some thoughts on the ambiguities of Christ's words
(is it money itself or undue attachment to it that constitutes evil?),
George encourages readers to rise above Madison Avenue manipulation and
neighborhood peer pressures and suggests specific steps people can take
to reduce consumption. Down-to-earth advice for the socially concerned
but essentially mainline Christian.

659. Hancock, Maxine. Living on less and liking it more. Chicago: Moody,
     1976. 158p. notes. LC 76-40220. ISBN 0-8024-4912-3. OCLC 2424864.
     pap. (o.p.).
Neither advocating poverty nor condemning prosperity, this explores key
principles (responsibility, realism, restraint) around which to build a
"modest" lifestyle. Hancock starts with the tithe as a basic step toward
systematic giving and a conviction that living with love means "sharing
the load." Covers contentment (which must be learned), getting off the
credit "merry-go-round," basic needs (for food, clothing, shelter, transportation), and other miscellaneous needs (how much insurance? etc.).
Closes with thoughts on the importance of creative fellowship for psychological security.

660. Mattison, Judith. Help me adapt, Lord: discovering new blessings while
learning to live with less. Minneapolis, MN: Augsburg, 1981. 96p.
photogs. LC 80-67797. ISBN 0-8066-1859-0. OCLC 7648600. pap.
Informal free-verse reflections for women that touch on themes associated
with scaling down expectations and discovering the value of simplicity,
together with the psychological processes involved. Prayers explore overcoming resentment, discovering recycling, needs vs. wants, neighborhood
work crews, awareness of ecological constraints, having garage sales, etc.;
a mix of concrete, homey detail and more general principles.

H. LIVING IN CHRISTIAN COMMUNITY

661. Vanier, Jean. Community and growth: our pilgrimage together. New York:
Paulist, 1979. 232p. notes. LC 79-91603. ISBN 0-8091-2294-4. OCLC
6447431. pap.
Based on long experience with L'Arche Communities, shared living situations
between normal and developmentally disabled individuals, this is a discussion of the processes by which community life deepens and grows or, conversely, is impeded. Vanier's discerning analysis and loving reflection
make this a truly unique book as he examines necessary attitudes of for-
giveness/patience/trust, the difficulty of leaving old networks to forge
new commitments, questions of celibacy vs. marriage, dealing with people
who have problems, developing and sharing gifts, welcoming the marginal
and vulnerable, holding meetings, cultivating spirituality in everyday
life, and more. This not only describes an ideal but really explores the
dynamics by which community grows. Extremely rich.

662. Gish, Arthur G. Living in Christian community. Scottdale, PA: Herald,
1979. 379p. bibliog. index. LC 79-11848. ISBN 0-8361-1887-1. OCLC
4832223.
The author, a former pastor in the Church of the Brethren, has been active
in social action movements and lives with his family in the New Covenant
Fellowship in Ohio. This is a substantive book, thoughtful and probing
in its reflections, grounded and realistic in its observations and guidelines. The focus is on community as a context for sharing (emotions,
material goods, etc.), discerning (through group decision making), and
discipling (with an emphasis on accountability, discipline, forgiveness),
with some thoughts, too, on different modes of community (voluntary, organized, worshipping, non-conforming, witnessing). Many useful guidelines
from experience and Bible study, but definitely on a more theoretical
plane than, for instance, Dave Jackson's highly concrete books (see annotations).

663. Jackson, Dave and Neta Jackson. Living together in a world falling
apart. Carol Stream, IL: Creation House, 1974. 304p. illus. bibliog.
LC 73-82857. ISBN 0-88419-055-2. OCLC 1009107. pap. (o.p.).
In contrast to the books that discuss community in somewhat general or
theoretical terms, this really gets down to the nuts and bolts. The
authors draw on visits they made to several Christian fellowships, as
well as on their own experience at Reba Place; they examine on a practical,
down-to-earth level different ways of managing relationships and leader-

ship, discerning God's will, handling housing arrangements, scheduling
daily living patterns, working out roles, dealing with finances, outside
jobs, etc. Extremely useful.

664. Jackson, Dave. Dial 911: peaceful Christians and urban violence. Scott-
     dale, PA: Herald, 1981. 150p. LC 81-2541. ISBN 0-8361-1952-5. OCLC
     7278154. pap.
Here are true stories of how members of Reba Place, an intentional Christian community on Chicago's north side, have sought creative alternatives
to coping with crime and criminals. The fellowship has had to cope with
vandalism, sexual deviants, and assorted other problems; they have tried
to keep a creative tension between Christian principles and healthy realism,
and Jackson discusses some of the distinctions they have learned to draw in
deciding what to do (e.g., is the offender a juvenile or an adult? was
the crime against a person or against property?). Most interesting.

665. Harper, Michael. A new way of living: how the Church of the Redeemer,
     Houston, found a new lifestyle. Plainfield, NJ: Haven-Logos, 1973.
     144p. notes. LC 73-180328. ISBN 0-88270-066-9. OCLC 800223. pap.
     (o.p.).
This is the story of Houston's Church of the Redeemer: how, under Graham
Pulkingham's leadership, there occurred a remarkable convergence of human
and spiritual resources, and a once dying church became revitalized into
a charismatic community experiencing deep renewal on the individual level
and reaching out into a radical involvement with the struggling people in
the church's local neighborhood. The chapters discussing the styles of
extended family living, resource sharing, and spiritual discernment are so
very useful as potential guides/models on community living that this is
included here even though, in its totality, the book is actually the history of one particular church.

666. Lee, Dallas. Cotton patch evidence: the story of Clarence Jordan and
     the Koinonia Farm experiment. New York: Harper, 1971. x, 240p. LC
     70-150593. ISBN 0-06-065219-5. OCLC 162962. (o.p.).
In 1942 Jordan, the translator of the "Cotton-Patch" versions of the New
Testament, established Koinonia Farm in Americus, Georgia, as a gathering
place for Christians desiring to rid themselves of worldly possessions and
to live a communal life of radical discipleship. This is the story of that
experiment—of the vision, the conflicts with segregationist neighbors, the
community life—as well as of its aftermath and Koinonia's evolution into
Koinonia Partners, Inc., after Jordan's death. (See also the annotation
for Millard Fuller's Love in the mortar joints.)

667. Ellis, Marc. A year at the Catholic worker. New York: Paulist, 1978.
     140p. LC 78-61722. ISBN 0-8091-2140-9. OCLC 4534253. pap.
In journal format, here are experiences and responses of a young Jewish
man—a recent college graduate—who spent nine months with Dorothy Day's
Catholic Worker community on the Lower East Side. A record of those Ellis
came to know—the wounded and flawed, both "givers" and "receivers"—as
well as of his own struggles to come to terms with the suffering he wit-
nessed, this documents a personal spiritual search in the context of a
unique Christian community. Preface by Robert Coles. (See also annotation
of Dorothy Day's Meditations.)

668. Schutz, Roger. Parable of community: The rule and other basic texts
     of Taize. New York: Seabury, 1981. 96p. LC 80-26412. ISBN 0-8164-
     2301-6. OCLC 6943608. pap.
Taize is an ecumenical community in France with an international membership:
some 80 or so brothers, representing many Protestant denominations as well
as the Catholic Church, and some twenty countries. The community has become
a place of pilgrimage for searching youth, holding international meetings
and engaging in world-wide correspondence. The present book offers the
community's basic rule, stressing guidelines of inner silence, the spirit
of the Beatitudes, and goods held in common, all set forth in a context of
spirituality rather than legalism. A very simple, profound statement with
additional appended texts from Itinerary for a pilgrim, God's love, etc.
(Note: while in general, rules for religious communities are not included
here, Taize has been so influential as a model and an inspiration that an
exception was made in this case.)

669. Jackson, Dave. Coming together. Minneapolis, MN: Bethany House, 1978.
     199p. photogs. LC 78-16123. ISBN 0-87123-087-9. OCLC 4056110. pap.
     (o.p.).
By a leader in the emerging network of intentional Christian communities,
this examines that network and the characteristics of the communities that
compose it--the nature of their ministries, why people seem to be entering
them (or not), trends in organization, family living, leadership, and personal implications for individual members. Very specific with many suggestions and guidelines, this includes appendixes containing "A selected list
of Christian communities" by state as well as photos/personal testimonies
of members of Reba Place Fellowship.

670. Rodes, Richard. Running free: new life in community. Valley Forge,
     PA: Judson, 1974. 64p. photogs. notes. LC 74-7514. ISBN 0-8170-0637-0.
     OCLC 994970. pap. (o.p.).
In large paper-back format with black and white photos, this discusses
representative examples of Christian communities plus some general dimensions of community. Rodes, a "minister-at-large to the disenchanted,"
looks at the Community for Creative Non-violence, Pinebrook Community,
Kittamuqundi Community (an experimental church), and healing communities
like The Ark and Innisfree Village. He then explores trends, e.g., "Cold
wants warm," "War wants peace," "Doing wants being," "Lost childhood wants
found," etc. Liberal and free-wheeling.

671. Whitehead, Evelyn Eaton and James D. Whitehead. Community of faith:
     models and strategies for developing Christian communities. New York:
     Seabury, 1982. xiv, 187p. bibliog. notes. index. LC 81-18411. ISBN
     0-8164-2370-9. OCLC 7948635. pap.
With renewed emphasis on the importance of Christian community, the Whiteheads argue, has come disillusionment with community as actually experienced
(in church settings, etc.). This is an attempt to clarify expectations by
making insights from the social sciences on the dynamics of community available to the lay believer or "reflective minister," and bringing these into
dialogue with the Christian tradition and people's actual experiences of
living together. Explores pluralism in Christian community, diverse manifestations of community, community vis-a-vis the larger social world and
as a context for integration/mediator of dreams, etc. Substantive and
rich; more theoretical than "self-help" in thrust.

I. CHRISTIAN SOCIAL ACTION

672. Ryrie, Charles C. What you should know about social responsibility. Chicago: Moody (Current Christian Issues Series), 1982. 117p. LC 81-16804. ISBN 0-8024-9417-X. OCLC 7923104. pap. A leading spokesman for biblical inerrancy argues that Christians are indeed to serve, but to serve Christ rather than "the world," and to offer "redemptive" rather than "social" service. Social service is to be practiced within the immediate community of believers, never in the context of political or economic systems. Theological interpretations of Christ's teachings on compassion are offered, all tending to narrow down their thrust and shift the focus to issues of personal salvation rather than concern for bodily well-being: e.g., the feeding of the masses is seen as an act to glorify God more than a compassionate response to the hungry. An "agenda" at the end stresses priorities of personal holiness, evangelism, building the church, and--after everything else--a "generous" lifestyle.

673. Christenson, Larry. Social action Jesus style. Minneapolis, MN: Bethany House, 1974. 112p. LC 75-44927. ISBN 0-87123-504-8. OCLC 2296822. pap. (o.p.). Grounded in the author's studies on the charismatic movement during a sabbatical at The Institute for Ecumenical and Cultural Research, this emphasizes that Christian social action should emerge from a specific sense of call by the Holy Spirit rather than a preconceived list of concerns, and that the context for discerning the call will always be a genuine Christian community. Christenson looks at the importance of spiritual as well as material well-being and suggests that a certain separation from the world is a prerequisite for the right kind of involvement in "agape" servanthood. Brief and clear. Originally published as A charismatic approach to social action.

674. Wallis, Jim. Agenda for biblical people. New York: Harper, 1976. xi, 145p. bibliog. LC 75-36745. ISBN 0-06-069236-7. OCLC 1992050. pap. Speaking out of the new evangelical movement toward "costly discipleship" and social justice, the editor of Sojourners magazine (formerly Post American) and founder of Washington, D.C.'s Sojourners community offers a critique of civil, conservative and liberal religion, calling on the church to rediscover the radical implications of the Gospel and to forge new styles of living. Wallis has a long chapter here on "the new community" in which he spells out some of the criteria, as he understands them, for authentic Christian lifestyles in groups.

675. Schaeffer, Franky. Bad news for modern man: an agenda for Christian activism. Westchester, IL: Crossway-Good News, 1984. vii, 183p. bibliog. LC 84-70082. ISBN 0-89107-311-6. OCLC 10607203. pap. Schaeffer is the son of Francis A. Schaeffer, theologian/author, and Edith Schaeffer, also a writer. As founders of L'Abri Fellowship in Switzerland and, more recently, vocal spokespeople on the conservative evangelical scene, the Schaeffers have been very influential as a family. This is son Franky's third book; angry, ironic, and willing to name names, he takes the evangelical community to task for accommodating to trends in the secular culture (the pro-choice and women's liberation movements; leftist politics and peace activism), citing in particular the Christian media

and educational institutions. Calling for a new "ecumenism of orthodoxy" that would unite Catholics and Protestants in a call to conservative social action, leaving doctrinal differences temporarily aside, he devotes one entire chapter to an annotated bibliography of "the literature of Christian resistance." See also Francis A. Schaeffer's final book, The great evangelical disaster (Crossway, 1984).

676. Falwell, Jerry. Listen, America! Garden City, NY: Galilee-Doubleday, 1980. x, 269p. LC 79-6279. ISBN 0-385-15897-1. OCLC 6485784. pap. (Bantam ed. in BIP).
A call to "moral Americans" to arise from apathy and save America from destruction, this looks first at what Falwell perceives to be liberty's imminent demise (the threat of communism, a faltering national defense) and next at issues of morality--"the deciding factor"--and trends he sees as threatening the basic unit of the family: the children's rights movement, feminism, abortion, homosexuality, TV programming, pornography, drugs, educational trends, etc. Closes with a call for revival as the highest priority. The original rallying call for the Moral Majority.

677. Jeremiah, David. Before it's too late. Nashville, TN: Thomas Nelson, 1982. 177p. notes. LC 82-18891. ISBN 0-8407-5818-9. OCLC 8907299. pap.
In the spirit of Jerry Falwell, Jeremiah offers a critique of liberal theologians and calls for biblical action, preaching, and solutions for America's problems. This is a sort of conservative evangelical consciousness-raising book that surveys various social issues and describes what the author sees as appropriate responses. In the section on "the home," Jeremiah discusses family roles, homosexuality, abortion, and pornography and urges action to uphold a traditionally moral stance; re "the nation" he suggests that God often uses wicked states to judge those that have once known the advantage of His blessing but have since fallen away, and he calls for America to repent and to pray for peace, but be militarily strong. Draws frequently on Francis Schaeffer and Aleksandr Solzhenitsyn.

678. Monsma, Stephen. Pursuing justice in a sinful world. Grand Rapids, MI: Eerdmans, 1984. 100p. ISBN 0-8028-0023-8. pap.
A former political science professor and eight-year member of Michigan's legislature, acknowledging the tension between Christian idealism and political realities, calls for believers to help bridge this gap. Mainly theoretical yet clearly written for the general reader, this distinguishes between political activity that fosters justice (which Monsma favors) and a more "totalitarian" style that seeks to impose some "moral" good on others (e.g., school prayer). The book explores, too, ways to redeem the political process and outlines models for citizen--and professional--involvement. Appendix lists organizations active on justice issues.

679. Sine, Tom. The mustard seed conspiracy. Waco, TX: Word, 1981. 246p. notes. LC 81-51225. ISBN 0-8499-2939-3. OCLC 7938509. pap.
Written by a Christian futurist, this stresses that God's way is always to change the world through a "conspiracy of the insignificant." Sine looks at contemporary examples (drop-outs from conventional success ladders who join Christian communities, etc.), analyzes the challenges of the '80's in very specific terms, then turns to explore creative lifestyles, creative vocations, and creative communities emerging in response. Closes with thoughts on potential missions in the "One-Third World" (industrialized

nations in the Northern Hemisphere) and the "Two-Thirds World" (less industrialized Southern Hemisphere nations). Combines biblical study with
a futurist approach, offering many specific examples and suggestions.
Discussion/action questions at the end of each chapter.

680. Coffin, William Sloane. The courage to love. San Francisco: Harper,
     1982. 100p. notes. index. LC 81-48386. ISBN 0-06-061508-7. OCLC
     8172179.
Urging preachers to acknowledge the moral ambiguities of our time, Coffin
offers a liberal alternative to the Moral Majority in these sermons on the
need to become fully alive (within human limitations), to use the tensions
of thorns-in-the-flesh creatively, to help alleviate pain by sharing it.
He explores homosexuality (gays "are different--that's all") and abortion
(too complex to make God-like pronouncements) but reserves his real passion
for the arms race, about which he is willing to take an absolute stand:
disarmament is imperative.

681. Wentz, Frederick K. Getting into the act: opening up lay ministry
     in the weekday world. Nashville, TN: Abingdon, 1978. 144p. notes.
     LC 78-17179. ISBN 0-687-14125-7. OCLC 4004002. pap.
This might best be described as applied liberation theology for the layperson. Referring often to the liberation theologians, Wentz makes suggestions on how ordinary people can find ways to serve, modify lifestyles,
and become more globally conscious. One can be a "liberator" in ordinary
life through financial contributions, prayer, political involvement, and
expressing attitudes even if one is not on the truly radical "front lines,"
he says, but in some way all Christians should contribute to social change.
Closes with a look at Brazil's Dom Helder Camara.

682. Fahey, Sheila Macmanus. Charismatic social action: reflection/resource
     manual. New York: Paulist, 1977. xvii, 174p. notes. LC 77-70633. ISBN
     0-8091-2014-3. OCLC 3040423. pap. (o.p.).
Fahey believes that Christians are called to transformation in the heart
as well as to be facilitators of social/institutional change. Active in
prayer groups since 1969, she has put together here a resource manual for
people and groups wishing to fuse the personal/social calls into one. The
book examines nine areas of social action (re the aged, prisons, drugs,
race relations, etc.), presenting in each case introductory background
information, a bibliography, theological reflections, questions for discussion, and suggested action steps. Concludes with an alphabetical list
of action organizations.

683. Scanzoni, Letha and Virginia Ramey Mollenkott. Is the homosexual my
     neighbor?: another Christian view. San Francisco: Harper, 1978. xi,
     159p. bibliog. indexes. LC 77-20445. ISBN 0-06-067076-2. OCLC 3853826.
     (pap. ed. in BIP).
This is written out of the conviction that, as neighbor and "Samaritan,"
the homosexual is entitled to love, understanding and honest concern from
the Christian community--and may even have a special ministry, since homo-
phobics are in need of help just as much as homosexuals themselves. This
surveys homosexual contributions to society (including homosexual Christian
contributions), explores biblical passages on the subject to expose what
the authors see as the false reasoning behind moralistic, legalistic interpretations, gives scientific evidence on the subject, and explores dis-

tortions growing out of homophobic thinking, the current debate in church
circles, and a possible homosexual Christian ethic. Questions the possibility that "born-again" Christians can be truly "cured" and favors an
ethic supporting commited love in homosexual unions if voluntary celibacy
is not chosen.

684. Lovelace, Richard F. Homosexuality: what should Christians do about
it? Old Tappan, NJ: Power-Revell, 1984. 160p. notes. LC 78-16686.
ISBN 0-8007-5168-X. OCLC 10613620. pap.
By a professor of Church history at Gordon-Conwell Seminary, this is a
widely respected summary of the church's traditional stance on the homosexual question and more radical approaches making in-roads in the Christian community today, together with a theological critique, a biblical
analysis, and suggestions for appropriate ministry to homosexuals, all
from the conservative evangelical perspective. Lovelace calls for dual
repentence--for gay Christians to renounce active homosexual expression,
and for straight Christians to renounce all forms of homophobia--and, in
the course of his wide-ranging analysis, manages to touch on most current
books on the subject that have been influential in the Christian community.
For this reason alone, the present work is an excellent resource, and
while it is definitely more scholarly than a standard "self-help" title,
it is easily accessible to the serious general reader. Appendixes include
questions and answers about homosexuality (a guide for theological dialogue)
and list ministries and support groups led by ex-gays.

685. Allen, Loyd V., Jr. Drug abuse: what can we do? Ventura, CA: Regal,
1981. 141p. LC 79-92950. ISBN 0-8307-0744-1. OCLC 7366615. pap.
A conservative evangelical pharmacology professor surveys the drug scene
and offers explicitly Christian guidelines for action. Allen discusses
the over-all dimensions of drug abuse, then devotes separate chapters to
alcohol, tobacco, marijuana, angel dust, LSD and other hallucinogens,
stimulants, sedatives/depressants, opium/narcotics, and volatile inhalants.
A mix of scientific research findings, sociological analysis, and exhor-
tation to witness, with a stress on abstaining from any drug use which
could possibly lead others astray. Includes glossary.

686. Lewis, Gregg A. Telegarbage: what you can do about sex and violence
on TV. Nashville, TN: Thomas Nelson, 1977. 164p. notes. LC 77-24093.
ISBN 0-8407-5628-3. OCLC 3089631. pap. (o.p.).
While the average Christian's attitude toward TV has remained static
during the '70's, says Lewis, the content of programming and the industry's subtle potential to manipulate views has changed drastically, along
with the values shift in the culture. This attempts to rouse parents to
action against TV's implicit promotion of sex, violence, and secular attitudes by exercising control in the home, making their views known at
large, and creating alternatives.

687. Rogers, Dale Evans with Frank S. Mead. Hear the children crying. Old
Tappan, NJ: Revell, 1978. 137p. LC 78-6703. ISBN 0-8007-0925-X. OCLC
3844122.
Adoptive mother of a child suffering brain damage as the result of a beat-
ing, Dale Evans Rogers looks at the widespread problem of child abuse in
its various contemporary forms, the characteristics and dynamics of abusive parents, and possible solutions, stressing the spiritual component

and Jesus Christ as resource for transformation. Includes data and case
illustrations, danger signals to recognize, and resource agencies. While
this could possibly be helpful to abusive parents, its main thrust is to
explore abuse as a social problem that demands attention--especially from
Christians.

688. Gallagher, Neil. The porno plague. Updated ed. Minneapolis, MN: Be-
    thany House, 1981. 256p. illus. notes. LC 77-21992. ISBN 0-87123-
    231-6. OCLC 8874064. pap.
A truly impassioned call for Christians to become actively involved in
fighting pornography with spiritual, civil and legal resources, plus a
look at pornography in the arts and media and at society's general attitudes. This is very concrete in describing both the extent and types of
pornography available and suggested strategies for action: conducting
anti-pornography workshops, protesting sex on TV, etc. Lengthy question
and answer sequences, sample forms and letters, arguments why it is not
enough just to "preach the Gospel," and more.

689. Gage, Joy P. Broken boundaries, broken lives. Denver, CO: Accent,
    1981. 160p. LC 81-66134. ISBN 0-89636-068-7. OCLC 8488992. pap.
A minister's wife with a special interest in the physical/spiritual welfare of children writes on the problem of eroded parental authority and
disturbing implications of the "children's rights" movement. State and
human service professionals are intervening increasingly in areas previously considered private, she explains, and she calls for more emphasis on
the concrete welfare of young people and less on abstract "rights" (that
may actually lead to the "wrongs" of pregnancy, abortion, etc.). Discussing ways of setting parental boundaries in the midst of legal/social
conflicts, Gage advocates getting support from the church community and
becoming involved with issues of advertising, peer pressure, etc.

690. Schaeffer, Francis A. and C. Everett Koop. Whatever happened to the
    human race? Old Tappan, NJ: Revell, 1979. 256p. photogs. notes. index.
    LC 79-12750. ISBN 0-8007-1051-7. OCLC 4932978. (available in Schaef-
    fer's Complete works; see BIP).
Various Christian books in recent years have set forth a "right-to-life"
perspective on the practice of abortion and have encouraged citizen action: e.g., John Powell's Abortion, the silent holocaust (Argus, 1981),
Jeff Hensley's The Zero People (Servant, 1983), and, most recently, Abortion
and the conscience of the nation, with President Ronald Reagan billed as
author (his chapter-length essay is included) and with Afterwords by C.
Everett Koop and Malcolm Muggeridge (Thomas Nelson, 1984). One of the
first and most influential books in this genre, however, was the present
title, a collaboration between noted evangelical philosopher/theologian/
activist Francis A. Schaeffer and Dr. C. Everett Koop. Based on a film
series by the same name, produced by Franky Schaeffer V Productions, Inc.,
and featuring large black and white photos, it presents abortion as a
contemporary "slaughter of the innocents" and explores implications. (See
also the authors' Plan for action: an action alternative handbook for
Whatever happened to the human race? Revell, 1980, which reviews principles
discussed in the first book and offers some suggestions for positive action.)

691. Whitehead, John W., ed. Arresting abortion: practical ways to save unborn children. Westchester, IL: Crossway, 1984. pap.
Scheduled for publication in October, 1984, this was not actually examined. According to pre-publication notices, it contains advice on how to work effectively for the pro-life movement, including techniques for picketing, reaching the media, contacting members of Congress, etc.

692. Blockwick, Jessma Oslin. You, me, and a few billion more. Nashville, TN: Abingdon, 1979. 128p. bibliog. notes. LC 79-170. ISBN 0-687-46759-4. OCLC 4591422. pap.
By the director of the United Methodist Church's Department of Population, Board of Church and Society, this explores in clear, readable language for the general reader issues pertaining to the population problem: the human dimensions, how awareness and efforts grew, what is and isn't working, changing theological approaches, ethical questions, U.S. policy and programs etc. Concludes with suggestions for personal involvement.

693. Sider, Ronald J. Rich Christians in an age of hunger: a biblical study. Downers Grove, IL: InterVarsity, 1977. 249p. bibliog. indexes. LC 76-45106. ISBN 0-87784-793-2. OCLC 2848063. pap. (also Paulist ed.).
First Sider, of Evangelicals for Social Action, analyzes the contemporary situation of an affluent minority (mainly Christians) and a billion hungry neighbors, and looks at some of the ways we rationalize (calling ourselves generous, etc.). He then offers a biblical perspective on the dilemma, citing God's identification with the poor, economic relations as set forth in the Law (the Jubilee Year, tithing) and in the New Testament (koinonia and the radical new community), and the carefree attitude toward possessions taught by Jesus. Finally he discusses implementation: the tithe and "less modest" proposals for sharing monetary and human resources. Appendix lists resource materials and organizations. (New ed., revised and expanded, published by InterVarsity in June, 1984.)

694. Simon, Arthur. Bread for the World. New York: Paulist, 1975. x, 179p. bibliogs. filmography. LC 75-16672. ISBN 0-8091-1889-0. OCLC 1622105. pap. (also Eerdmans ed.).
Simon is executive director of Bread for the World, a Christian movement to combat world hunger. Here he analyzes the plight of the world's hungry in economic and political terms, stressing the need for a U.S. commitment to ameliorate the situation. In the final section of the book he presents a "program for action" which includes suggestions for involvement on both the individual and group levels. Many books exist which analyze the hunger crisis from a Christian perspective, but this one has more specific guidelines than most. Includes resources for follow-up: e.g., literature, filmstrips, lists of concerned groups.

695. Hutchinson, Robert. What one Christian can do about hunger in America. Chicago: Fides/Claretian, 1982. xi, 115p. LC 82-18499. ISBN 0-8190-0651-3. OCLC 8827592. pap.
The Bible, says Hutchinson, is one long diatribe against human arrogance in which God sides with the oppressed. He looks at the extent of hunger in America, at "politics of hunger" (past, present, and future, including Reagan's policies), and at what the church has done (Dorothy Day, etc.). The only real "how to" part of the books is in the epilogue, which touches

briefly on fasting and possible parish programs, including such traditional activities as Thanksgiving dinners for the surrounding community.
All in all, the title promises something different from what the book actually delivers.

696. Freudenberger, C. Dean and Paul M. Minus, Jr. Christian responsibility in a hungry world. Nashville, TN: Abingdon, 1976. 128p. bibliog.
LC 75-43764. ISBN 0-687-07567-X. OCLC 1975249. pap.
Addressed to comfortable Christians by a former agricultural missionary
and the past chairman of The United Methodist Church's task force on
hunger, this analyzes (in Part One) the extent of the world's food shor-
tage, causes, the need for rural community development, and the Bible's
stress on "daily bread." Part Two suggests ways Christians can tackle
the problem: by heightening awareness (a consciousness-raising grid is
offered), mobilizing resources, developing responsible lifestyles, and
helping to reorder priorities. Various examples of effective church action are described, and additional study/action resources--books, addresses,
AV tools--are provided.

697. Sprinkle, Patricia Houck. Hunger: understanding the crisis through
games, dramas, and songs. Atlanta, GA: John Knox, 1980. 142p. bibliog.
LC 78-52451. ISBN 0-8042-1312-7. OCLC 6040549. pap.
A resource/handbook for all age groups offering lifestyle evaluations, experimental exercises, quizzes, Bible activities, songs, etc., to nurture
participants' understanding of issues pertaining to world hunger. All activities are cross-referenced according to type of game, time needed to
play, number of players, suggested ages, and special preparations or features required. Intended primarily for established church groups, but
clearly adaptable to informal gatherings of family/friends also.

698. Fuller, Millard and Diane Scott. Love in the mortar joints: the story
of Habitat for Humanity. Chicago: Assoc. Pr./Follett, 1980. 190p.
illus. notes. LC 80-13426. ISBN 0-695-81444-3. OCLC 6195733. pap.
(New Century ed. in BIP).
Fuller is a former millionaire/businessman/lawyer who left his wealth to
start a housing project in Zaire; the story of this transition is told in
his Bokotola (Assoc. Pr., 1977). The present book tells of additional
African housing projects plus similar activities in Central America and
the U.S. Includes a look back at some experiences set forth in the first
book--e.g., meeting Clarence Jordan of Koinonia Farm--as background to
the on-going story. Considerable exploration of "Kingdom economics"
(based on sacrificial sharing) and entries from one volunteer's journal;
a case study in alternative Christian ministry based on radical personal
transformation. Photos, maps, and appendixes.

699. Wright, Nathan, Jr. Let's face racism. Camden, NJ: Thomas Nelson (Youth
Forum Series), 1970. 92p. LC 77-127079. OCLC 132268. (o.p.).
One of the "Youth Forum Series," a joint venture of Youth Research Center,
Inc. of Minneapolis and Thomas Nelson, designed to discuss with young
people some pressing concerns as indicated by research surveys, this explores issues surrounding racism: how it starts, how it affects blacks
and whites respectively, the dynamics involved, its relationship to religion, and living with change. Uses the imaginary experience of two ghetto
young people in the school setting as catalyst for discussion.

700. Angeles, Peter A. The possible dream: toward understanding the black
     experience. New York: Friendship Pr., 1971. 140p. notes. LC 78-146633.
     ISBN 0-377-01211-4. OCLC 145201. pap.
A white philosophy professor, long active in the civil rights movement,
sets out here to help nonblacks get a glimpse of the black experience and
transcend racist attitudes via transcripts of blacks sharing their own
responses re issues of ghetto housing, the need for jobs, the educational
process, and ego/identity questions. Not explicitly religious in approach,
but grounded in the assumption that true peace and freedom for whites can
only come by breaking through prejudice. Foreword by Floyd B. Barbour,
a professor of black literature/culture.

701. Barndt, Joseph. Liberating our white ghetto. Minneapolis, MN: Augs-
     burg, 1972. 128p. text, plus 12 page study guide. LC 70-176477. ISBN
     0-8066-1206-1. OCLC 278146. (o.p.).
A white community organizer shares his views that all whites are--uninten-
tionally if not intentionally--enslaved in racist attitudes nurtured by
the culture, trapped in "comfortable prisons" behind "unseen bars." The
intentional Christian racist, he says, is called to repentance, but for
the unintentional racist the proper response is anger, which can then be
used in co-creative partnership with God to break down walls on behalf of
the oppressed.

702. Perkins, John M. With justice for all. Ventura, CA: Regal, 1982.
     208p. notes. Foreword by Chuck Colson. LC 80-50262. ISBN 0-8307-
     0754-9. OCLC 8169456.
The founder of Voice of Calvary Ministries challenges the evangelical com-
munity--white and black both--to live out Jesus' radical message so that
the poor and oppressed can become self-sufficient through the Gospel's
power. Perkins explains the three principles of VOC--relocation to a
place of service so your neighbors' needs become your own, reconciliation
between races through love in action, and redistribution of resources as
God's stewards--and how they took shape for him through his own experiences
of discrimination and call to service. Provocative and challenging.

703. Adjali, Mia. Of life and hope: toward effective witness in human
     rights. New York: Friendship Pr., 1979. 90p. notes. LC 79-10324.
     ISBN 0-377-00084-1. OCLC 4775228. pap.
Based on the belief that Christians are called to confront critical struggles in the world, this is organized around articles drawn from the U.N.
Human Rights Covenants. Section One presents statements on specific sorts
of human rights, re self-determination, torture, migrant labor, aliens,
voting rights, and racial justice. Section Two explores political action
in pursuit of human rights. Section Three examines "universal" human
rights--for health care, food availability, free assembly, etc. The focus
throughout is on peoples' concrete experiences and activities. Includes
spiritual reflections and "additional resources."

704. Hessel, Dieter T., ed. Energy ethics: a Christian response. New York:
     Friendship Pr., 1979. 170p. bibliog. notes. LC 79-19345. ISBN 0-377-
     00095-7. OCLC 5333958. pap.
Hessel, who is Associate for Adult Resources and Social Education with the
United Presbyterian Church's Program Agency, has a special interest in
education for social change. This book grew out of a seminar with the NCC

Energy Study Panel and has chapters on nuclear energy, eco-justice for the
'80's, energy and society, the moral, religious and political dimensions,
and ways to influence policies. Appendixes cover theological questions,
individual/institutional conservation, study resources, and sample options.
Includes a list of organizations and resources.

705. Grannis, J. Christopher, with Arthur J. Laffin and Elin Schade. The
     risk of the cross: Christian discipleship in the nuclear age. New
     York: Seabury, 1981. xiv, 110p. illus. bibliog. filmography. LC 80-
     29281. ISBN 0-8164-2305-9. OCLC 7176756. pap.
Here is an exploration of some central issues in the Gospel of Mark (who
is Jesus? what constitutes the journey of discipleship?) and their spiritual implications for responding to the nuclear threat. The authors,
members of the Covenant Peace Community and Sisters of the Cross and Passion, offer the best of their personal discoveries as they searched Scripture for guidance. Their answers emphasize community as a necessary context for activity, and the role of the Eucharist as basis and source of
authentic community.

706. Freund, Ronald. What one Christian can do to help prevent nuclear
     war. Chicago: Fides/Claretian, 1982. 185p. LC 82-15584. ISBN 0-8190-
     0650-5. OCLC 8762923. pap.
Freund first traces his personal journey and sets forth a theology and
politics of responsibility to encourage everyone to assume a personal
role in peacemaking and to integrate personal faith with public action.
Thereafter he touches on a wide range of issues: jobs and their implications; the biblical dilemmas surrounding tax resistance and obligations
due to God vs. Caesar; stances within various churches in the Christian
community; the possibility of a World Peace Tax Fund Bill (for legal conscientious objection to war taxes); budgetary trade-offs; draft resistance;
just war criteria, and much more. Includes profiles of representative
figures in various careers who are integrating stands of conscience with
their work and lists of national religious peace organizations with descriptions.

707. Vanderhaar, Gerard A. Christians and nonviolence in the nuclear age:
     Scripture, the arms race, and you. Mystic, CT: Twenty-Third, 1982.
     128p. bibliog. LC 82-82388. ISBN 0-89622-162-8. OCLC 8941269. pap.
Opening with a brief look at how he came to his present stance, Vanderhaar stresses that nonviolence takes two forms: a "no" to the forces of
destruction and a "yes" to peaceful visions of worldwide human dignity.
In six chapters he explores the present dangerous state, attitudes of
idolatry underlying reliance on nuclear weapons, scriptural passages in
the Old and New Testaments that address the war/peace issue, dynamics of
nonviolent action with concrete examples (Gandhi, Martin Luther King, Jr.),
ways of demythologizing the enemy, and the way of personal nonviolence.
Includes a look at spirituality, communication, peace groups, etc.; discussion questions as well.

708. Wallis, Jim, ed. Waging peace: a handbook for the struggle to abolish
     nuclear weapons. San Francisco: Harper, 1982. xiv, 304p. illus. bib-
     liog. index. LC 82-47759. ISBN 0-06-069240-5. OCLC 8627775. pap.
The essays here assess the present state of the arms race and biblical/
theological issues surrounding it. The book itself is designed as an edu-
cational/informational tool for individuals, churches, and informal groups.

Part One deals with the current dilemma; Part Two explores biblical/theo-
logical dimensions; and Part Three suggests specific guidelines for action
and visions about which to dream. A complementary title is Wallis' Peacemakers (Harper, 1983), which consists largely of personal testimonies.

709. Sider, Ronald J. and Richard K. Taylor. Nuclear holocaust and Christian
     hope: a book for Christian peacemakers. New York: Paulist, 1982. 368p.
     illus. bibliog. notes. index. LC 82-18844. ISBN 0-8091-2512-9. OCLC
     8866472. pap.
Grounded in the premise that all Christians must say "no" to the posses-
sion and use of nuclear weapons, this explores the nuclear threat, bibli-
cal/theological perspectives (including the "just war" theory and the way
of the Cross), concrete steps toward peace which Christians can take, and
the conflict between biblical faith and reliance on national defense. Appendixes include lists of peace organizations and AV materials, plus extensive notes and indexes.

710. Sheerin, John B. Peace, war, and the young Catholic. New York: Paulist,
     1973. viii, 109p. bibliog. LC 72-91458. ISBN 0-8091-1733-9. OCLC
     572233. pap. (o.p.).
Written for young people and draft counselors, this is a guide for dealing
with issues of conscience vis-a-vis the military. The first chapters delineate a context, exploring realities of war, potential conflicts of
conscience involving family and governmental loyalties, the plurality of
attitudes toward war in the Christian community, and the just war theory.
Subsequent chapters look at the peace movement (with special reference
to Catholic protesters), some obstacles to sound judgment (e.g., neurotic
anti-Communism, on the one hand, or worship of revolutionaries, on the
other), and issues surrounding the draft. Stresses the importance of
conscience and the legitimacy of differing views.

711. Steiner, Susan Clemmer. Joining the army that sheds no blood. Scott-
     dale, PA: Herald (Christian Peace Shelf Series), 1982. 155p. illus.
     bibliog. notes. index. LC 82-81510. ISBN 0-8361-3305-6. OCLC 8966913.
     pap.
Designed for young people who must decide on their stance toward war, this
book, from a Mennonite perspective (but reaching out to all Christians)
considers Jesus' words and life as the standard for peacemaking, pros and
cons of typical arguments against pacifism, and specific activities and
beliefs of Christian peacemakers. The style is informal and colloquial,
with appealing cartoons ("Pontius Puddle") by Joel Kauffmann. Includes
Scripture index, resource list, bibliographies, review/reflection questions.

712. Durland, William. People pay for peace: a military tax refusal guide
     for radical religious pacifists and people of conscience. Rev. and
     expanded ed. Colorado Springs, CO: Center Peace Publishers, 1982.
     vii, 104p. illus. notes. OCLC 8127752. pap.
By an attorney, theologian, and military tax refuser, this discusses general background and principles regarding military tax refusal (including
Jesus' and Paul's words about obligations to Caesar and issues of civil
disobedience), specific steps in refusing to pay a military tax, likely
actions the I.R.S. will take, the process of going to court, and issues of
conscience and constitutional law. This is a greatly expanded update of

an earlier edition, featuring specific legal precedents and helpful guidelines. Large paper format with line drawings; appendixes on resources,
sample I.R.S. letters/notices, war tax resistance counselors and centers,
and alternative funds as of October, 1982.

713. Drescher, John M. Why I am a conscientious objector. Scottdale, PA:
     Herald (Christian Peace Shelf Series), 1982. 73p. bibliog. LC 82-894.
     ISBN 0-8361-1993-2. OCLC 8169834. pap.
Drescher teaches at Eastern Mennonite Seminary. In this book he shares an
interpretation of Scripture which has led to his pacifist stance: the
Lordship of Christ necessarily disarms us; the church is universal and its
callto reconciliation global in scope; the command to submit to government does not mean secular authority   should supercede God's clear call to
peace. Brief and readable, this includes an annotated bibliography of
Christian peace literature (mainly Mennonite).

714. Schaeffer, Francis, and others. Who is for peace? Nashville, TN:
     Thomas Nelson, 1983. 112p. notes. LC 83-17482. ISBN 0-8407-5878-2.
     OCLC 9919229. pap.
Three independent essays by an influential evangelical Protestant (Schaeffer),
a Russian dissident (Vladimir Bukovsky), and a Catholic historian (James
Hitchcock). Schaeffer denounces unilateral disarmament as he emphasizes
the need for military preparedness in a fallen world, while Bukovsky offers an ironic expose of Soviet hypocrisy, and Hitchcock gives a critique
of the Catholic Bishops' 1983 pastoral letter. Like Who are the peacema-
makers? by Jerram Barrs of England's L'Abri Fellowship (Crossway, 1983),
this is a work of political analysis rather than a guide to action; it is
included to illustrate the thinking of Christian conservatives who are
convinced that a strong nuclear deterrent is necessary.

715. Yoder, John H. What would you do?: a serious answer to a standard
     question. Scottdale, PA: Herald (Christian Peace Shelf Series), 1983.
     119p. bibliog. LC 83-12811. ISBN 0-8361-3346-3. OCLC 9756779. pap.
By a Mennonite theologian, this explores the implications of a pacifist
response in three sections. First, Yoder offers his own thoughts on the
issue and the various options available. Next, he presents reflections
from the writings of others (Tolstoy to Joan Baez). Finally, he gives us
statements from such well-known Christians as Tom Skinner and Gladys Aylward testifying to instances of creative non-violence in encounters with
others.

716. Lamont, Victor. Hungry for peace. New York: Friendship Pr., 1976. 63p.
     illus. LC 76-4779. ISBN 0-377-00056-6. OCLC 2072814. pap.
A Methodist minister active in Third World concerns and media ministries
explores problems surrounding the peace issue (are we born aggressive?
what about pacifism or peace by force?) and examines data on the arms race
and ways of moving toward peace according to insights embodied in Jesus'
life and teachings. Includes photos, cartoons, quotes from public figures,
games to stimulate experiential learning, discussion questions, etc.

717. Halvorson, Loren E. Peace on earth handbook. Minneapolis, MN: Augsburg,
     1976. 128p. illus. LC 75-22718. ISBN 0-8066-1516-8. OCLC 2164580. (o.p.).
Described as "an action guide for people who want to do something about
hunger, war, poverty, and other human problems," this offers suggestions
and guidelines based on programs or activities already set in motion by

others. Emphasizes that peace building is everyone's concern, the importance of working with resources presently available or in nearby, unexpected
places, and the power of many small people when they work together. Chapter Five focuses specifically on the hunger question. Includes a "Whole
earth confession checklist," plus models for local action and educational
helps (contact people, specific programs/resources/study materials, seminars
etc.).

718. Hinton, Pat Corrick. Images of peace. Minneapolis, MN: Winston, 1983.
     88p. photogs. notes. LC 83-60407. ISBN 0-86683-748-5. pap.
With introductory quotes from a variety of well-known figures (Martin
Luther King, Jr., G. K. Chesterton, Kahlil Gibran, Dr. Helen Caldicott,
Pope John Paul II, etc.) this presents forty meditational themes in the
broad areas of listening and thinking about peace, speaking peace to one
another, and working for peace. The reflective passages in each meditation
are, again, drawn from various sources (words of children; the writings
of Jim Wallis), and close with the author's free-verse prayer thoughts.
The integrating theme is a call to take up the challenge of building peace,
on the faith that one person can make a difference.

719. Miller, Ella May. The peacemakers: how to find peace and share it. Old
     Tappan, NJ: Revell, 1977. 179p. LC 77-1625. ISBN 0-8007-0865-2. OCLC
     2818517. (o.p.).
Gently evangelical, stressing that God intended the family to be a "labora-
tory" for living, this explores ways to maintain peace on personal, family,
and community levels by living to avoid conflicts and finding peaceful solutions whenever possible. Guidelines for personal relationships are high-
lighted (sharing feelings, sticking to the issue at hand, being patient,
cooperative, affirmative) along with bridge-building in the community (a
child sharing peanuts with Chicano friends). Miller stresses respect for
authority and discourages any civil disobedience, though she does have good
words for conscientious objection (a "legal" alternative).

720. Berrigan, Daniel and Robert Coles. Geography of faith: conversations
     between Daniel Berrigan, when underground, and Robert Coles. Boston:
     Beacon, 1971. 179p. LC 70-159844. ISBN 0-8070-0539-8. OCLC 239919.
     pap. (o.p.).
These transcribed conversations are extremely significant, given the Berrigan brothers' impact on America as radical Catholic activists before such
behavior was widely "fashionable," and Coles' influence as an articulate,
prolific writer and psychiatrist with a remarkable ability to communicate
the complexity of reality, transcending stereotypes. In the early parts of
the book Coles is mainly an interviewer, skillfully drawing Berrigan out;
as their talk unfolds, however, Coles the individual--deeply concerned for
his personal integrity, honestly questioning both some of Berrigan's methods
and some of his own--emerges more clearly. A stimulating exploration of
spiritual/strategic issues.

721. Schaeffer, Francis A. A Christian manifesto. Westchester, IL: Crossway-
     Good News, 1981. 157p. bibliog. index. LC 81-69737. ISBN 0-89107-
     233-0. OCLC 7948807. pap.
This book, says Schaeffer in the Preface, is the natural outgrowth of all
that he has written before: over twenty titles affirming the objective
truth of God's presence, the Lordship of Christ over all phases of the

Christian's life and, by implication, over the culture as a whole. Following Whatever happened to the human race? (entry 690), the present work
examines what Schaeffer takes to be the need for civil disobedience as a
bottom-line mandate when the Christian is faced with secular authority
demanding behavior antagonistic to his/her faith: e.g., the importance of
protesting against the use of tax money for abortion, say, or of resisting
the use of tax rulings to interfere with Christian schools. A conservative
evangelical statement by a noted spokesman. For a theologically broader
discussion that considers liberal perspectives/agendas as well as conservative ones and explores evolving approaches to civil disobedience in the
Christian community, see Holy disobedience by Lynn Buzzard and Paula
Campbell (Servant, 1984).

722. Day, Dorothy. Meditations. Selected and arranged by Stanley Vishnewski.
    New York: Paulist, 1970. 104p. illus. LC 73-133570. ISBN 0-8091-1636-7.
    OCLC 98861. pap.
Culled from the Catholic Worker, these pieces are Vishnewski's choices as
to the most representative of Day's writings in that paper. Many are autobiographical and concern the Catholic Worker movement; others are reflections on family life, war and peace, laymen/clergy relations, etc. Those
which reflect on simple living, identifying with the poor, and the importance of voluntary poverty make a good introduction to Day's thinking on
such community-building themes, and the compiler was active with the Catholic Worker movement for many years. (Note: Another recent collection
of Day's writings is By little and by little: the selected writings of
Dorothy Day, ed. and with introd. by Robert Ellsberg, Knopf, 1983.)

723. Schutz, Roger. Afire with love: meditations on peace and unity. New
    York: Crossroad, 1982. 192p. tr. by Emily Chisholm and the Taize
    Community. LC 81-71392. ISBN 0-8245-0474-7. OCLC 8710623. pap.
Brother Roger, who founded the Taize Community in France to be a "parable
of communion," pleads for a wider ecumenism grounded in love rather than
bureaucratic strategies. Stressing the need to bridge gaps between all
kinds of people and to recognize the relationship between global and inner violence, he shares journal entries reflecting on the many who bring
their concerns to Taize and points to the possible partnership between
spirituality and social action. Highly recommended.

AUTHOR INDEX

Includes authors and joint authors.
Numbers refer to entry, not page, number.

Spande, Norma, 624
Sprinkle, Patricia Houck, 697
Stafford, Tim, 177, 181
Stanger, Frank Bateman, 502
Stapleton, Ruth Carter, 113
Stedman, Ray C., 635
Steiner, Susan Clemmer, 711
Stern, David E., 482
Stern, E. Mark, 005
Stewart, Charles, 397
Stigger, Judith A., 297
Stoop, David, 049
Stoop, Jan, 049
Stott, John R. W., 579
Stout, Martha, 599
Strunk, Orlo, Jr., 131
Sullivan, Barbara A., 030
Sutherland, S. Philip, 214
Swihart, Judson J., 382, 454
Swindoll, Charles R., 219, 275
Switzer, David, 409
Switzer, Shirley, 409

Taylor, Richard K., 709
ten Boom, Corrie, 484
Tengbom, Mildred, 333
Thielicke, Helmut, 166
Thomas, Joan, 435
Thompson, Andrew D., 349
Thornton, Edward E., 121
Timmons, Tim, 276
Tomczak, Larry, 321
Toohey, William, 189
Tournier, Paul, 095
Towner, Jason, 232. See also Smith,
   Harold Ivan
Trobisch, Ingrid, 178, 265
Trobisch, Walter, 176, 178
Trudinger, Ron, 628
True, Michael, 395
Truman, Ruth, 164
Tubesing, Donald A., 566
Tubesing, Nancy Loving, 566
Twomey, Gerald S., 465

Umphrey, Marjorie, 022

Vanderhaar, Gerard A., 707
Vanderwall, Francis W., 137
Vanier, Jean, 661
Van Kaam, Adrian, 158
Van Vuuren, Nancy, 598
Vaswig, William L., 102
Vaughn, Ruth, 127, 175
Vecchio, Holly Lee, 415

Vigeveno, H. S., 436, 455
Vishnewski, Stanley, 722
Vitz, Paul C., 010
Vogel, Linda Jane, 516
Vredevelt, Pam W., 300

Wagemaker, Herbert J., Jr., 323,
   630
Wagner, C. Peter, 608
Wakin, Edward, 065, 327
Wallis, Jim, 573, 674, 708
Walter, James Lynwood, 016
Walters, Richard P., 055, 216
Ward, Patricia, 599
Warner, Paul L., 066
Watson, David, 574
Wayne, David J., 187
Weir, William, 076
Welter, Paul, 398
Wentz, Frederick K., 681
Westerhoff, John H., III, 357
Wheat, Ed, 264
Wheat, Gaye, 264
Wheeler, Bonnie, 368
White, Jerry, 192, 521, 593
White, John, 408
White, Mary, 521, 593
Whitehead, Evelyn Eaton, 152, 671
Whitehead, James D., 152, 671
Whitehead, John W., 691
Wicks, Robert J., 129
Wilder, Garnett M., 051
Wilkerson, David, 182
Wilkerson, Don, 413
Williams, Strephon, 136
Wilson, Earl D., 141, 247
Wilson, J. Christy, Jr., 589
Wilson, Ken, 230
Wittman, E. C., 160
Wolff, Pierre, 094
Woods, Richard, 253
Worthington, Everett L., 643
Wright, H. Norman, 258, 292, 303,
   330
Wright, Nathan, Jr., 699

Yancey, Philip, 090, 261
Yoder, John H., 715
Yohn, Tick, 612
Youngren, J. Alan, 390

Zehring, John William, 582, 602
Zimmerman, Martha, 294
Zlotowitz, Bernard, 289
Zwack, Joseph P., 450

TITLE INDEX

Includes titles and, if needed for
clarification, partial or full sub-titles.
Numbers refer to entry, not page, numbers.

SUBJECT INDEX

For best results, consult entries for target groups defined by age, sex, or condition (e.g., Women, Teenagers, Single living, etc.) as well as entries for conceptual or purely abstract topics (e.g., Faith and doubt, Anger, Loneliness, etc.). Index includes institutional and personal names appearing in annotations if these are deemed theologically or theoretically relevant, but denominational affiliations are not indexed. Numbers refer to entry number, and in two instances discussion in the "Preface" is cited.

Ambivalence, 140-142. See also
Wholeness
American Friends' Service Com-
mittee, 652
Amniocentesis, 307
Amputees, 488, 491
Anger, 046, 048-051, 053-055, 060,
068, 074, 077, 145, 160; and
creativity, 095; at God, 094,
236; in marriage, 272, 438. See
also Child development, and
feelings
Annulment, 450, 465
Anorexia nervosa, 088, 102. See
also Bulimia
Anxiety, 048, 049, 051, 056, 073
074, 077; acute neurotic, 075.
See also Fear; Worrying
Aphasia, 492
L'Arche communities, 661, 670
Archetypes. See Jung, Carl, theory
of; Shadow archetype
Ark, The. See L'Arche communities
Assertiveness, 221-223. See also
Conflict resolution
Authority relationships, 161, 607.
See also Family living, and
relationship patterns; Marriage,
and male/female roles
Automatic writing, 126
Avocational interests, 602. See
also Ministry, personal modes
of; Spiritual gifts
Aylward, Gladys, on non-violence,
715

Baptism in the Spirit, 149-151,
291, 377. See also Charismatic
movement; Tongues, speaking in
Beatitudes, implications of: for
community living, 668; for
evangelism, 623; for family relationships, 382
Beauty, 210, 211; and aging, 535
"Beginning Experience" workshops,
449
Behavioral psychology. See Psychology, the discipline of
Benedictine rules and family
living, 391
Bereavement, 093, 160, 508-513;
counseling for, 646. See also
Death, of a child; Death, explaining, to children; Death,
by suicide and its aftermath;
Grief, types of; Widowed

Berne, Eric, theory of. See Trans-
actional analysis
Bible reading: for personal study,
147, 164, 574; as therapy, 012,
159, 160. See also Introspection
and self-examination, via Bible
reading
Bible study, home groups for,
624, 627
"Biblical Attitudes Survey," 130
Big-Brother, Big-Sister programs,
604
Biofeedback, 111
Birth control. See Family planning
Birthmarks, 487, 488
Birth order, 030
Birthright, 293
Blindness, 487; in a child, 368
Body/mind relationship. See Mind/
body relationship
Boone, Pat, 088. See also Author
Index
Boredom, 051, 159
Born again experience. See Conver-
sion
Bread for the World, 588, 694
Breast feeding, 265, 307
Bulimia, 087. See also Anorexia
nervosa
Burn-out, 119, 129, 480. See also
Stress

Camara, Dom Helder, the example
of, 681
Campus Crusade for Christ, 174
Campus Life magazine, 177, 181,
186, 188
Cancer, 102, 494-497, 506, 509,
510, 549, 550; and teenagers,
497. See also Circumcision and
penile cancer
Careers in religion, 585, 586.
See also Vocation
Caring for self and others, 566,
567. See also Compassion; Fel-
lowship dynamics; Friendship
dynamics; Intimacy (in general)
Catholic Worker community, 667,
722
Catholic Worker newspaper, 722
Celebration as corporate disci-
pline, 551
Celibacy as a call, 249, 606, 661.
See also Single living
Cell groups. See Small groups
Centering and centering prayer,

About the Compiler

ELISE CHASE is a reference librarian at the Forbes Library, North-ampton, Massachusetts. She has been a columnist for *Library Journal* in the field of popular religious literature since 1980.